THE MONSTER THAT ATE MY MOMMY

A MEMOIR

JESSICA AIKEN-HALL

THE MONSTER THAT
ATE MY MOMMY

A Memoir

Jessica Aiken-Hall

ISBN-13: 978-0-9993656-7-0 (paper)

ISBN-13: 978-0-9993656-8-7 (cloth)

ISBN-13: 978-0-9993656-0-1 (e-book)

Library of Congress Control Number: 2017913595

The events, places, and conversations recreated in this work are based on the author's memories. *The Monster That Ate My Mommy* is written from the author's perspective and based on stories as told to the author. To maintain the anonymity of characters, names of individuals, locales, identifying characteristics and details such as physical properties, occupations, and places of residence have been changed in most instances.

Rogena Mitchell-Jones, Literary Editor

RMJ Manuscript Service LLC www.rogenamitchell.com

AmiLynn Hadley, Cover Design by Ami www.coverdesignbyami.com

To George—thank you for waiting.
To my children—you are stronger than you know.

In Memory of my gram,
Murrium Aiken.
My soulmate and best friend.

"Something Good Coming"
Tom Petty and The Heartbreakers

Jessica A. Hall

CHAPTER 1

"*J*'m not your mommy. I'm the monster that ate your mommy!"

The words echoed through my head as my tiny body went limp with fear. I clung to my mother's side as we lay together on the mountain of blankets on her bed. In spite of my terror, I needed to save my mommy. I buried my head deep into the monster's belly as I talked to her. *"Mommy! Mommy, please don't leave me. Mommy, I need you."*

Her muffled voice cried, *"Help me. Help me."*

I burrowed deeper as I attempted to rescue her. "Mommy! Mommy, I'm here! I'll save you, Mommy." Crying between my pleas, I was determined to get her out. The more I yelled, the more the muffled voice shouted out for help. I could not free her. She was trapped deep inside the monster. I had failed her. Tears turned to sobs as I nuzzled my face into the monster's soft round belly, my arm draped over her side.

The muffled voice returned, "Be a good girl, Jessie, and go to sleep."

I wanted to please her. My eyes closed tight, and my breathing slowed as I listened to my mom's heartbeat. Panic turned to exhaustion and sleep engulfed me. The room went silent as we napped together. I didn't know it then, but this was part of her plan. She didn't want to answer the inquisitive questions of her three-year old. She wanted to sleep and let the world go quiet while depression took her over.

I don't remember much else about that time—only how the fear consumed me and led me down the path to be wary of others. It taught me no matter how much love I could give another person, it might never be enough to save him or her from themselves or make them love me back. A painful and difficult reality to face at three years of age—but it was only the first in my journey through mental illness, grief, and loss.

I was born into chaos. The consistency of it made it comfortable. It made *normal* look crazy. For many years, I existed in a toxic environment mere inches from death. As a child, I didn't know any different. I assumed all parents plotted to kill their children. All mothers had their kids keep a lookout for their father while they had sex at a strange man's house. The chaos was so comfortable anything else looked frightening. I was scared to leave it...I guess that in itself explains a lot.

As I got older, I began to notice the differences in other families. I didn't understand why my life was so different. To understand, I blamed it on luck. I concluded I was unlucky in every aspect of my being.

In the backseat of our rusty Volkswagen Beetle, I pushed my face against the glass as we passed by houses through our rural Vermont town. I looked inside their windows and saw happy families sitting together. Mothers laughed and hugged their children. Families sat around dining room tables, smiling as they passed the mashed potatoes. And kids were running around having fun. I longed for what I saw. I imagined a family waiting for me to arrive to love me and welcome me with hugs and kisses. I didn't understand what I had done to be stuck in this life. A dark cloud always followed me, and I hated it. If something *could* go wrong, it *did* go wrong. Other people always appeared to be happy. I got angry and then sad as I watched everyone else have what I wanted.

I was overcome with depression as I reflected how much effort it took to survive. It hurt even to breathe some days, all because nothing *ever* went the way I expected. Jovial occasions ended with gloom and misery—never what I had hoped for. The excitement built as I imagined how it *could be*. I envisioned how it was for people who always smiled and how it happened on TV. I ruminated about everything, anticipating that maybe *this* time was my turn for life to go as I planned. For once, it was going to be my turn to smile and be happy. Time after time, my turn never came. A jubilant event ended as the next dive into depression began.

I struggled each day to find a reason to keep going. I wondered if I could ever make my mom love me. Negative thoughts took over my mind. There was no *quiet* in my head. *Your own mother doesn't love you, so what makes you think anyone else will?* These words haunted me and affected every decision I made. Would I ever find love? Would I ever be good enough? Would I ever learn to love myself?

My closet is open, and my skeletons are ready to meet you.

CHAPTER 2

a hot summer day in July, Wendy mowed the thick, long grass with her mother's black, rusty lawn mower. Flecks of metal dug into her palms as blisters formed. "God damn piece of shit!" she bellowed as she leaned onto the handle and clutched her stomach. "I need to finish this fuckin' lawn before Mom gets home," she yelled as she gave it another push. The mower stalled, and Wendy began to cry.

Wendy fell to her knees, her blue floral sundress ripped as she tried to get up. She *hated* that dress, but it was the only thing that still fit her. She was overdue with her second child. "Great, now I'll have to go naked until this kid decides to show up." Her swollen hands covered her chocolate brown eyes as she continued to sob.

Her mother, Theresa, pulled into the driveway in her white Audi 5000. The keys still in the ignition, she ran to Wendy. "What on Earth are you *doing*? You're going to kill that baby." She extended her hand to help her daughter up.

"I don't give a damn anymore. I am so sick of this thing."

"Get on into the house. I bought you some vanilla ice cream. Let's go cool off."

As Wendy stood up, she grabbed her mom's hand as she screamed. *"Ahhhhh!* It's...time to go..."

Theresa rushed her daughter to the hospital. It was a twenty-minute drive. They arrived in ten. At the hospital, Wendy's contractions continued to intensify. She was admitted and waited for her midwife to come. The pain was excruciating—more pain than she experienced with her first child six years earlier.

The labor lasted for hours into the next day. Wendy was exhausted, but it was time. I was coming. Wendy was fully dilated and ready to push. After I made my arrival, the midwife panicked when she looked at my mom's face.

"Wendy. *Wendy.* Come back to us. Don't you dare leave this beautiful baby girl without a mother," the midwife shouted as she hit my mom in the face with a wet washcloth.

My birth was a traumatic experience for her. I was eleven pounds, six ounces, and her blood pressure was dangerously low. She lost a lot of blood during the delivery. "We need a doctor in here STAT," the midwife yelled as she watched the monitors continue to drop.

My mother lost consciousness and was steps away from "the light." She walked up to two large doors, her hand on the handle ready to tug it open. "Wendy, honey, come back to us and meet your baby girl."

My mom picked me. She opened her eyes when she heard I was a girl. She spent my life telling me I killed her. However, if I had been a boy she would have opened those doors, and her life would have ended when mine began on July 3, 1981. She survived but always held me responsible for taking her life—literally for a few seconds and figuratively for the rest of it.

Living in such a small town, it wasn't long before Ralph found out about my birth. He arrived at the hospital with convenience store flowers and a teddy bear. Ralph brought the gifts as a peace offering. His blue eyes sparkled as he made his way up the elevator. He fixed his driving cap and straightened his button down plaid top.

"Excuse me, ma'am. I'm here to see my daughter. She was just born. Can you tell me what room her mother's in?" he asked with a beaming face.

"What's your name, sir?" The nurse looked down her glasses at him, shifting her eyes to the note on the desk.

"Ralph. Ralph Hall. My lady's name is Wendy Aiken. We didn't make it to the altar just yet." He chuckled at his own joke.

"I'm sorry, sir. I am not able to give you that information."

"What do *you* mean? *You* can't give me *that* information? That's my fuckin' daughter. You better fuckin' tell me you mother fucker."

"Sir…"

"Don't you sir me, you dumb cunt. Where the fuck is she? Where is that fuckin' whore?"

"Sir…"

"It's just like that fuckin' whore to pull this shit." His voice continued to rise and spit flew with each word. "That's *my* fuckin' kid, and I'm *not* leaving until I get to see her."

The nurse called the police to escort Ralph out of the hospital. He didn't get to meet me or see my mom. She heard him. She knew he was there. She didn't know what he was capable of doing. Only hours old, and I had experienced my first immersion in chaos.

Theresa picked up the bundle of pink out of the plastic hospital bassinet and rocked me from side to side. "Look how beautiful she is." She loved me from the moment she saw me. "Finally, a chance to do it *right*," she whispered as she kissed my forehead. From that moment, I became hers, and she became mine. She was always disappointed in her daughter. In Theresa's eyes, Wendy was a failure. As far as Theresa was concerned, my birth was the only thing Wendy had ever done right.

Gram strapped my car seat into the back of her Audi and drove us home. Our apartment was in the basement of her house. The back wall was covered with shelves of books. Across from the book shelves was Mom's queen-size mattress and box spring that sat on the cement floor with an old wooden crib beside it. Down the hall, past the bathroom and boxes, was my older half-brother's room. Peter was six years old and wasn't sure if he wanted his new job as big brother.

Mom was overwhelmed with having an infant and a six-year-old boy who was no longer an only child. Gram jumped in and took care of me in almost all aspects except for breastfeeding me—the one thing she couldn't do. One of my earliest memories is snuggling into Gram's lap, drinking milk from my bottle, gazing up into her blue eyes as she read to me. I was safe with Gram. She was my only constant source of love.

Gram was sixty-two years old when I was born. She was divorced after thirty years of marriage when she learned her husband had been having an affair with his much younger secretary. The whole town knew what had happened, and she wasn't ready to be the center of anymore gossip, so she invested her time in my mother, and later, us kids.

Mom described herself as a free-loving hippy. She had long brown hair always in a braid down her back. She wore denim overalls with tie-dyed shirts or no shirt at all. She had multiple sexual partners who often came to visit. Mom left me in my playpen as they smoked joints in the bathroom and drank beer in front of me.

Martin was one of the visitors. He had long, dark hair and a bushy beard and mustache to match. He wore ripped up, faded denim jeans and a light blue button-down shirt exposing his hairy chest. He took a liking to me. He sat on the floor with me and repeated the words *pizza and beer* until I finally mimicked him. It became a family joke that those were my first words.

My brother's dad, Jake, was still friends with Mom. He was a gentle soul and treated me like his own. He visited often and spent holidays with us. When Jake was around, it felt like we were a family. Mom was nicer and calmer in his presence. Peter lit up with excitement when his dad visited. Jake always gave us change to put into our piggy banks. I carried my pink, plastic pig as I crawled up the stairs and made my way to his lap where he deposited a few coins into the bank. I giggled with excitement as I heard the coins clank together.

Jake knew my dad and offered to give me his last name and be listed as my father on my birth certificate. Mom contemplated the idea but didn't take him up on his offer. Jake was ill. As time passed, he got sicker and needed dialysis. His treatments were two hours away, which meant we saw less and less of him.

Just before I turned three, Mom got the call. Jake had passed away. They had planned to make the two-hour drive to the hospital the day before but had to cancel due to a snowstorm. Jake asked to have all of his machines and tubes taken off so he wouldn't scare Peter for their visit. Jake decided to leave them off.

"How am I going to tell Peter?" Mom asked Gram after she hung up the phone.

"I don't know." Gram paused as she thought. "He's just a boy."

Peter made his way up the stairs. A somber smile on his face.

"Peter, honey, come sit down," Mom said as she patted the kitchen chair between them.

"Dad's all better." He rubbed the sleep from his eyes. "He came and saw me last night and told me he doesn't hurt anymore."

Mom's and Gram's eyes locked together. "What, honey?" Mom managed to ask.

"Dad said goodbye and told me to be a good boy. He is with the angels now. I'm not sad. I know he's okay."

Mom's eyes filled with tears as she hugged Peter. She stroked his dark brown hair as her tears hit the top of his head. "It's okay, Mommy. He's better now."

CHAPTER 3

*A*fter Jake's death, Mom and Ralph became involved again. Within six months, Ralph's name was added to my birth certificate, and my last name became hyphenated. After a few months of dating, they bought a piece of land in the next town. They dreamed of building a house, but neither had credit to do so. Mom asked Gram to co-sign a loan to purchase their dream home, but she refused. She didn't like the idea of us moving in with Ralph, and neither did I.

Ralph had a way of making things happen. He was a master swindler. He knew just what to do and say to get what he wanted. Within a few weeks, an old, rusted, white trailer was placed on the land, and we began the move. I was afraid to leave the security of Gram and be left alone with Mom and Ralph. Neither one of them knew how to be a parent. Living with them was like living in Neverland, where no one grew up—except the kids.

The tiny trailer had three bedrooms. Mine had been a storage closet, so small my twin bed and a few toys were the only things to fit in it. Peter had the suite, three times as big as mine with a bathroom. I wanted *that* room as soon as I saw it and had the perfect plan to claim it as mine. I pulled down my pink pajama bottoms and peed on the mustard yellow shag carpet. I was sure he would want to trade after that. I was wrong. The only thing it got me was a spanking. They banished me to my closet for the rest of our first night.

Inside our decrepit trailer, comfort and love were a rarity. Abuse ran deep throughout the home, circulating between the walls as strong as the smell of animal urine. The abuse was the norm, expected, and had even become comfortable. I was desperate to be loved and cherished, but those were luxuries on only the good days.

The unpredictable treatment became expected, but I never knew who might hurt me next. Did I want to make a mess or be naughty so there was a reason someone might hurt me? Or did I want to be on my best behavior so I might miss the next hair pulling or belt lashing? It was a decision I made every day, sometimes every hour.

Ralph was a ticking time bomb. We were all cautious not to provoke him. It was impossible to know what might set him off since it was ever changing. One day, he would share his Dinty Moore beef stew, giving us a bowl. The next, he would swing his arm out to hit us away as our bellies growled while he ate the whole can.

"Get the fuck out of my way, you little vultures. This is *mine*. You can starve until you earn your keep."

Ralph and Mom's relationship was just as sporadic. Nothing was ever the same. One day, I heard Mom groan as I walked into the living room. She was on her back on the filthy carpet floor, piles of dirty laundry surrounding her, and Ralph's naked body on top of her. "Scream for me, baby." Frozen, I stood and watched. "Get the fuck outta here, you little pervert." I ran to my room, threw myself onto my bed, and hid under the covers as I waited for my punishment.

Other times, I walked in as Ralph's hand was around Mom's throat. "You're gonna die, you fat whore." Again, frozen, I watched until I was noticed. "What the fuck are *you* looking at?" Ralph let Mom go and came after me. He pulled off his belt, held it between his hands, and made it *snap*. "You're gonna get *it* now, you little bitch." The buckle stung as it met my bottom. Ralph didn't hit me often, but when he did, the pain was intense. He used the buckle or other times just his hand. When he became enraged, he lost control. One spank quickly turned into five. He became a different person when rage was in his blood.

The psychological abuse was more constant. When I wet my bed, Ralph called me *pisser* or *cunt lapper*. It was embarrassing when I had my accidents, but I couldn't stop. The more I tried, the more I woke up wet. The days Mom felt kind, she did the laundry quick so Ralph wouldn't know. Other days, she announced, "She pissed again." Ralph took me into my room, grabbed me by the head, and rubbed my nose into the urine soaked bed, just as he did to our dogs when they had accidents in the house. "Does that smell good, you little pisser? Huh? Huh? Smarten the fuck up, you animal. We piss in the toilet, not the bed, you dumbfuck."

Ralph antagonized me. It was as though he wasn't happy unless I was scared. He often threatened to beat me, but luckily, he rarely followed through with the threats. There were times he got inches from my face, and in a quiet, deranged voice, repeated words over and over again until they were ingrained in my head. "You're just a stupid little cunt lapper. You're just a stupid little cunt lapper. You're just a stupid little cunt lapper."

When I closed my eyes to go to sleep, the words he spoke swam around my head. Dreams led to nightmares as his words became my beliefs.

12

I was scared of him, but I loved him. He was my dad. I believed the words he spoke to me—they became who I was.

Despite how Ralph treated me, there were times he was proud of me. I was his only child. When he had someone to show me off to, I became his princess. I was the cute, little blonde girl with a smile on her face. I looked like a happy, well-adjusted girl. No one could see my scars inside or out. They had trained me to behave, so the skeletons remained in the closet. I followed the rules, stayed quiet, and maintained the constant ruse of happiness.

When it came to Peter, Ralph despised him. Peter turned ten soon after the year anniversary of Jake's death. Living with Ralph made it hard for Peter to mourn his father. "You're lucky that piece of shit, queer father of yours is dead. He can't see what a fuck-up you are." Ralph muttered as the back of his hand cuffed Peter's face. Peter stood tall, his face red and hazel eyes wet. He remained silent as Ralph continued. "What's the matter? Are you a *queer* too? *Queer boy, queer boy, queer boy.*" Ralph chanted as his hands pushed into Peter's chest.

Peter fell to the floor, and his nostrils flared as he sucked back his tears. "Fuck you," he whispered as he stood up.

"What's that, *queer boy?*"

"Nuttin," Peter grunted as he walked away.

Ralph's abuse toward Peter far surpassed mine. When Ralph started hurting Peter, I was afraid he wouldn't stop. I hid as I watched, squeezing my eyes closed when he made contact with Peter's body, then opened them to make sure he was still alive. I loved Peter, and I didn't like when he was hurt. Peter blamed me for the abuse. Ralph was my father, and because of me, he was in our lives.

Peter and I had a simultaneously close yet distant relationship. When Ralph wasn't around, Peter reenacted the abuse on me. I didn't tell on Peter because I didn't want him punished. I wanted him to love me. He needed me as much as I needed him.

At times, Peter played with me. He taught me how to ride my bike. Every day, after Peter got off the bus from school, he took my baby blue, banana seat bike down to the dirt road and had me sit on it while he held the back. He was never frustrated when I fell.

"Get back on it Jessie. You can do it."

After a few falls, he was right. I did it. He was proud of our accomplishment. Riding my bike allowed me to leave the yard with him. We rode our bikes up and down our long, winding driveway and then the road. Cars rarely drove past us, but when they did, they slowed down and waved.

Now that I could ride my bike, playing cops and robbers became easier. Peter was always the robber, and I was always the cop. My legs were not as long or as strong as his, and I never caught him. I had fun just the same. I loved the time he gave me. It was an escape from the darkness I was trapped in.

Alcohol took the remaining pieces of Mom depression had left behind. Like Peter and me, Mom needed to escape. Living between those walls took pieces of us and shaped us into different people. The air was thick—toxic to breathe, but essential for survival.

When a Budweiser can wasn't in Mom's hand, she was asleep in her room. She was absent from our lives the majority of the time. To spend time with her, I had to sit on her bed. Sometimes, she ignored my presence while other occasions, the monster that ate my mommy came out to play. I tried to break through the wall surrounding her. On rare occasions, I found an opening and was able to feel the love I craved.

During the good times, Mom sang Peter, Paul, and Mary to us. She sang like an angel, her voice mesmerizing. Snuggled next to her on the couch, she sang "Where Have All the Flowers Gone?" It was my favorite because Mom brought beauty to the sadness of the words. Our life was like that song. When would *we* ever learn? When would we find our flowers? I hoped not in graveyards.

When Mom sang, she was herself. It was the only thing stronger than her depression. In those moments, as her voice filled my soul, I knew she loved me. I begged her to sing all the time. She didn't realize her talent and often was annoyed at my request. I wanted time to freeze so I could steal my mom back from the depression that held her hostage.

Like a flower that needs water, her love nourished me. It gave me strength. When she loved me, I felt warm and safe, and I forgot about the pain she caused me. During those moments, I let go of the fear and the memories that caused it. She was my mom, and more than anything, I wanted to be enough and to make the feelings last.

They didn't. Mom yelled and called me names. "You stupid little bitch. You dumb little whore." I couldn't get out of the firing range fast enough. Her words seared my soul, reaching the same places her songs did. The damage her words left was covered by scar tissue. She unleashed bottled up anger on me—a rage bottled inside her from a lifetime of never being good enough.

She started fights to justify hitting me. In the beginning, I stood in front of her while I received her wrath. My world went black as the mother I wanted love from beat me until she was tired. As I got older, I attempted to outrun her and hid on my bed, my hands locked over my butt, my head pressed into my pillow. She caught up to me. "You think you're pretty smart? Not like I can't see you," she wailed as she pried my hands away from my bottom. She slapped me until my skin was raw, yelling between each blow. I shriveled up inside myself to create a distance between where I was and where I wanted to be.

Other times, she pulled my long, blonde hair by my bangs and smashed my head against the wall. "Look at what you made me do.

I hope you're happy." My head bounced off the wall after each blow. "If you just behaved, this wouldn't happen. Why can't you be a *good* girl?"

I didn't know. Why *couldn't* I just be a good girl? I didn't know what I did to make her hate me. I didn't know why some moments she loved me while others she tried to kill me. *I didn't know.*

Mom never hurt Peter. She loved him. Peter did things to be helpful, and she praised him for it. When Mom knew Peter had hurt me, he never got into trouble. She often spanked me for making Peter *have* to hurt me. I wasn't upset she loved Peter. I was grateful someone loved him. I loved him, but I was *nobody*.

CHAPTER 4

*W*e acquired pets of all kinds—dogs, cats, ducks, geese, chickens, rabbits, guinea pigs, a goat, and pigs. We were overrun with animals. At least seven large dogs were living inside and another seven outside. In the living room, there were two incubators used to hatch duck and goose eggs. When it was too cold outside, livestock came inside. At times, there were rabbits, chickens, geese, ducks and a goat roaming the trailer along with the dogs and cats that always lived inside.

Peter helped Ralph build a huge barn, a way to contain the continuous flow of animals. I lost count after five hundred geese and one thousand ducks. It sounds excessive, and at times unbelievable, but it was true. When people hear about our animals, I can almost guarantee they think I am exaggerating. I wish I were.

Weekends were often spent at auctions buying yet another breed of duck or goose. We were almost in competition with ourselves, not satisfied until the money was gone and our yard was full of animals. After the auctions, we wouldn't have money left for the things we needed—like food. When this happened, we gathered into the car and went to the local grocery store after hours to go dumpster diving.

We sang a song as we drove there, as though this was a joyful family outing: *"Dumpster diving, dumpster diving, you can bring your mother and your brother! If you need it, you will find it dumpster diving. Come on, everyone. Let's go dumpster diving!"* As a child, this was fun and helped us not be hungry. It was a regular part of our lives, something I assumed others did as well. We thought it was normal.

Mom encouraged Peter and me to climb into the filthy dumpster to dig out food. The smell of rotting flesh overpowered our senses. Black flies buzzed around our heads. We swatted them away as we scoured for treasure. We took all we found, the trunk of our car full. Mom and Ralph never climbed in but always took what we handed them. I was proud to be able to help.

When the food was too rancid to eat, we fed it to our pigs. They squealed with excitement as they gobbled down the food. I spent a lot of time in the pigpen. Many times, I curled up on the wood shavings inside the pen and took naps as I hugged the pigs that would let me. They were babies when we got them. They each had a name and were some of my favorite pets. As they got bigger and older, they took up more space in the pen, and I had less room to play. I continued to spend time there, often volunteering to feed them.

One morning, I heard the beeping of a box truck backing into the yard. I peeked out the window and saw Ralph and a man dressed in navy blue coveralls. As they walked closer to the pigpen, I yelled to Mom, "What's going on out there? Why are—"

"Your friends are leaving."

"What do you mean, Mommy?"

"Oink, oink." I heard her laugh as she taunted me.

My face still pressed against the window, I watched as Ralph and the other man chased my friends. I could hear the blood-curdling squeals as they avoided capture for as long as possible. One by one, they boarded the slaughter truck. "Mommy, please, make them stop. Mommy, *please*."

"Stop your nonsense, Jessie. Pigs are to *eat*."

I ran to my room where I placed my pillow over my head. I didn't want to hear my friends scream, but it was so loud I had no choice. I didn't get a chance to hug them goodbye. My heart hurt as I imagined how afraid they were. I knew what being afraid felt like and didn't want anyone else to experience that.

A few nights later at dinner, Ralph snickered as he looked at me. "Jessie, how does Wilbur taste?"

My fork dropped. "Wha...what do you mean?"

"What do *you* think I mean?" His head tilted back as he laughed.

My throat closed as I looked down at my plate. Had I just taken a bite of him? They were feeding me pieces of my friend I couldn't save.

I ran from the table to my room, but they soon forced me to rejoin everyone. Peter made pig noises while Ralph laughed. Mom told them to stop as she held back her laughter. *How was this funny?* I refused to eat my dinner, but they forced me to sit at the table until my food was gone. After hours of protesting, Mom scraped the food into the garbage and pretended I had eaten it. Otherwise, I would have stayed there all night if it meant not eating Wilbur.

In an attempt to heal my wounds, Mom let me pick a kitten from our Siamese cat's litter. I choose a white girl with dark ears and blue eyes. I named her Sapphire. She was a sweet kitten, playful and full of love.

One afternoon Ralph yelled from the end of our driveway. "Jessie, get yur ass down here." He laughed from his belly. "Get the fuck down here."

I giggled with excitement as I ran to him. "What's so funny?"

He pointed under the wheel of one of his junk cars. "Look. Look at *that*." Laughter returned as he saw my face.

"*No*." Sapphire's mangled body was lifeless. I kneeled and stroked her dirty fur. "Please, no."

"Get the fuck away from her, you sicko. She's *dead*."

I ran back up the driveway and begged Mom to call Gram. I had to see her. She could make it better for me—she was the only one.

Gram came right over and took me to her house. She was disgusted at what had happened and demanded Ralph remove the kitten before she brought me back. She knew things were not *right* at home, but she had no idea what was really going on. The incident with the kitten had Gram asking questions, but I didn't answer them. She knew I was hiding something.

"Pull your pants down, Jessie. I want to see what you're not telling me."

I paused as I unbuttoned my pants and let them drop.

She lifted up my shirt and gasped. I was covered in bruises and handprints. She sighed as she discovered the secrets I had tried to keep.

"Jessie, who is hurting you? Who is hitting you? I'll kill them."

I stayed quiet and began to cry.

"Come on, honey. I need to know so I can make them stop."

I didn't speak. I was embarrassed. Gram wasn't supposed to know I wasn't strong enough to protect myself or that sometimes, I was naughty. I was terrified. What was going to happen to me when Mom and Ralph found out someone knew?

Gram rushed to the phone. I could hear her yelling, "God damn it, Wendy! Who in the hell has been laying their hands on Jessie? You tell me right now!"

She was quiet as she listened to Mom explain.

"She didn't say anything. I was giving her a bath when I saw the marks." A wave of relief washed over me. She saved me.

I stayed with Gram longer than normal that time. Peter came to visit her too. He wasn't able to stay long. He had to get back home to help with chores and the barn. He was now—at eleven years old —in charge of building. When he arrived at Gram's house, she quizzed him. She asked him all the same questions she had asked me, and he tried to take the blame. "Nah, Gram, it's me. Jessie's so annoying. Sometimes I just smack her to keep her away." His eyes went to the floor as he tried to hide his lies. She didn't believe him but stopped the interrogation because she sensed our fear.

When Gram brought me home, I was afraid Mom was going to be angry. I sat in Gram's car while she talked to Mom.

"I will be coming to get Jessie and Peter on the weekends. You two need a break."

"We're fine, Mom." She crossed her arms tight against her denim overalls. "We are doing just fine."

"I'm not asking. I'm telling. The kids will be with me on weekends."

"What? You don't think I know what I'm doing?"

"For God's sakes, Wendy. I just want to help. I want these kids safe."

"They are safe, Mom. Jessie is accident-prone, you know that."

"It's not a choice, Wendy. I'll see you next weekend." Gram got back in her car and told me to call her if I needed her to come back.

I took my bag of clothes and walked over to Mom. She wrapped her arms around me and kissed the top of my head. Confused, I pulled away and waved as Gram left.

"You're safe, Jessie. *Right?*"

I nodded as I walked inside.

Todd, our eight-year-old neighbor, was playing with Peter in the yard. He asked if we wanted to come over to play. Peter and I spent as much time as possible at his house. He had an older brother and sister who we also played with. In the summer, we swam in their pool and rode bikes together. They had snacks, and sometimes, they invited us for lunch.

Todd liked to play house. He had different rules and got upset when I questioned him.

"I don't havta play wit you. If you be a jerk, I can play house with my other friends."

"What do I have to do?"

"I told ya. We havta be married. We havta kiss. You havta kiss me."

"I don't wanna."

"Then I don't wanna be friends."

"No. Please be my friend."

"Then you havta kiss me." He puckered up his lips and stuck them in my face.

I quickly kissed his lips.

"Now we can be friends."

Each time we played house, Todd had more rules. I didn't want to make him mad, so I did what he asked, even when it didn't feel right. Like at home, Todd told me what we did was our secret. He said if I told anyone, he would never talk to me again.

"You know what else married people do?"

I shook my head no.

"They fuck. And I wanna fuck you."

"I don't wanna do that."

"You havta, or else."

I closed my eyes tight as he rubbed his hand over my chest, and then between my legs.

"You havta let me if you wanna play."

His pants fell to the top of his shoes, and he fumbled with my button. "Take 'em off, or else."

I unbuttoned my pants and let them fall around my ankles. He walked closer to me until his penis touched my skin. He pressed his body into mine as we stood together. He grunted as he tried to figure out what he was supposed to do. My stomach churned as I waited for him to stop, and I kept my eyes clamped shut so I didn't have to watch.

"You needa make noise too, or it ain't gonna work."

I mimicked his noises as I wished for it to end.

"I think I'm done." He pulled up his pants.

I pulled mine back up, and he left. Ashamed, I walked home through the wooded path. I just wanted to be his friend.

Another skeleton added to the closet.

CHAPTER 5

"*Jesssss-ica.*"

The angelic voice woke me from a sound sleep. I sat up in bed as I looked for the loving woman who spoke my name. I tiptoed into Mom and Ralph's room to find them asleep. I walked to Peter's room. He was out cold. It wasn't them.

I felt warmth in my heart as the voice echoed in my mind. I walked around the trailer some more to be sure I wasn't missing someone who wanted to love me. There was no one there. I crawled under my Rainbow Bright sheets and tried to fall back asleep. I smiled as I imagined who it might have been. Hearing the kindness and love made me desperate to find her. I yearned for the comfort she offered.

When Mom woke up, I asked her, "Did you hear someone calling my name last night?"

She looked at me with a puzzled expression. "No. What are you talking about?"

"A nice lady called my name. I looked for her, but—"

"Stop it, Jessie. It's too early for this bullshit."

"Mommy, it's not bullshit."

"God damn it, Jessie. *Drop it.*"

When I went to Gram's, I told her about the mysterious woman. Gram smiled as she listened.

"Do you know who it was, Grammy?"

"I don't, honey, but I bet it was your guardian angel. Everybody has an angel watching over them, but only the special ones ever meet them."

"But I didn't meet her. I couldn't find her." Sadness replaced my excitement.

"Yes, but she found *you,* and you heard her. That makes *you* special, Jessie."

"Do you think she sees *everything?*"

"I think she sees what she needs to. Just know, when you need her, she is there. Don't ever forget that."

It brought great comfort to know I had someone watching over me. My angel wasn't the only one who watched over me. I had a group of imaginary friends who presented themselves as ghosts. They lived in my bedroom closet and came out to play when I was in my room. When I cried after being hurt, they comforted me. I spent many hours talking to them, telling them the secrets I couldn't tell anyone else. They were the only friends I had until I started school.

After I turned five, I started kindergarten. I was timid during my first few days at Westville School, but I was the only child out of the seven in my class who didn't cry when their mom left. I was relieved to have the break from the chaos.

I grew to love school and adored my teacher, Ms. Farmer. I wanted to make her proud, so I paid close attention. I was a quick study, and the more I learned, the more I loved her.

With such a small class, we all became friends. I was invited to birthday parties and was never excluded. As I spent time with my classmates and their families, I began to see how our lives were very different. I was embarrassed by Mom and Ralph and how we lived.

Summer vacation took me by surprise. I didn't want a vacation from school. I wanted a vacation from home. Ms. Farmer hugged me goodbye. I clung tight to her as she stroked my hair.

"Thank you for being such a good girl this year, Jessica."

"I love you, Ms. Farmer. I don't want to leave you."

"Oh, honey, enjoy your summer. We will see each other next year when you are a first grader."

"But I don't wanna be a first grader. I wanna be with you."

She laughed as she gave me a squeeze. "Oh, you'll be fine next year." She let go and looked in my tear stained eyes. "You're a smart girl, Jessica. You have made me proud."

Goose bumps grew on my arms as a smile took over my face. She really meant what she said. She *believed* in me. "I'll see ya next year, Ms. Farmer. I promise."

That became a promise I couldn't keep.

CHAPTER 6

*W*hen Ralph left for work, Mom started bringing Peter and me to her friend Bill's house. Bill lived on top of a steep hill in an old, worn down white two-story house. The inside of the house was meager, just big enough for a bachelor. It was dingy but spotless.

Bill was six inches shorter than Mom was. His thinning, dark brown, curly hair covered his glasses. His eyes were blue but bloodshot. "Hey, man, it's mighty nice to meet you guys." He toasted the air with his Budweiser can. "Yur mom's a real great lady. Yur some lucky kids." He stumbled to give Mom a hug.

I had never seen this side of Mom before. She was happy. Bill handed her a Budweiser. As she cracked it open, she looked over at us. "Don't you darlings go telling Ralph about this." She took a sip from the can. "Not unless you wanna die. He'll kill me, and then you."

"He wouldn't."

"Oh, don't be an asshole, Jessie. This is our secret. You cannot tell anyone. Got it?"

I nodded as I looked up at her. Ralph was mean, but he wasn't a murderer. Ralph was my dad, and it upset me to think Mom was so happy with someone else.

Peter and I sat downstairs on Bill's lime green vinyl couch while Mom went upstairs with him to have sex. We heard them and were unsure what to do, so we sat in silence and looked at each other waiting for them to finish. As they walked down the stairs, Bill buttoned his shirt while Mom kissed him. "Hey, man, I got some really cool shit up here. Com'on. Take a look-see."

Peter stood up, itched his head. "Yeah, sure man."

I grabbed Peter's hand and followed. At the top of the steps, there were rooms on each side. To the right, there was a pinball machine, and to the left was a three-foot stuffed panda bear, which sat on top of a double bed covered with a light blue blanket.

"Whoa. That's cool, man. Can I play with it?" Peter pulled his hand away from mine.

"Sorry, dude. It ain't workin'."

"That fuckin' sucks."

Mom giggled as she watched Peter and Bill interact. I tugged on her shirt. "Mommy, I wanna go home."

She slapped my hand off her. "Stop it, Jessie. Be polite."

"I wanna go home. Ralph will be home soon."

Mom looked at the clock on the wall. "Shit. She's right. We gotta get outta here."

Peter and I walked out to the car and waited for Mom. She took forever. In the car, she reminded us how important it was for us not to tell Ralph where we were. We agreed. After all, what was one more secret? It took us ten minutes to get home from Bill's house. We were late. Ralph was already home. My heart raced, and butterflies took over my stomach as I planned my next move.

Ralph met us at the car. "Where in the fuck were you?"

"We...we...we were just going for a r-ride, right, kids?"

Peter and I shook our heads in unison and scattered. Ralph was out of control. He hated it when he didn't know where we were at all times. I didn't want Ralph to hurt Mom. *Was he going to kill her? Was she right? Was he going to kill me?* I swallowed hard as I tried to think about something else. I didn't want to die, not at six. I wasn't ready. I needed Peter too. He couldn't die. And Mom, I needed her.

Hours later, Peter and I huddled together on the kitchen floor with Mom, hiding from Ralph. With all the doors locked, we waited for him to leave. My fear at that moment was one I had never experienced before. It was paralyzing.

I winced with every knock, kick and sound Ralph made. We held each other closer. The last thing I remember was seeing Ralph's large hand break through the tiny glass window of the trailer door, and his hand fumbling for the doorknob. My memory stops there. As hard as I try to relive that moment, I cannot. I remember the terror like it happened yesterday, but I don't remember if he got in or what happened next. I imagine there are many memories forever wiped from my memory bank as a way to protect myself and for that, I am grateful.

The fear from that night inspired Mom to leave Ralph. "Start packing your stuff, and hurry before Ralph gets back home."

Peter and I looked at each other. "Where are we going this time?" Peter asked.

"Back to Grammy's?" I hoped I was right.

"No, don't be silly. We're going to move in with Bill. No more questions. Now get packing."

We shoved our belongings into trash bags and stuffed them into the back of Mom's car.

Bill assured us we were safe with him. He didn't have a gun, but he had nunchucks. He took them out and showed us how he used them—although in slow motion because of all the beer that he had already consumed. He also had throwing stars he demonstrated. He said if Ralph came near us, he would kill him with one. Bill didn't make me feel safe. I was still scared—scared for Ralph and scared for us.

All of the animals we had collected were now just an inconvenience. Mom found homes for all of them. The only animal we could take with us was one of our dogs, Zuul. She was a doberman pit bull, and she was my protector.

It didn't take long for Bill to change his mind. He didn't want Zuul to stay. He antagonized her. He snuck up behind her and pulled her tail. She growled at him, which gave him the leverage to get rid of her. I was heartbroken as we drove her to her new home. I didn't want to say goodbye. With Zuul gone, I had lost everything that mattered to me.

It got worse… When it was time to enter first grade, I was outraged when I learned the move came with a new school. "But Mom! I promised Ms. Farmer I'd see her again. She'll think I lied to her." I couldn't stop crying. I disappointed one of the only people who loved me.

"Don't be ridiculous. She doesn't even remember *you*."

"Fuck you."

Her hand hit my face. "How dare you talk to me that way, you little bitch."

I spat in her face. "*You* talk to me *that* way."

She grabbed my bangs and hit my head into the door casing. "You little bitch. Get into the car. It's the first day of fuckin' school."

I put my backpack on and walked to the car. We rode in silence to the new school. It was less than five minutes away. Once there, I slammed the car door and walked into the crowd of strangers alone. There were many more kids at this school than at my old one.

A kind, older woman walked over to me. "You must be Jessica. I'm Mrs. Bess." She reached her hand out to shake mine. "Don't be scared, honey. We're all friends here."

I wiped the tearstains off my face and stood next to the first-grade door. I watched as kids played while I tried to figure out who was in my class. Mrs. Bess blew her whistle and kids ran toward me forming a line by each door. I walked to the end of the line, as I attempted to blend in.

Mrs. Bess was right—everyone was nice. I was soon friends with all twenty-one kids in my class. School was the only thing I was good at, and I excelled in both reading and math. I beamed with pride when I received my work back with smiley faces and stickers. For a few hours a day, I was a normal six-year-old. I played, didn't worry, and I wasn't afraid.

I settled into the new chaos at Bill's house. I had visitations with Ralph every other weekend. On the opposite weekends, I went to Gram's house. Mom said it was better if I went away on the weekends because she and Bill had parties at the house. I didn't need an excuse to go to Gram's house—I couldn't wait to get there.

One Friday, I was so sick I couldn't go, though. I had a migraine that kept me home from school. If I was too sick to go to Gram's, I was *very ill*. Mom came up to my room to tell me about what was going to happen. "A lot of people are on their way here. Don't leave your room. Just keep sleeping, don't pay any attention to the music."

My head was killing me. It was about to burst from all the pain. Even the thought of noise made me cry. I stayed in my bed as people started to arrive. As the night went on, the noise grew. The music was blaring, and the people downstairs were just as loud. My bedroom was en route to the bathroom. Drunken people stumbled through my toys, and some even sat on my bed and talked to me. I didn't know these people. They were Bill's friends.

One woman stayed with me and rubbed my back. "It's okay, honey. I'll try to make them keep it down." Her brown eyes were so kind, I wished she were my mom. She cared that I was in pain. When she went back down to the party, I heard her ask them to turn it down. They just laughed at her.

I heard Mom say, "She'll be fine. She's just trying to ruin our fun."

Hearing her say that stung more than usual. A stranger loved me more. By three o'clock in the morning, the last person had passed out, the stereo clicked off as the cassette tape ended, and I was in too much pain to sleep. After that, I made sure I was always away on weekends.

Bill was a hard person to read. One minute, he was fun, and the next, he was someone you didn't want to be around. He watched porn on the living room TV after he got home from work, often making Peter watch it with him. The noises from the women on the screen made me look, and when I did, I saw too much. I was careful not to let Bill see me. I didn't want him to make me watch too.

Bill started taking an interest in me—paying particular attention and giving me things. He was very sexual and always wanted to see me naked. He took a shower every night when he got home from work, and sometimes, he volunteered to have me join him to "help" Mom. I didn't want to take showers with him. It felt weird. He touched himself under the water and made me watch. I told Mom, but she said to stop making up stories.

This kind of thing continued. At night, Bill was in bed next to Mom, and he would call me to their room to say goodnight. Often he'd pull his penis out of the side of his underwear, so I had to see it. He stroked his penis while he looked at me. Mom said and did nothing.

One night, he made me sit on his face. I didn't know what to do, but I wanted to keep him happy. As I contemplated how to do what he asked, Mom rolled over with her book. I wanted her to get me out of it, but she didn't offer any help. I climbed onto their bed and stood over him. He stuck his tongue out and patted his face as he smiled. I squatted over his face with my Care Bear underwear on with my nightgown over them. When I felt his breath, I jumped off and ran to my room.

Bill would force me to touch his penis. He wouldn't let me leave until I did. I kneeled by the edge of the bed, my eyes closed and my hand hovering over his briefs. He pulled his penis to the side and placed my hand on top of it. I wanted to squeeze it, to hurt him, but I was afraid.

I tried to avoid their room at night and hollered good night from my bed. Bill demanded I say it in person. Once in there, he asked me to kiss his penis. My stomach cringed at the thought. *When was Mom going to do something?* She sighed as I stood there. She folded her arms and rolled over. I did as I was told. I quickly bent down, kissed him on the top of his underwear, and then hurried to bed.

The next morning before school, Mom took me by the collar of my shirt. "You better leave my man alone. He's mine, not yours. Don't you *ever* forget that." She tightened her grip and pressed me into the wall. "We'll be homeless if you keep it up."

I was confused. I didn't like what Bill did yet I was being blamed for it. "Make *your man* stop touching *me*."

She slapped my face. "If you didn't like it so much, he wouldn't do it!"

"I'm gonna tell Ralph what Bill does to me."

"If you tell anyone, *you* will go to jail for being dirty. Normal little girls *don't* do that kind of stuff. You're crazy just like your father."

Another skeleton added to my closet.

Soon after this, Mom found out she was pregnant. I had mixed feelings about the news. I was excited to have someone to play with, but I was also upset this meant we were tied to Bill. There was no way out if Mom had a baby. Everything would change, and I wasn't sure if the change would be for better or worse.

The pregnancy made Mom quit drinking. She gave Bill an ultimatum—stop partying or lose his family. To our surprise, he complied and never looked back. Life began to calm down. Bill became more like a dad to Peter and me, and Mom settled down as she prepared for the baby.

As time got closer to the baby's birth, I became more excited. I couldn't wait to meet my sibling that was growing in Mom's belly.

I turned seven that summer, and the anticipation grew. I spent more and more time at Gram's house as the baby took Mom's energy. On July 31, as Gram tucked me in, I told her, "I'm gonna wake up and have a baby sister!"

That next morning, Gram woke me with exciting news. My new baby sister had been born that morning. I didn't fully understand what having a baby meant or how fragile they were. I wanted to go to the hospital to meet her and see Mom, but Mom wasn't up to having visitors. The excitement overpowered the disappointment, and I patiently waited for Mom and my sister to arrive home.

After what felt like an eternity, Gram took me home to meet the baby. "Katherine Joan," Mom announced as she moved the soft, pink blanket off my sister's face. I was so excited. I wanted to hold her. I wanted to play with her. Overwhelmed by my excitement, Mom asked Gram to take me back to her house. She was worried I might hurt the baby. Her words crushed me—I was sad I wasn't welcome at home to be a part of the new family.

Gram saw how upset I was and tried to explain how exhausting new babies were. "You're lucky you don't have to be there, Jessie. Babies aren't any fun at this age. All they do is sleep, eat, and cry." I began to have second thoughts about this baby. I was glad to stay with Gram where it was quiet, and I had all of her attention.

After my sister's birth, it became apparent to me Gram was my family, and I was an intruder anywhere else. She was always there for me and never turned me away. When someone hurt me, she did her best to fix it. Gram was my rock and my best friend. At seven years old, I knew she was where I could find love anytime I needed it. All I had to do was be myself—she never asked for anything in return. This piece of knowledge kept me alive more times than I can count.

CHAPTER 7

Mom and Ralph shared a mutual animosity for one another. Being with them was toxic. The hatred oozed from their skin. Mom didn't let me talk about Ralph when I was with her unless I wanted to say negative things about him, and Ralph spent all of our time together bad-mouthing Mom. I had a hard time knowing what was real and what was made up, who to trust and who to love.

After one of the many conversations with Mom, I asked her, "If you hate Ralph so much, why did you have me?"

"It wasn't my choice." She paused as her face turned red. "He delivered wood to Gram's house when Peter and I lived there. He fooled me."

"Fooled you? How?"

"With his coke bottle glasses, his greasy comb-over under his golf hat, and the missing teeth. I thought he was an old man. I felt sorry for him, so when he asked me out, I said yes. I didn't want to be rude."

"Huh?"

"He's a liar. He wasn't old, he was twenty-five, he was a year younger than I was. He schemed me into it."

"But I don't understand."

"God damn it. He raped me. Are you happy now?" She stared into my eyes. "You're only here because I didn't have an abortion. Everyone wanted me to kill you, but I said no. I fought for you."

My mouth dropped open as I looked at her. I fought back the tears. "*Everyone?*"

"Yes, even your perfect Grammy."

Hearing this as a child made me question many things. It made me wonder how Gram, someone I loved so much, wanted to *kill* me. I wondered why Mom, who often acted as if she didn't love me, fought so hard to have me. It just didn't add up.

When I saw Gram, it was hard to hide how upset I was. It was as if I didn't even know her. I loved her so much I didn't know how to handle the news. "Grammy, why'd you want Mommy to kill me?"

"Oh, honey, what are you talking about? I never wanted your Mommy to kill you." She caressed my curly, blonde hair and wiped the tears from my cheeks.

"Mommy said you told her not to have me, that you didn't want me."

"Honey, when I told your mom that, I didn't know you. I know you now, and I love you. I'm so glad your mommy didn't listen to me."

With her explanation, it all clicked. People didn't want to kill *me*. It wasn't *me* they didn't want, but the situation. The whole world was not against me after all. I later found out Mom and Ralph went to Atlantic City, New Jersey, for a mini-vacation and that was how I was conceived. I think it was easier for Mom to say she was raped than to admit she liked Ralph enough to agree to have consensual sex at least one time before I was born.

Ralph had Marfan syndrome, a genetic disorder that affected his connective tissue. He was six foot three, with a large frame, and a rounded chest, almost like a reversed hunch back. His blue eyes were huge when looking through his thick glasses and his thinning, dirty-blond hair stuck to his head from lack of hygiene. Most of his teeth rotted away, leaving just a couple dangling from his gums.

He was picked on as a boy due to his appearance, so he learned to trust no one. When I was five, he had his first heart attack due to his condition. Mom called an ambulance, and they told her she had saved his life. After their break up, she regretted that decision. She wished for his death and reminded me the doctor had given him ten years to live, adding a countdown at the end. "Only seven more years."

Ralph also had paranoid schizophrenia. He didn't agree and refused all medications related to his mental illness. Some days, his anger was out of control, and he couldn't see beyond it. Fixated on a thought, he acted without being present.

One afternoon, Mom picked Peter and I up from school early and rushed us to the community mental health center. Ralph called her earlier and threatened to kill her, Peter, and me. He had made similar threats before—this time was different. This time he said he had a gun.

The staff at the center called Ralph. "Ralph? This is Diane from Kingdom Mental Health."

I heard his voice blast through the receiver. "What the fuck do you want? Is that fat whore there?"

"Ralph. Can I help you? I want to—"

"Shut the fuck up! That bitch and those bastards of hers need to die."

"You don't mean that."

"Shut the fuck up! You don't know what she's done. What

they've done. They need to die, and I'm not gonna stop until I see blood."

As I listened, I felt nauseous. He didn't love me. He *did* want to kill me. I was scared. I didn't want to die. I thought about never seeing Gram again, or my friends, or my toys. I thought about never growing up and being a mom.

"Mommy, I'm gonna be sick. My belly hurts."

Mom brought me to the bathroom. "See, Jessie, I told you he was a monster."

The emotions boiled out through my eyes. I wanted a daddy who loved me. I wanted a mommy who cared about me. I had neither. "I just wanna go home, Mommy."

"Don't be silly. We can't go anywhere with that lunatic out there. Unless you'd like to die. Is that what you want? To die?"

I was too upset to respond. I collapsed on the floor and sobbed. I wanted the nightmare to be over. We stayed at the center for hours, until Ralph admitted he didn't have a gun and he wasn't going to kill us. I don't know if the police intervened or why they believed him, but we were free to go.

Despite this threat, Mom still sent me on my scheduled weekend visitation. I was on guard the whole time. I wasn't sure if he was going to kill me when he had the chance or if I was safe. The hours passed so slowly that weekend as I sat wondering if my life was going to end before my eighth birthday. Ralph, on the other hand, acted as though nothing had happened.

I never knew what Ralph was capable of and Mom fed that fear. "Make sure you keep your room clean. Ralph goes through our things when we're gone."

"What do you mean, Mommy?"

"He's always watching us. He's probably up on that hill peering into the window." She pointed behind me.

"Why would he do that?"

"Because he's crazy. He wants to prove I'm unfit so he can steal you from me."

I lived in a constant state of fear. I never knew if someone was watching me or going to jump out of the woods to kidnap me. Although it was nerve-racking, I wasn't sure it would be a bad thing if someone stole me. Since Mom and Ralph split up, he didn't hit me anymore, and he never called me names when I was with him. He was always on his best behavior.

He took me out to eat every night we were together to McDonald's or for pizza. We went to the movies often, and every weekend ended with a new toy. He was fun to be with, and most of the time, I would have his undivided attention.

It was so difficult to shift between being afraid of Ralph when we weren't together and loving him when we were. I always had to change who I was and who I loved. Fear always lingered as I worried what might happen if Ralph and Mom ran into each other. The unknown haunted me.

Mom and Ralph fought a gruesome battle in court—I was the grand prize. Neither one of them had money to pay for lawyers, so their mothers picked up the tab. Both of my grandmothers spent thousands of dollars to protect me, but neither saw the big picture.

Both of my grandmothers spent their life savings to protect me. They both loved me very much. I was Gram's favorite grandchild and my grandmother's only. Their hearts were in the right place, but thousands of dollars were wasted as their children fought a war unable to be won.

One Christmas Eve, I was with Ralph at his cousin Stan's house. I was scheduled to return home so I could wake up Christmas morning with Mom, Peter, and Kate. The lawyer Mom hired to stack visitations in her favor made an error when she wrote up the documents for court. All past documents stated I was to return home on Christmas Eve. This time she forgot to add that detail. She also added I was to stay with Ralph over the whole Christmas break. Mom didn't notice this mistake—Ralph did. He noticed everything. He kept the secret quiet and pounced at the right moment. He was an intelligent man and always came up with ways to be ahead of Mom and the rest of the world.

Ralph unleashed his plan. "You're staying with me tonight, Jessie."

"Why? It's Christmas Eve. I wanna be home for Santa."

"What? You don't love me enough to stay with me?" His voice rose louder. This had been the first time he yelled at me since my visitations started.

Not able to look into his eyes, I hid behind my hair as the tears fell.

Stan saw how upset I was as I pressed my face against the window. "Come on, Ralph. It's Christmas. Let her go home to be with her family. It's not her fault you hate her bitch of a mother."

"Mind your fuckin' business."

I listened as Ralph called Mom to tell her the news. "I'm keeping her from you like you keep her from me."

I imagined Mom tried to talk him out of it, but I was too far from Ralph to hear.

"Merry fuckin' Christmas." The phone slammed into the receiver as he laughed.

I wished for Santa to save me. I begged him to make Ralph see what he was doing. *Santa, please take my presents back and get me home.* As the night went on, I knew I wasn't going home. Ralph took me to his mom's house where he was living. My grandmother was surprised to see me. "Ralph, what's going on? Why is Jessie still here?"

"Mind your own fuckin' business. She's *my* kid. I can do what I want with her. Her mother doesn't own her. Shut the fuck up! Go to fuckin' bed. It's late. Tomorrow's Christmas." The words rolled off his tongue so fast, so loud my eardrums rang.

My grandmother got up out of her chair and walked me into the bathroom to get me ready for bed. She took a warm washcloth and washed the dirt and tears off my face. She tucked me into bed, kissed my forehead, and whispered, "Sweet dreams, Jessie."

I fought sleep in protest. I listened as my grandmother tried to talk Ralph into returning me home. "She's just a little girl. She doesn't understand why she can't go home. It's Christmas, Ralph. Take her home."

Exhaustion won, and I fell asleep. When I woke up early the next morning, Ralph had my stuff by the door. "Merry Christmas, Jessie. Get in the car. You're going home." Maybe Santa helped, or maybe it was my grandmother, or maybe Ralph saw how much he was hurting me. It didn't matter what changed his mind, only that he was taking me home. As he pulled up to Bill's house, he got out of the car and gave me a hug. "Be a good girl. I'll see you in two weeks." He didn't say a word about the night before. It was as though it had never happened.

When I got inside, everyone was already downstairs opening their stockings. "Why didn't you wait for me?" I started to cry.

"It's Christmas. It's not their fault *your* dad's an asshole. Why should they be punished too?" Mom looked up at me with anger. "Stop crying and go get your stocking."

I was devastated. I wanted more than anything to be home with my family, but it appeared they didn't even care I was missing. I *really* was just a pawn. From that moment on, I understood I was a possession to fight over. My parents were not fighting to protect me. They were fighting to hurt each other. I was the prize that no one wanted.

Ralph said he would fight for me until my mom was dead. Mom said the same about him. The threats from Ralph were to kill all three of us, and Mom's plan was to kill Peter, me, and then herself. I believed the rest of my childhood, however short it may have been, would be spent in a constant battle of tug-of-war. I was wrong. My world was about to be forever changed.

Again.

CHAPTER 8

Soon after Kate was born, we ran out of space at Bill's house. Mom and Bill didn't have money to buy a bigger house, but Gram did. Mom asked Gram if she wanted to look for a place big enough for all of us. Gram knew our house was too small and wanted to help. Mom and Bill found homes to show her, but Gram wasn't happy with their choices. The houses they found had just a tiny room for Gram, and she wanted more space. "Wendy, if I'm buying it, I want to be happy."

"God, Mom, you're never happy with anything I do."

"Stop it, Wendy. If you didn't mess everything up, I'd be happy."

By spring, they found the perfect solution—a house with a trailer on seven acres of land in Johnsville. I was excited to be able to visit Gram anytime I wanted, but I was upset I had to change schools again. When I returned from April vacation, I was the new girl again. There were four times as many kids at this school than in my previous one. I had my first taste of cliques and popular kids

—I despised both. I spent the rest of the school year looking for others who felt the same. It was a hard task, and I failed.

Ralph also moved. He asked his new girlfriend, Ann, to marry him, and I lost the majority of his attention. I hated Ann. She looked like a witch. She had long, straw black hair and a pointy nose. She was as mean as she was ugly. For whatever reason, she made Ralph happy—that was the only thing that made her tolerable. Ralph spent less time with me and left me at my grandmother's house for most of our weekends together.

By the end of fifth grade, I was antsy for summer vacation. I was staying with Gram, and she walked me over to Mom's house where we sat in her living room, in the dark, waiting for her to return from taking Bill to work.

The kitchen door flung open, and Mom rushed down the hall to Peter's room. "Let's start planning the party. Ralph's dead!"

I sat in shock as the words circled in my head. Gram hollered, "Wendy, you better quiet down this instant!"

I turned to look at Gram with tears running down my face. She reached over and held onto me. Mom made her way to the living room and the excitement left as her face lost color. She hadn't intended to give me the news that way—she had no idea we were there.

Her words continued to bounce around my head. I had always been afraid of losing Gram, but never did I think I should worry about losing anyone else. "Is he really gone?" I whispered through the tears and looked up at Mom as I waited for her to say it was a joke.

She looked down her glasses at me. "Yeah, he's gone. Ann met me at Bill's work and said Ralph died last night at the hospital." She paused for a minute, putting her hand on my head in an attempt to comfort me. "Ann said he was up on the roof working on the addition, and he fell to the ground. She said he was bleeding from his mouth—"

Gram stopped her before she went on. "God damn it, Wendy! Would you just shut up? She's a *child*. She doesn't need to hear all this." Her anger was camouflaged by her sadness. At that moment everything shifted. The order of life and death became obscure, and I realized anyone could die at any time. My obsession with death and all it encompassed was born.

The minutes, hours and days that followed are a blur with particular moments forever etched into my memory. The feel of the warm grass between my toes as I moped through the front yard to Mom's garden. Anger and sadness were out of my control. I watched *My Girl* over and over again and cried as Thomas J. passed away. I felt Anna's pain. I was aware of everything and yet nothing.

I wanted to go to sleep, then wake up and have it be over. I wanted to go back in time and get another hug from Ralph. I wanted to tell him I loved him and call him Dad. That was something I never did. The last few years of his life, I barely spoke to him. I was afraid to say something that might get Mom and Bill in trouble.

Regret replaced my thoughts. *What if I had called him Dad? What if I had talked to him? What if I were there when he fell, could I have saved him? What if seeing me could have made him come back to life? What if he didn't know I loved him? What if he thought I hated him? What if…?* These questions seemed endless, and the more I ruminated, the more I took responsibility for his death.

I walked into the bathroom as Mom brushed her teeth. I paused at the door. "Mom, do you think Ralph went to Heaven or Hell?" I kept my eyes on her, waiting for confirmation Ralph made it to Heaven. I wanted to hear he was safe and loved where he went. Mom took the toothbrush out of her mouth and spit into the sink.

"He was a bad, bad man. You figure it out," and went back to brushing her teeth.

"How do you know anyway?"

"You shouldn't have asked if you didn't want an honest answer."

I ran outside and over to Gram's house. She was sitting in her recliner watching the morning news. "Gram, do you think Ralph went to Heaven?"

She didn't hesitate. "Of course he did, sweetheart." A thousand pounds of fear lifted as I heard her answer.

"It's weird we were in your bed talking when Ralph died. I didn't even know he was...dying."

"You know what, Jessie? Remember all those fireflies that came to the window on Sunday night? I bet that was him, coming to say goodbye and to tell you he loved you." The smile on her face was magical.

I remembered the fireflies. She was right—it *was* him coming to say goodbye—it had to be. Now, whenever I see a firefly, I think about Ralph. She exchanged my sorrow for joy in a simple sentence —she always did.

The next day, I rode to the funeral home with Mom. We stopped at the flower shop to get what Gram ordered. A single red rose with "Dad" written in black on the long, white ribbon tied to it. I held the rose as I looked out the window the rest of the way. I watched the world go by in slow motion. I noticed every branch, every leaf, other cars, and the people in them. The world was still going on as if it were a typical day. How could I feel so much pain when no one else did? Warm tears turned cold as they ran down my cheeks. My stomach knotted. A lump in my throat made my breath rapid as I wiped the sweat from my palms onto my jean shorts.

When we pulled into the parking lot at the funeral home, I saw

Ralph's mom on the porch crying. I saw other people I didn't know. I stayed close to Mom as we walked up to my grandmother. She grabbed me by my arm and hugged me. "We dressed him up real nice for you. Go see him, Jessie."

I didn't know what she meant. I walked into the building through the massive white doors. I felt so small and insignificant as I entered this beautiful sorrow-filled dwelling. The weight of the air sat on my shoulders as I stepped inside.

The funeral director led me to the room where Ralph was. He opened the door, "Go ahead. Say goodbye to Daddy." I made my way to the door where I saw a bunch of colorful flowers around the big, long box. Ralph was inside that box. He was dressed in a suit and tie. The light reflected off his glasses, and his hands were folded on his chest where he held the rose I brought for him. It all happened in a matter of seconds, but it seemed like an eternity. I bolted out of the room, out of the building, and onto the porch. My grandmother followed me. "Jessie, we got him ready for you. You have to go see him, you have to."

The funeral director came out next. "He looks really nice. We worked really hard to make him look nice for you. Your grand-mother wants you to see him, she did this for *you*."

I didn't have sympathy for my grandmother. I didn't understand her pain. I didn't even understand mine. She had lost her only child. All she wanted was for me, her son's only child, to see her daddy at his best. At his *last* best. I couldn't do it. I didn't understand how important I was to her. The fear of the unknown and the reality of his death was too much for me to handle. I didn't yet understand how permanent death was.

Mom butted in. "Leave her alone. She's a ten-year-old child. Can't you see how upset she is?"

The funeral director took a step back, put his arm around my grandmother, and walked her back into the building. Mom and I followed. Mom asked for a minute alone with Ralph. She went into the room and shut the door behind her. I found a corner to wait in while Mom was in there. Time stood still as I tried to remain invisible.

After Mom came out, she took my hand to walk me out to the car. On the porch, Mom asked Ann about the services. They were holding a wake that night and the funeral the next day at the cemetery. Mom asked her what I should wear to the funeral.

"It's not a fashion show. She can wear what she has on."

A wizard with his staff covered the front of my black t-shirt, and my denim shorts cut into my chubby legs—this was the outfit Ann wanted me to wear to say goodbye to Ralph?

After we pulled out of the driveway, I looked over at Mom. "I have to wear *this* tomorrow? My wizard shirt?"

"Just do as she says."

"Why did you go in with Ralph?"

"He's a sneaky mother fucker. I wanted to make sure he's really dead."

"Was he…really dead?"

"Yup."

The rest of the ride home was silent.

The next day was the funeral. A few metal folding chairs were placed around the casket at the back of the cemetery. Green, plastic grass-covered a pile of dirt. As I got closer, I saw where the dirt had come from. Under Ralph's casket was a deep hole. A group of people stood around his casket along with the priest, who wore a long, black robe and had a bible clutched to his chest. I had never gone to church before, and this was my first interaction with religion of any type. The priest walked over to me. "Jessie, I am holding you close in prayer. I'm very sorry for your loss." He was a large man with a commanding presence. His words comforted me —it helped to know someone who didn't even know me cared about how I was doing. Mom and I found a place to stand by Ralph and waited for the service to start.

The sun beat down on my black t-shirt, and the crowd began to recite the *Lord's Prayer*. I had never heard it before. I didn't know any of the words and wasn't able to repeat any of it with the group. I squirmed in my skin as I looked around. I was the only one not reciting it. Shame and guilt lingered as the words filled the air. I was a complete failure as a daughter. Even in death, I let Ralph down.

After the funeral, I told Mom I wanted to go back to Ralph's house to be with my grandmother. As I got into Ann's car, I regretted having Mom leave me behind. When I got to Ralph's house, I was uncomfortable. The only saving grace was Ralph's dog, Candy. She was sad too. When she was outside on her run, she sat at the corner of the lawn waiting for Ralph to return. It was heartbreaking, but I knew how she felt. Her love was all that kept me sane during my stay there.

Inside the house, Ann talked to my grandmother about the day. The next words she spoke have stayed with me ever since. "I can't believe people wore shorts to a funeral! Can you believe how disrespectful that was?"

Ann's son saw me start to twitch on the couch as I tried to hide my bare legs. He said, "What people wear isn't important. It's that they came."

Ann didn't get the hint and continued to talk about how rude it was. I should have known better, but Ann was the one who told Mom the day before it wasn't a fashion show and to wear what I had on. Ann was trying to pit my dad against me, even in death.

The next day, we went back to the cemetery because my grandmother wanted to see what it looked like after he was buried. When we arrived, we all got out of the car. I walked over to the gravestone and stood atop of where Ralph was. For that moment, I felt close to him. Ann rushed over and pushed me. "Get off of him. Don't be so disrespectful!" I did as she said and stood by the car. A whirlwind of emotions washed over me. I was angry, confused, sad, and lonely. No one there cared about me. I was being yelled at for every little thing. Maybe I was overly sensitive, but her words stuck with me.

The next few days were the same. I was out of place, and I wanted to go home. Mom finally came to pick me up. I couldn't wait to see Gram so I could be myself. I needed to be away from Ann and the pain that surrounded my grandmother.

My sadness softened as the summer went on. I had lots of questions and couldn't sleep at night. In Gram's chair, I ate carrots and watched old reruns, and when they ended, I turned to QVC, the shopping channel. I didn't want to be alone, and I was scared if I went to bed, Ralph might visit.

In the silence of the night, the ticking of the clock made me think Ralph was around. The heart attack he had six years earlier left him with a pacemaker that ticked. When he was angry, it ticked louder and faster, but it always ticked. *Tick. Tick. Tick.* It reminded me of Captain Hook and the crocodile from Peter Pan.

When I heard it, I couldn't stop thinking he was around. With the television turned up, I cast my attention to the next item for sale. These people never slept, and they talked to me! It was incredible. Gram came out to check on me and to ask me if I wanted to go to bed, but I didn't. She joked about seeing my blonde head barely poking out of her chair watching QVC, but she let me be.

Gram was the only person who let me be sad and understood I had suffered a tremendous loss. She gave me love and support I didn't get from anywhere else. She let me know it was okay to cry and to be sad, but she also encouraged me to go on with my life and not let Ralph's death consume me.

The amount of fear that followed his death almost outweighed my sadness. I was afraid of everything. I was scared I would never know when the last time I would see someone would be. I was afraid I was defective because I no longer had a dad. I was afraid I would see Ralph's ghost, and if I did see his spirit, I would know for certain he was dead. I was scared I would die. I was afraid I would forget him. I was terrified of everything. Every thought that entered my head turned into something to be scared of, and fear kept my sadness at bay.

Summer soon came to an end, and it was time to return to school. I hadn't faced many people since Ralph's death. I didn't want anyone to treat me differently, and I didn't want to talk about it. I wanted to ignore it every way possible. I soon created a story in my mind that Ralph had not actually died but was hiding until my eighteenth birthday so he wouldn't have to pay child support. I never shared this with anyone, but it was how I dealt with the loss.

CHAPTER 9

*R*alph's death heightened my awareness of Gram's mortality. For as long as I can remember, my greatest fear was losing her. She provided the best gift anyone could ever ask for—unconditional love. As she loved me, she taught me how to love others, even the ones who might seem undeserving. She loved without expectation and gave to all who needed it.

Gram was my safety zone. I sat in her lap for as long as I was able, later squeezing myself into her chair next to her. Her age-spotted, wrinkled hands brought me comfort. They had seen the world as she traveled with my grandfather before my birth. On one of her trips, she purchased a jade ring she wore every day. The oval stone was pale green with daisies carved on it, set in a simple gold setting. She claimed it was her good luck charm—to me, it was *her*.

As I got older, she continued to grow older too. Gram's health began to decline, and my anxiety escalated. Since Ralph's death, I had been staying with Gram because I didn't want to be away from her. I wanted to soak up as much time with her as possible.

One November morning, as I rolled over in bed, I felt a washcloth hit my face. Gram was standing above me. In the shadows, I couldn't tell what was wrong. Frantic, she hit my face again until I got out of bed.

"Help...me..."

I swallowed the panic that bubbled inside of me. "Gram... what's wrong? Gram?"

Terror replaced her pupils. Her eyes bulged as she continued to swat me with the washcloth. Her mouth moved, but no words escaped.

There was no time to coddle myself. Gram needed *me*. I took her hand and led her to the bathroom. She sat on the toilet, her eyes still wide open.

"Gram, I'm going to get help. Please don't try to move." My heart echoed in my ears as it beat against my chest. My hand shook as I dialed Mom's number. *Please, God, let Grammy be okay. I'll do anything. Please don't take her. Please.*

Peter answered the phone.

"I n-need Mom quick!"

"She's not..."

"Peter, please come quick, Gram's...Gram's sick."

"Jesus, I'm taking a shower, leave me alone."

"Peter, please I need..."

Click.

He hung up on me. I called back. No answer. The little bit of calmness I had channeled to try to get help vanished. I paced the floor. *What am I going to do?* Mom wasn't home yet from taking Bill to work. I had to wait. *What if Gram can't wait?*

I ran to the door to watch for Mom. My heart thumped louder as time went on. "Gram, I'm waiting for Mom. Please, be okay." As I looked out the window, negative thoughts flooded my head. *You're going to kill her. You can't do anything right. Gram is going to die. It's all your fault.* "Any minute now, Gram."

Mom's maroon Subaru wagon made the corner and pulled into the driveway. I threw the door open, ran into the driveway, and waved my arms for her to see me. "Mom! Mom! I need you. Gram…she's sick. Mom."

Mom parked her car halfway up the driveway, left her door open and walked toward me.

"Mom…hurry…please…"

"What's wrong?"

"I don't know. She can't talk or smile. She's in the bathroom."

"Oh, I'm sure she's fine. Stop overreacting"

Mom gasped when she saw Gram. Gram had fallen into the bathtub. Mom got her up and helped her get into her bed. She told me to get Peter and stay with Kate.

"No, I don't want to leave her."

"If you don't want her to die, you *will* go *now*." Mom called 911 as I ran to the house.

"Peter…Mom needs you. Gram needs you…Hurry."

Peter could tell something was wrong. He pushed past me and ran out the door.

The house was too quiet. Kate was still asleep. I went into her room, kneeled on the floor, and rubbed her back until she woke up. "Kate, you have to get up. Grammy's sick, and I need to get over there." She sat up and threw her arms around my neck.

"Grammy sick?" She locked eyes with mine and saw my concern. She was only three, but she knew how scared I was. "Grammy be okay."

"I hope so, Kate."

I found her jacket and slipped it over her pajamas. She grabbed her teddy bear as we rushed out of her room. "Where are your shoes?"

"I don't know. I no need 'em."

I sighed as I searched the kitchen. "You do too."

Kate ran into the living room. "Here them are." She fell as she tried to put them on.

"Come on, Kate. We have to go." I helped her get them on, took her hand, and we rushed out the door.

"Ohhh, big truck, big truck. Beep, beep." Kate giggled when she saw the ambulance.

"It's *not* funny, Kate. This is serious. Grammy's sick. Now *stop it.*"

Two EMTs had Gram on a stretcher. Mom and Peter followed. I let go of Kate's hand and ran over to them. "What's wrong with her? Where are you taking her?"

They ignored my questions as they rushed past me. Gram tried to smile as she passed by. The floodgates opened as I saw how vulnerable she looked. "I love you, Gram." She disappeared out of sight as they loaded her into the ambulance. As the door shut, I swallowed hard as reality hit—it might be the last time I saw her.

Peter scooped up Kate, and Mom walked over to me. "I told you to watch your sister."

"I know...but...I had to see Gram."

"Oh, so you want your sister dead too?"

Dead too? "What's wrong with Gram? Is she going to be okay?"

"I don't know. They are taking her to the hospital to find out. Go get ready for school."

"No, Mom, I can't. I can't go. I'll wonder all day if she's okay."

"You need to go to school. I need to get to the hospital."

"But Mom!"

"No buts. *Now.*"

There was no convincing her. I got ready for school while Peter stayed home to take care of Kate. When I arrived at school, my emotions took over. My teacher sent me to the guidance counselor's office when he saw I couldn't stop crying. That's where I was when the call came.

Mom called to say she was coming to pick me up early. I got my backpack and walked to the office where I waited for Mom to arrive. The worst scenario played in my head as the clock ticked. *Gram was dead.* I tried to talk myself out of that thought, but I couldn't shake it. When Mom walked through the door, I ran to her.

"Where's Gram?"

"She's going to Dartmouth."

I couldn't hear her. The voice in my head was louder. "Can I say… goodbye to her?"

"She's not dead. She's going to the big hospital. I think she'd like to see you."

Relief filled my body. "I can *see* her?"

"Yes. It's about a two-hour drive."

I sat in the back of the car as I rehearsed what I would say to Gram when I saw her. *Gram, I love you. Please, get better.* I didn't want to make things worse for her or make her feel guilty if she couldn't, but I wanted her to know I needed her. *Just tell her.* I felt sick as I thought about what might happen. I pulled the *Boxcar Children* book out of my bag and tried to read to get my mind off the *'what ifs.'*

Mom broke the silence. "You know, Jess. The doctor said if you weren't there, Gram would've died. You saved her life."

"I did?" I put the book down. "The doctor said *that?*" A smile took over my face.

"Yup."

"So, is she going to be okay?"

"That's what we're going to find out when we get there."

Snow began to fall as we approached the hospital. It was the biggest building I'd ever seen. Mom parked the car, and we walked in through the front doors. The size of the building was over-whelming. I didn't have time to look around. I needed to find

Gram. The attendant at the desk gave us directions to where Gram was.

We climbed three flights of stairs. At the top were halls on each side of us. Mom took a right, and I followed. We walked down the long hall to find Gram. At the nurse's station, they gave us her room number.

Down another winding hall, we found Gram in bed. I stood at the door as I looked at her. I expected her to be back to normal and was shocked she was still so sick. She *had* to get better. *She had to.*

Gram held her hand out for me to take. I hesitated. She looked so fragile. I was afraid to hurt her. Mom nudged me closer to Gram until we touched. The warmth of her surrounded me. She stroked the top of my hand with her thumb as our eyes connected. She still couldn't speak, but the love behind her eyes said all I needed to hear. "I love you, Grammy."

The doctor came in and told us Gram had a massive stroke and gave her two weeks to live. He suggested she get her affairs in order and say her goodbyes. The words rocked me out of my skin. *Two weeks.* That was only fourteen more days. How was I going to prepare for this?

Mom called her brother, Doug, to let him know. He booked a flight and arrived as they discharged Gram from the hospital. Gram was able to speak again and gained some strength back. She was almost back to her old self, just with a countdown.

Uncle Doug spent Thanksgiving with us. In the short time he visited, he knew Gram was the only person I could count on, and he sensed my fear of losing her. "Jess, have you ever thought about going to school in Colorado?"

Before I had a chance to answer, Mom dropped her fork. "What in the hell do you think you're doing, Doug?"

"Nothin, just know Jess will be lost without Mom, and I—"

"What? Lost without Mom? What the fuck am I?"

"Wendy, that's enough. Let your brother speak."

I sat in the middle as my uncle and Mom fought over me. It brought back memories of the battle between Ralph and Mom. I wanted to go home with Uncle Doug, but I couldn't leave Gram. "I-I want to stay here for Gram."

"Don't be silly, Jessie. Your uncle could give you things we can't," Gram said.

"What the fuck do you think you're doing? She's my fuckin' kid. No one is taking her anywhere."

"I'm just trying to help. She's a smart kid. Vermont doesn't have a lot to offer. That's all," Uncle Doug explained.

"God damn it, Wendy, Doug just wants to help." Gram was getting angry.

Tension filled the empty spaces as we finished our dinner. Spoons clinked against porcelain at what could be Gram's last holiday. Sorrow replaced joy as the afternoon ended. Uncle Doug didn't visit often, but we shared a special connection. He was Gram's favorite, the child she was proud of. He was nine years older than Mom was and had a successful career and a family back home. The following day, he had to get back to his life. I watched as Uncle Doug kissed his mom goodbye. The finality of the moment was not lost on me.

"Don't forget my offer, kiddo. Your mom will come around, just give it time." I hugged him tight, not wanting to let go of the safety he offered. "I love you, kid." And he was gone.

Two weeks came and went, and Gram was still alive. She outlived the doctor's prediction, and I looked at every passing day as a gift. Having her at Christmas was all I had asked for that year, and I got my wish. As we got further away from the two-week mark, the fear went to the back of my mind, always present but quieter. We enjoyed our time together.

After six months of Gram waiting to die, she decided she

wanted to live. Since her stroke, she had depended on Mom for everything. The doctors had advised Gram not to drive and she followed those orders until she just couldn't take it any longer. "Jessie, let's go for a ride. I'm stir-crazy in this place! I want to go get some snacks at the store."

"But...you're not supposed to drive."

"Ah, who cares! You only live once." She grabbed her car keys and purse and started for the door. "Come on, Jessie."

I followed, unsure about her decision. We got into the car and fastened our seat belts.

"This one right here is the brake. If I die, just hit this one." I held onto my seat and kept my eyes on her feet the whole time making sure I remembered which pedal was the brake. When we arrived at the store after the two-mile trip, I wiped the sweat from my brow and got out to go into the store with her. The ride home was the same, my eyes glued to Gram's feet.

When we pulled into the driveway at home, Gram looked over at me and saw how scared I was. "That was fun, wasn't it, Jessie?" She tried to make light of the situation to ease my fear. She giggled and said, "We didn't die, honey. We made it in one piece!" I couldn't help but laugh. It was always an adventure with her.

That was her last time behind the wheel. When she saw the fear in my eyes, she decided it wasn't worth putting anyone's life in danger. Peter had recently gotten his license, so she gave him her car. Our adventures in a car alone together ended until I got my license, but I tagged along when Peter took her out. Gram had done a selfless thing by giving up her freedom. She said she would have felt terrible if she had gotten into a car accident and hurt someone. Since I was her riding companion most of the time, she didn't want to risk hurting me.

The adventures ended, but our fun together did not. We were always together. It didn't matter what we did. I watched TV with her every night, and we had conversations about what we were watching. In bed together, we read. Sometimes, she read to me, other times, I read to her, and at times, we read together separately.

Gram was the greatest gift life gave me. She said the same about me. I often wished I had been her daughter so we could have had more time together. The time we had could never be enough. She was my happy place, my safe place—she was everything to me.

CHAPTER 10

I was used to spending most of my time with Gram and never with friends my own age. I loved the time I had with her and didn't want anything to get in the way of it. She was the only friend I needed, but she encouraged me to branch out. I was nervous to think about letting someone else in. I worked hard to keep people at a distance and was unsure how to juggle friendship and secrets.

Since I was still the new girl, finding friends wasn't an easy task. I was shy with no self-confidence. *Who would want to be my friend?* Two girls in my class did. Emily and Lizzie let me become the third wheel. Emily had a twin brother, Ethan, but they didn't look anything alike. Ethan and I could have been twins, actually. We were both tall and blonde with blue eyes. Against Emily's wishes, Ethan and I soon became friends too.

When Lizzie and I both stayed over at Emily's, I felt left out. I didn't know their inside jokes and didn't really fit in with them. We were different. They lived happy, carefree lives while I struggled to survive. I gravitated toward Ethan. He seemed to understand me. He was kind of a misfit like me.

Emily made it clear to both of us we were not to be friends and definitely nothing more. That was enough to make Ethan irresistible. He soon became my closet best friend. When Emily found out, she was livid, and I no longer received invitations to her house. Little by little, they pushed me completely out of their group.

Eventually, I lost my room at Gram's house too. Peter ran away after he got into a fight with Mom and Bill. When Gram found out, she offered to have him live with her—the catch was I had to move back to Mom's since there was only one extra bedroom. I understood why, but I wasn't happy about it.

I packed up my things and walked across the yard with my arms full, my comforter dragging behind me. I dumped my belongings on Peter's bed and let out a sigh as I scanned the room. *Here we go again.* I wasn't ready to live under Mom's roof again, but I had to try to make the best of it. I still spent time at Gram's, having dinner with her and Peter most nights. Mom called to tell me they were about to lock the doors and that was my cue to go home.

At home, I spent much of my time in my room reading or writing poetry. I didn't like associating with Bill, and Kate took all of Mom's energy, so it wasn't even worth trying for. My room was my sanctuary. When I wasn't reading or writing, I longed for love and connection.

My desire to be loved filled all of my waking hours, at times seeping into my dreams. One dream stayed with me:

I walked onto a grass-worn path, through the trees behind my house. The twists and turns of the path guided me as tears overtook my eyes. Desperation grew inside of me as I searched. Searched to belong and to feel loved. These things were unknown to me, but I needed them. One foot in front of the other, I continued on, not knowing the way, but trusting I'd find it. The babbling of a brook grew louder as I reached a clearing in the woods. Through the evergreen trees, I saw him. Kindness beamed from his chocolate, brown eyes, a golden hue surrounded him as he sat on a boulder in the water. The light around him expanded, casting a shadow over me as my eyes locked with his. Warmth radiated from him, filling the coldness within my body. "It is me you are looking for." His words reached the core of my soul, fulfilling all I had been lacking. Awestruck, I could not find words. Tears remained in my eyes, replacing sadness with hope. From the tips of my toes to the crown of my head, my body tingled. His love, even from a distance, encased me. "It's not time yet. But I will wait for you."

I awoke to an unknown feeling lingering inside myself. I closed my eyes to get back, but I couldn't summon him. The warmth from the dream remained as I stared at the ceiling of my room. A smile took over my face as the words he spoke replayed in my mind. I believed he *existed*, and I would find him. His eyes were like no other I had seen before, and I knew they were how I would *know*.

Until I found him, I had to find new friends. Between losing Emily and Lizzie and moving back in with Mom, I needed something to look forward to at school. I didn't know where to look. It was an act of God I found friends in the first place. I still had Ethan, but in seventh grade, kids were mean. We didn't want anyone getting the wrong idea thinking we were more than friends, so our friendship stayed in the closet.

At recess, I stood alone at the corner of the brick building, in line ready to go back inside. Sweat boiled on my top lip as the most intimidating girl in seventh grade came up to me on the playground. Hannah was husky. She wore a denim jean jacket, black stretch pants, and leather biker boots. Her long, dark brown hair covered her face as she walked over to me. "You don't hang out with those losers anymore?"

"Nah...Emily's such a bitch."

"No shit. I wondered why you were friends with them."

"Yeah, I don't know."

"Wanna come over to my place after school? Abigail will be there." She took my hand and wrote her phone number on my wrist. "Call me."

Until then, I had been afraid of Hannah. I thought of her as a bad girl and someone I didn't want to get mixed up with. She smoked cigarettes, and so did Abigail. They had been best friends for years, always connected at the hip. I never saw room for me in their friendship and proceeded with caution. I thought they may be playing a joke on me, but curiosity won.

Hannah's number had washed off my wrist by the time I got home. Just faint numbers remained. I picked up the phone, closed my eyes to try to recall the numbers, and dialed. I got it right the first try.

Hannah asked me to come right over. Mom drove me the two miles to Hannah's house. She didn't question me about who she was or why I was going. She welcomed the break of my evading her. When I got out of the car, I took a deep breath, closed the door behind me, and walked down the dirt driveway where Hannah and Abigail were waiting. They welcomed me into their group, and a friendship was born.

Hannah soon became my best friend. Abigail was generous and allowed me to join in everything they did. I wanted all of Hannah's attention and tried my hardest not to be the extra. I liked Abigail, but we didn't connect as Hannah and I had. I was jealous of Abigail and what they shared. Abigail brought in more girls to our group. She started spending more time with some of her new friends, which left more time for Hannah and me.

Eighth grade almost slipped by us. The end of the school year meant graduation and a dance to celebrate the end of junior high. I was headed to high school with the kids I had spent the last four years with. Childhood was coming to a close as we prepared for the next phase of our lives. I didn't want to grow up, but at the same time, I wanted my freedom. Becoming a teenager was hard.

The dance was all everyone talked about. They talked about who they were going with and what they were wearing. Things I had never thought about before now consumed me. *What was I going to wear? Who was I going to go with?* These problems replaced the usual chaos that made up my life. I was depressed when I thought about my options. Mom noticed my glum new demeanor.

"What's wrong with you lately?"

"Nothing." I looked down at my stomach and pulled my t-shirt out of my rolls. "It's just I don't have anything to wear to graduation."

"Well, we can go shopping before then."

"And…I don't have…a date."

"A date? You like boys? I thought you'd be a prude forever."

"*Mom.*"

"What? You're Miss Perfect. I didn't think there was room for boys."

I thought about asking Ethan to go with me but changed my mind, fearful it might ruin our friendship. Maybe he'd say yes because he felt obligated, or worse, maybe he'd say no. Either way, it wasn't a chance worth taking. As I walked the halls at school, I looked around at the boys in my class. There were a lot of them, but no one I wanted to go to the dance with. They were all immature jerks, who snickered at the word *boob*. I far surpassed that level of maturity. I deemed the situation hopeless.

A few days later, Mom sat at the kitchen table, her eyes upturned in her large, brown framed glasses, her tie-dyed shirt poking out of her denim overalls. "Hey, Jess, I have a surprise for you."

"What, Mom?"

"You have a date for the dance."

"I do? Who? How?"

"Max. He said he'd go with you."

"Max? Peter's friend Max? Why would he do that?"

"How about *thank you*. God, just be happy."

Max was seventeen. I still had six weeks before I turned fourteen. He lived down the road from us and was always at our house. We hadn't paid attention to each other before the setup. He was just Peter's friend. But now he was *Max*. He was six feet tall with dark, bushy hair and a pencil mustache. His dark brown eyes appeared magnified behind his rectangle glasses. A loud, goofy, hyena laugh announced his presence.

As graduation approached, I grew more confident because I had a date! And it was with an older boy. I was elated someone actually liked me. This was the first time a boy had paid attention to me.

When graduation arrived, the ceremony was long and tedious. I couldn't wait to get to the dance. When the parents finally left, my classmates and I entered the gym. This was *our* night. Max sat against the wall with his head on his knees almost the entire evening. He was no fun at all. The pit of my stomach burned as disappointment washed over me.

A group of my friends snuck outside beyond the basketball court to smoke cigarettes they had smuggled from their parents. I didn't smoke, but most of my friends did. I managed to get Max to come with us. Ethan was at the picnic table we all surrounded. He sat with his back to us and didn't turn to see who was there. His head hung down as he looked at the grass under his feet.

I walked over to him and put my hand on his shoulder. "Ethan, what's the matter?"

He pulled away, and my hand fell to my side. "I'm fine. Why don't you get back inside?"

"Come with us. It'll be fun."

"I'd rather die."

I had never seen Ethan upset before. He didn't like Max, and I wasn't sure why—they didn't even know each other. I wanted to stay outside with Ethan to help, but Max didn't want to. As we walked back into the gym, I turned around to get one last look at Ethan. Our eyes met, and I saw the sadness his anger had hidden. It all made sense. Ethan didn't like Max because he *liked* me. I had a crush on him, but he never acted as if he felt the same. My heart broke for what could have been. I wished Max had never come with me. I wished I had gone alone as I always did. Why did life have to be so complicated? I was unaware how complex and difficult life could really be, though. This was the beginning of dating for me.

I didn't want to hurt anyone. I didn't want Ethan to be sad, and I didn't want Max to be upset. I wanted life to be simple again. I wanted the night to be over and summer to begin. I left that night confused. I didn't understand how I could have missed that Ethan liked me or why Max acted as if he didn't.

The next morning, Mom asked how the dance was. "Did you have a good time?"

"No, it was awful. I wished I hadn't gone."

"I need to get my money back then."

"What are you talking about, Mom?

"I paid Max to give you a good time."

"You what?" The lump in my throat began to grow. "You paid him?"

"Yes. I wanted to make sure you had someone to go with you."

"Why would you do that?" I screamed as I began to cry. "Why would you do *that*? I had someone I could've gone with. I had someone I could'had fun with! Why would you do that?" *She* had ruined my night. Max didn't really like me. She had to pay him to like me. *Was I so disgusting boys had to be paid to date me?*

A little while later, Max came into my room. He sat on my bed next to me and stroked my hair. "I gave it back to her. I told her I didn't want the money."

"Why not?" I wailed between sobs.

"Because I *do* like you."

"You didn't act like you liked me last night. You just sat there by yourself." I looked up at him.

"Because I was sad. I felt bad for hurting my ex-girlfriend. I thought I could go back to her after this, but I knew I couldn't. I knew I liked you." His head dropped down as he spoke. "I was just so confused. I didn't think I would like an eighth grader."

I believed the words he spoke, and I fell for him. I forgot about Ethan. I forgot about the awful night before. I forgot about the money. All I could do was believe I was worth it. Feeling as though I mattered was addicting because it was so rare. I liked it, and I wanted more.

That summer, Max introduced me to music. I had grown up listening to Mom's music and liked it, but I never felt it before. When I started listening to the radio with Max, I could *feel* the music. I could hear the words. The one song that stuck with me was "You Don't Know How It Feels" by Tom Petty. I couldn't get enough of that song. I related to the lyrics and ran to the living room to listen when it came on the radio. Nothing else mattered while the words touched my soul. There was something about it that reached deep inside of me. The song found the words I had been unable to find. Tom Petty was right—no one knew how it felt to be me. And with that, my love for Tom Petty was born.

His music gave me peace. For my fourteenth birthday, Mom bought me *Wildflowers*, the album with the hit from the radio. I listened to it over and over. Tom Petty became my artist of choice. If I felt sad or depressed, or angry or alone, I listened to his songs. I was never alone when I had Tom's music. For the first time in my life, I felt like someone understood.

Max began to spend more time at my house than he did his. Mom let him camp on the front lawn with Hannah and me. She never thought twice about it. I was partially hoping she would say no because I didn't know what to do. I was nervous but excited. When we got into our sleeping bags to go to sleep, he snuggled up to me, but I pulled away to try to get closer to Hannah. She was sleeping with her head by our feet, I wanted her to be close by in case things escalated.

When Max ran his finger over my lips, I kicked Hannah in the head to try to get her attention. It didn't work. When that tactic failed, I pretended I was asleep. His warm finger kept tracing my lips. My body tingled as I fought off the urge to roll over and kiss him. I was embarrassed because I didn't know how. The warmth of his body next to mine was intoxicating. After a few more minutes, Max stopped trying to kiss me and rolled over. I was disappointed he didn't want to fall asleep with me in his arms and knew I might lose him altogether if I didn't start letting him do what he wanted.

The next morning, when we woke up, Max kissed my lips as I stretched. Hannah got up, unzipped the tent door and went inside the house. I didn't expect his lips to touch mine. A rush of warmth surged through my body as I took in the feel of his mouth. I stared up into his dark brown eyes as he pulled away.

"I wanted to do that last night, but you were sleeping." His hyena laugh filled the tent. "You sure do fall asleep quick!"

I giggled and hid my face under the covers. "Yeah…"

"What I really wanted to do was this…" His eyes closed as his lips touched mine. His tongue licked my lips and then poked into my mouth.

Unsure what to do, I met his tongue with mine. The warmth I had felt intensified, and my heart beat faster as I gasped for air. My eyes remained open to watch what he was doing, his face a blur as he was so close. When his eyes opened, I closed mine tight.

His fingers traced my face and continued down my neck as they stopped where my breasts started to form. He kissed my lips again and made his way to my neck. The moisture from his lips on my neck sent goose bumps down my body, my nipples hardening under his hand. I shivered as I craved more. I didn't want him to stop. I liked how it felt... how it felt to be desired.

"You like that, huh?"

I nodded my head, not wanting my voice to pull me out of the pleasure I was feeling.

"It gets better. My tongue can do other things too."

I gulped hard as I thought about what he meant. *How could it get better?* I wasn't even fourteen and had visions of being with Max for the rest of my life. Max *liked* me. I was worth his time. I was falling for him. He was my first love.

Max had to have heart surgery because he was born with congenital heart disease and needed a valve replacement. He told me he might not make it through the surgery and suggested we have sex before he went. I couldn't bear the thought of losing him. I loved him and didn't want to live without him. I thought if I did lose him, I wanted him to be my "first" so I could at least have the memory.

Two nights before Max's scheduled surgery, we were in the living room watching *Quantum Leap*. Everyone else had gone to bed, and it was just the two of us. I imagined we were married and the only ones in the house. It felt perfect. During the commercial, I leaned over and kissed Max. I put my hand on the top of his pants and rubbed until I felt the hardness of his penis. I continued to kiss him as I unzipped his pants. I placed my hand under his boxers and stroked his hard, warm penis. He pulled his pants and boxers down around his ankles and pulled his penis out. He put his hand over mine and guided me up and down at the pace he wanted.

"Put it in your mouth."

I continued to stroke his penis and kissed him as I tried to ignore his request.

"Come on. Don't be a tease. Just suck it."

"I can't," I whispered as I felt his penis expanding in my hand.

"Awe fuck. Just try. *Please.*"

I was nervous. I wanted to please him, but I didn't know how. "I can't."

"Just make me come then." He put his hand back over mine and tightened my grip around his penis. I continued to stroke him until his body convulsed and white, thick liquid shot out.

"Just like that baby." He kissed me as he pulled up his pants.

"I'm sorry, I..."

"Don't be sorry. It's fine."

"I wanna have sex with you before...you...you go."

"No one can find out if we do. It'll be our secret, okay?" He pushed my hair behind my ear.

"I won't tell anyone."

The next morning, when Mom went to take Bill to work, I woke up and found Max asleep on the porch. I shook him awake and told him I was ready.

He started to kiss me, then took off my pants, and pushed me down on the bed. He stepped out of his pants, his penis erect and warm as it brushed against my thigh.

I covered my opening with my hand. "Do you have a condom?"

"No. We don't need one. Stop worrying." He continued to kiss me and press himself against me.

"I don't wanna get pregnant. We can't do it without one."

Frustrated, he kissed me harder. "Come on baby, just don't worry. *Trust me.*"

Images of a pregnant belly flashed in my mind while my hand still covered myself. "No, Max. I can't. Not without protection."

"Jesus." He stood up and put his pants back on. "You're giving me blue balls."

"I'm—"

"Whatever. I'm going back to bed."

The next morning, I woke Max up again. This time I had a condom. He said he wasn't in the mood and wanted to sleep. I went back to my room and cried. He had tried so hard to have sex with me before. Then, when I was ready, he didn't want me. He must have figured out I wasn't good enough for him. Later in the day, Max had to leave to go home so he could get ready to go to the hospital. I kissed him goodbye and told him I loved him. I cried as he walked home. I didn't know if I'd ever see him again—his operation was the following morning.

I couldn't sleep. I was so worried. The next morning, Peter told me he heard everything went fine, and Max would be home the next day. The wait seemed like forever. Once he arrived home, I walked to his house to see him. His parents showed me to his room, and I gave him the gift I had picked out for him—a small Lego set and the card I made him. He seemed different. He was distant. There was something he was keeping from me. He told me he was tired and asked me to leave.

When he recovered enough, he started to come to my house again. He took me aside. "Jess, I can't be with you anymore."

With those words, he broke my heart. I ran to my room, but he followed. "Get out!" I screamed. "Leave me alone!"

"Jess…Jess… Please, don't cry." He sat next to me on my bed.

"I said *get out!*"

"Jess, it's not you. I just… I just want to go back to my ex-girl-friend. I feel—"

"Get out! I *hate* you!"

And with that, he was gone. My heart hurt so badly. I didn't want to see or talk to anyone. I listened to "Cryin" by Aerosmith on repeat as I sat on my bed crying. I didn't know when the pain would end. I wanted things to return to normal. I second-guessed everything I had done. I should've had sex with him when he wanted to. I should've done anything he wanted to do. I should've been prettier. I should've been older. I should've been anyone except me. I was the real problem. I'd never find anyone to love me.

That was all I ever wanted.

CHAPTER 11

*W*hen I was able to shake the pain a little, I went to Hannah's house where we ate Doritos and chocolate ice cream and watched *Legends of the Fall* and *Wayne's World* and just talked.

"You're so lucky, Jess. Max is stupid anyway...I mean, look at him...he looks like a giant monkey!"

We laughed together. Hearing what she said took some of the sting away. She was right. I was lucky. I had just turned fourteen. My whole life was ahead of me. Max wasn't worth the heartache. The next time I saw Max, I held my head up high and walked past him. He tried to talk to me, but I kept walking. He didn't understand why I was ignoring him. He assumed he had a hold over me. I felt so powerful in that moment.

Hannah and I got closer, and she was my best friend. We spent all of our free time together. We took turns spending the night at each other's house, and sometimes we lied to our parents and stayed out in town all night. We were growing up, and the world was ours. We were invincible… we were unstoppable… we were teenage girls.

Our invincibility ended suddenly one hot July afternoon. I received a frantic call from a friend, Tina, who told me Abigail had been in a car accident. My body went numb. I must have heard wrong. "What? She what?" I paused as I waited for the news to change. "Tina, are you sure?"

"Yes, you need to get to the park and find Hannah. Now! I'm worried about her."

I ran to the living room and asked Mom for a ride to the park. I told her what was going on, and she looked worried. She didn't want to take me, but I pleaded. I needed to make sure Hannah was okay. I didn't even know if she knew yet. Hannah and Abigail had been friends forever. In my world, it was Hannah and me, but in Hannah's, it was her and Abigail.

I felt guilty that I had been jealous of Abigail in the past. In my anger and jealousy, I wished for Abigail to disappear. I hoped it wasn't my wish that had caused this. I felt guilty I was alive, and Hannah had lost her best friend.

When Mom dropped me off at the park, I couldn't find Hannah. I found Ethan sitting on a park bench with a solemn look on his face. "Did ya hear?"

I shook my head and sat down next to him. We didn't speak. We sat for a while, quietly looking at our feet. After a few minutes, I told him I had to find Hannah to make sure she was okay.

He reminded me that she was working at the community pool. We walked there together and found Hannah finishing her shift. She knew. She was in shock, but she knew. She didn't know if Abigail was going to make it or if she had died. Rumors were circulating in our small Vermont town. Ethan and I walked with Hannah the two miles to her house. There were two messages on her answering machine from Tina. The first message said, "Hannah, don't worry. Abigail's at the hospital, and she's gonna be okay."

For a split second, Hannah's body went limp with relief. Until the second message played. "Ummm, Hannah, this is Tina again. Uhhh….ummm… Abigail's dead. Uhhh…I mean… she… uh… didn't make it. I'm really sorry…"

Hannah ran out of her house to the woods across the road. Ethan left so we could be alone. I followed Hannah, not knowing if she wanted me there or not. I went anyway. We sat on a dead tree in the woods while she cried. I cried with her—I didn't know what else to do.

This wasn't something I could fix. I stayed with Hannah even though she probably wanted to be alone, but all I could give her was my time. We spent the next few days together while the reality of what had happened sunk in. A small group of friends stayed at my house so we could all be together to mourn and grieve. We had to camp out since there were four of us. We were all scared. Our imaginations ran wild. Tina told us she thought Abigail's spirit would be in the tent, so we were all too afraid to get in it to go to bed. We sat up most of the night talking and crying. We had one of Peter's friends check the tent to make sure there was nothing inside so we could try to sleep.

Abigail's wake was the next day. The last time I went to a funeral was when Ralph died. All of the emotions I had kept hidden came bubbling to the surface. Abigail's family decided to have an open casket, and they warned us before we entered. I hadn't gotten over seeing Ralph's body—although brief, the image still haunted me. Hannah wanted to look, so I did too.

We walked into the room and saw the casket. Abigail's elderly father stood above her yelling, "No! No! No!" He placed his hands under her armpits, lifted her body out of the casket, and shook her. "Abigail! Abigail! Come back!" Everyone froze at this raw expression of grief. The funeral director saw what he was doing and escorted her father out of the room while another worker rearranged Abigail in her casket.

For weeks after that, whenever I closed my eyes, all I could see was Abigail's father shaking her lifeless body. I couldn't erase the image from my mind. I didn't understand why she had to die. She was only fourteen years old. We were supposed to start high school together. I didn't know why life worked the way it did. Her death was a reminder that some things are out of our control. Some things happen, and there is nothing we can do about them except continue living.

Abigail's death brought Hannah and me closer. Our friendship blossomed as we realized tomorrow is not promised. We had to live in the now or we may miss out. Her death also began my fascination with "the other side." Hannah and I attempted to make contact with Abigail. We spent hours working with the Ouija board asking if she was okay. We sat in front of the scrambled television trying to talk to spirits like in *Poltergeist*. We never had much success, but we kept trying. We became obsessed with contacting the dead. We were hoping we could get a sign to prove death did not end our existence.

With our interest in the afterlife, our curiosity grew, and we wanted to try more things. We heard about witchcraft from Abigail's older sister, and we wanted to try it. Hannah and I both bought books and started to research it. Everything we read emphasized how dangerous magic was and warned not to cast spells without experience. Hannah and I never used any of the new information, but I kept my book—just in case.

CHAPTER 12

*A*fter the summer we'd had, I was ready for high school to start. A mix of terror and excitement filled me. I was nervous to be the youngest class in a new school. I was scared of all the people I'd meet and of getting lost on campus. I was worried, as freshmen, we'd be the target of pranks like they show in the movies, but I was excited for the change and for the opportunity it brought.

After a while, I knew my way around, and there were enough familiar faces that my fear faded. Confidence replaced my worry, and school became a place I couldn't wait to go. I enrolled in all of the classes required for college. I wanted to be able to have my pick of colleges and worked hard to do well. I dreamed of being a journalist, anywhere but Johnsville. I imagined the world had a lot to offer and couldn't wait to explore.

There was a boy I had my eye on who was in tenth grade. The confidence I felt took over, and I asked Hannah to see if he'd be my boyfriend. Hannah walked back over to me after she talked to him, a smile spread across her face.

"Danny said he'd do it!" She squealed as she took me into her arms to hug me. "You sexy bitch!"

I giggled in her embrace. I had a boyfriend. Again. I couldn't believe another boy wanted to be with me. Danny was as shy as I was. We stood together and just looked at each other. I wanted him to kiss me, but I was too nervous to make the first move. He never kissed me or even held my hand.

Max found out I had a new boyfriend and he was jealous. "Jess...I'm sorry about before."

"It's okay. I'm fine."

"I made a mistake, Jess. I should've never..."

"Don't, Max. You know I have a boyfriend."

"I know, but I still love you." He leaned in and kissed me. "Dump him, Jess. I know you want me."

All my feelings for Max came rushing back. I wanted to be with *him*. I didn't know what to do or how to tell Danny. I was sick at the thought of hurting anyone. I tossed and turned all night. I couldn't sleep. I had to break up with Danny, but I didn't know how. I wrote him a letter and asked Hannah to give it to him. I watched as he read it, hoping he didn't see me. He didn't seem to care. He folded the letter up and threw it on his lunch tray. I ran to the bathroom and cried. *What had I done?* He was a nice boy. But I loved Max. And he loved me. This was the only way we were going to be together again.

I was anxious to let Max know I did what he asked. He didn't come over that night. I tried to call him, but his mom said he was out. Days went by. When he finally came to see Peter, I told him I was single. He shrugged his shoulders and walked away. He broke my heart. Again. I regretted what I had done. I was angry with myself. I was mad at him. I was just angry. I asked Hannah to see if Danny would take me back. When she asked, he said no. I was alone again.

Consumed by rage, I was angry at how I'd been so stupid. Everything made me angry, and I took my anger out on all the people around me. I was trying to clean the kitchen and asked Kate to clean up her toys. She didn't listen to anything I asked, so I yelled at her. Bill watched, and he kicked my small dog, Toby.

Toby let out a cry, and my rage turned to fury. I got in Bill's face and yelled at him. "Don't you *dare* touch my dog, you asshole!"

He pushed me out of his face. "I just wanted you to see what it's like for someone bigger to hurt someone smaller."

"Fuck you, you sick fucker."

He grabbed me by my shoulders, pushed my body into the counter, and pulled his fist back to punch me. His fist connected with my cheek. The moment he hit me, all of the abuse I had endured as a small child came rushing back. I dug my nails into his arms and pushed him away from me. He opened the front door and pushed me down the three stairs. "Get the fuck out, you whore."

It was a cold November evening, and I was barefoot. He slammed the door in my face. I banged on the door demanding he give me Toby. He threw Toby out the door, and he whimpered as his body hit the landing. I scooped Toby up and ran to Gram's house through the snow with no shoes or jacket on.

I tried to catch my breath as I shut the door behind me. "Bill... Bill just hit me! He kicked Toby and then hit me." I couldn't stop the tears from coming.

"He did what?" Gram was furious. "He better not have touched either one of you."

"Can I call Hannah? I need to get out of here," I asked as I wiped the tears from my face. She said I could. As soon as Hannah's dad heard what happened, he told her he was coming to get me. I let Gram know, and she called Mom. Gram demanded they send my shoes and jacket over and told her I was going to

Hannah's house for the night to cool down. Peter did as she asked while I waited for Hannah and her dad.

Hannah had another friend over that night. Mindy was in our class too, and they were already having a sleepover. When I got into the car, Hannah's dad said he wanted to show Bill what it was like to pick on other people. The three of us girls begged him not to, and thankfully, he listened. That night, I told Hannah and Mindy about what Bill had done to me and then the secrets spilled out. I told them he had touched me and made me touch him when I was little. I told them he always felt my breasts and pinched them and said inappropriate things to me. Everything I held so close poured out. I didn't have anyone to protect anymore. Mom and Bill didn't want to protect me, and I was no longer going to protect them. After I spilled out seven years of secrets, Mindy told me she had to tell her stepmother, Deb. Mindy said Deb worked at the courthouse and could help.

When Mindy got off the phone with her stepmother, she said, "Deb has to report what happened to you. She said she has no choice."

Mindy asked me not to call or talk to my mom. She told me it would be best if I stayed at Hannah's house until things were figured out. Hannah's parents agreed. I called Gram to let her know what was happening. She promised to let Mom know I wouldn't be coming home for a while. Deb arrived at Hannah's house and said she had to take me to talk to someone that could help me. I was scared. I didn't know what was going to happen. I had no idea my life was going to be forever changed.

Again.

CHAPTER 13

*D*eb came the next day, and Mindy introduced us. She seemed nice, but I wasn't sure I wanted to tell anyone else my secrets. I hadn't been able to sleep since Bill hit me, and my body was filled with adrenaline. The lack of sleep had caught up with me—I was exhausted.

"Do we have to do this today?" I paused as I looked at my feet. "I'm really tired. I just wanna go to sleep."

"Honey, I'm sorry, but we have to go today. They're waiting for us at social services."

I let out a sigh and looked up at Hannah. She came over to me and took my hand. "Can I go with her?"

"No, I'm afraid not. No one else can go. She'll be fine. There's nothing to worry about."

She was wrong. There was *everything* to worry about. Hannah hugged me and said she'd see me soon. Mindy stayed with Hannah as I left with Deb. Riding alone with Deb in her shiny silver BMW convertible was uncomfortable. We didn't make small talk. I sat silently in the passenger's seat as I fidgeted in my seat of black leather interior. My eyes focused forward as we got onto the inter-state. The cold, fall day sent chills through my body as the heat from the car only warmed the surface.

Deb and I pulled up in front at the big brick building with a small white sign with green writing above the door—*State of Vermont Department for Children and Families*. Deb held the glass door open for me. As I entered, I saw a steep flight of stairs. I stood on the bottom step as I looked up and cleared my throat before I walked to the top. At the top of the stairs was a solid, heavy brown door. A piece of white paper taped to the door read "DCF: Social Services. Please check in with Receptionist."

My heart raced as we entered the small white room. At the desk, Deb said, "We're here to talk to the trooper."

The receptionist used her finger to push her glasses up on her nose and pointed to a wooden bench. "Have a seat. Someone will be right with you."

Trooper? What did she mean? Was I in trouble? The more I thought, the more nervous I became. Tears welled. This wasn't the time or place to fall apart. I had to stay strong. The image of Bill kicking Toby flashed before me, and the anger returned. Anger kept my tears away.

The fear of the unknown circled in my mind. I sat silently as Deb picked up a *People* magazine and started reading it. She was so calm as she flipped through the pages. She didn't notice my state of apprehension.

Finally, a closed door opened and a woman in a business suit came out. "We're ready for you now." She held the door open as I walked through. She pointed down the hall and directed us to the conference room. There was a long, rectangular table with maroon padded chairs pushed in around it. A police officer sat near the head of the table and asked me to sit down next to him. *I was going to go to jail. Bill must have told them I scratched him. This was it. Mom*

*always threatened to send me to juvie or the psych ward—whichever would
take me. It was actually happening.*

I was unable to hold back my fear. My body trembled as I pulled
out the chair. The trooper saw my hands shaking and knew I was
upset. "Jessica, I'm Trooper Clark. I just have a few questions
for you."

I began to cry. "I only scratched him because he was hurting
me. I won't do it again. I promise."

Trooper Clark looked at me and said, "You're not in any trouble. You did nothing wrong."

"Really?"

"Really. We just need to hear from you what happened the
other night with your stepfather and the other stuff you disclosed
to your friends."

I told Trooper Clark what took place when Bill hit me and
threw me out of the house. I stopped there. I felt uncomfortable
telling him what had occurred in the past. I wasn't ready to re-
release those secrets. I wished I hadn't let them spill out to
anyone. I wanted to rewind time and leave that part out. I couldn't
turn back, though— too many people knew now. If I didn't tell
Trooper Clark, someone else would.

I cracked my knuckles as I held my hands in my lap. My eyes
almost closed as I took a deep breath. Trooper Clark saw I was
uncomfortable. "I know it's not easy to talk about, but it's important. Take your time, and go as slow as you need. I'm not in
any hurry."

His compassion eased some of my fear. I told him what had
happened when I was younger. He stopped me and asked for
details. *Every little detail.* My stomach knotted as I relived those
moments. Vivid images of that time replayed in my mind. I became
angry as I said the words aloud. My voice echoed in the quietness
of the room.

No one protected me then, but these people, who didn't even know me, were trying to protect me now. I became united with them, and the repulsive things I had held in for so long poured out. I was torn between loving my family and being outraged at them. Everyone except Gram knew my secrets, but they made me keep them. They didn't want to help me. They only wanted to protect themselves. I loved them, and I wanted them to love me, but what if they never could?

After talking to Trooper Clark, I was told I couldn't go home. I was now in state custody. I was a foster kid. The social worker, Joan, talked to Deb, and she agreed to take me back to her house until they could figure something else out. I wasn't going home. I wasn't going to be able to have any of my things. I wasn't going to be able to have Toby. Or my clothes. Or anything.

When we left the big brick building, I went back to Mindy's house. Deb set up an air mattress on Mindy's bedroom floor, and that was where I stayed when I wasn't at school. Joan agreed to ask Mom to give her some of my things. The first couple of days, I had to wear my dirty clothes, and I didn't have my backpack or anything I needed. Mindy's family was nice, but it wasn't home. I wanted my bed and my stuff. I wanted Toby and Gram. Since Gram lived next door to Mom, I wasn't able to see her either. I felt like they were punishing me.

Within a few days, I had some of my clothes and my backpack. I had so much homework to catch up on, but I wasn't up to it. I was depressed. I didn't know what was going to happen from one day to the next. My world turned upside down. Trooper Clark said I didn't do anything wrong, but I was the one suffering.

Thanksgiving was only days away. I hadn't considered spending it without family. I had never been away from home for Thanksgiving. I didn't want the day to come, but sure enough, it did. For Thanksgiving, I went with Mindy's family to her grandmother's house. The house was full of people. So many people I didn't know. I was an outsider. Even though they tried to make me feel welcome, it wasn't the same. There were too many strangers and too many eyes looking at me.

I wanted my old life back. The desire inside me was so strong. I had never wanted anything as much as I wanted to go home. Two weeks passed, and I hadn't seen Mom or Gram. That was the longest I had been away from Gram my whole life. I didn't like how it felt. Depression took a stronger hold over me, and I started to withdraw. Life was too hard.

Hannah's parents saw how sad I had become. They understood how hard this change had been for me. I wasn't comfortable where I was staying. They talked it over and decided to take me in. They took foster parent classes, and within two weeks, I was living with them. They let me have Toby too. I felt like I was home. Life was starting to look up.

Soon after the move, I was allowed to have a supervised visit with Mom, Kate, and Gram. Peter didn't come to see me. Mom said he was working. I was so happy to see them. Gram was glad to see me too.

"I've missed you so much, Jessie." She had tears in her eyes as she took my hand. "I just want you home. Wendy will get you home soon. Won't you, Wendy?"

Mom didn't say anything, and Gram didn't wait for her to answer. "I love you, honey. How have you been? How's school? Do you need anything?" Her questions filled the room. I knew she was sad. I could see how much she loved me, and it made me miss her more.

"I miss you too, Gram. I just want to go home." I wiped my nose with my sleeve and sniffled in hard to try to make the flow stop.

"Awww, honey, you'll be home soon. Right, Wendy?" Our eyes

went to Mom. She shook her head and played with Kate's mousy brown hair. "See? Your mother will get you home."

I knew Gram wanted me home as much as I wanted to be home, but I also knew she still didn't know the whole story. I knew Mom hadn't told her the secrets. I wanted to let Gram know, but it wasn't the time or place to tell her.

Kate played with the toys in the room and ignored me for most of the visit. There was something between us now. We were strangers. "Mommy, I wanna go home. I'm hungry."

"Hush, Kate." Gram put her finger to her lips and shushed her. "We are here to see Jessie. Don't you want to talk to your sissy?"

"No. I wanna go home." Mom put Kate on her lap and hugged her as she rocked her back and forth.

I longed for my mother's love as much as I ached to go home. I wanted her to see me, to see the pain I was in. Rage boiled the blood that ran through my veins as I saw the love Mom gave Kate. Why can't she just love me?

"We should get going. I have to make supper." Mom stood up and took Kate's hand.

Gram stood up too and grabbed me into a hug. "I love you, honey. If you need anything, call me." She kissed my cheek and squeezed me tight.

"I love you too, Gram. I don't know if they'll let me call you."

Gram looked at the mirror in the room and talked into it. "Jessie can call me, right?"

"Who are you talking to, Gram?" I raised my eyebrows as I looked at her.

"Joan. She's on the other side of that mirror." She pointed to the mirror and explained how the two-way mirror worked. I knew our visit was supposed to be supervised, but I didn't know how.

Mom didn't talk much during the visit and didn't make eye contact with me. She occupied herself with Kate. She seemed upset with me, and the lack of emotion made me ache. Gram told Mom to hug me as they were leaving. When Mom held me, tears escaped from my eyes. Being in Mom's embrace, even forced, felt good. As Mom hugged me, she whispered, "You know Bill never did those things to you."

She would *never* pick me over him. I was afraid I'd never go home again. I became sad and angry. I changed. I was no longer a child. Once again, Mom made it clear she didn't want to love me. She didn't care if I came home, she just didn't want Bill to get into trouble. He *was* more important than I was. I'd always believed that, but now I was sure. Gram was the only family I had. Gram and Hannah's family. Hannah became my sister, and we were closer than ever.

People at school saw Hannah and me dropped off, and picked up together every day, and began to make fun of us. They had no idea what I was going through. They started calling us lesbians. I didn't need that on top of everything else. I loved Hannah, but I was not in love with her. She knew I was having a hard time with it, so she suggested we just go with it. She thought we should agree with them and hold hands when we walked together. "If we don't let them bother us, they'll stop."

We began holding hands when we walked to class or when we walked around town. We smiled when people called us lesbians. We were going to win this battle. And we did! People stopped calling us lesbians to our face. However, behind our backs, the gossip spread. I could handle the gossip. I just couldn't take the constant ridicule.

Life at Hannah's was good. We acted like sisters, and her family treated me like their daughter. I felt loved. They included me in everything. They bought the things I liked to eat, and whenever they brought Hannah something, they gave me one too. They treated us equally. It was nice there, but I missed Gram. I missed my old life. I still wanted more than anything to go home. Even though Mom picked Bill over me, it didn't stop my desire to be with my family. Every day, I hoped I would hear Mom had kicked Bill out, and I could go home. I hoped, for once, I would matter enough for her to pick me. For her to love me. That day never came.

The more Mom proved to me how insignificant I was, the more I wanted her love. That was the way it had always been. She pushed me away, and I chased after her harder. Part of me hoped I would be enough, that she would realize she loved me, and change her mind. I remembered a conversation we had when I was seven. We were sitting in the car in the parking lot at the school, and I asked, "Mom, if you had to choose between Bill or us kids, who would you pick?" I think I surprised her with my question.

She looked at me and said, "I'd pick you guys. I'd always pick you guys." She lied. She picked him. She always picked him.

The court proceedings started to see if Bill would be charged criminally for what he had done to me. I had to testify. I had to sit in the witness stand and answer questions. My heart thumped so hard and high in my chest, I thought I was going to swallow it. I didn't want to repeat my story. I didn't want to relive all that stuff. I wanted it to be over with. Bill insisted he was innocent, and Mom told them I was crazy. She said I was mentally ill like Ralph, and I didn't know what I was talking about. Those words hurt. She wanted people to believe I was a sick person who didn't know what actually happened. She asked the judge to send me away to a psychiatric hospital for tests to prove I was crazy. She said she was told by a therapist when I was younger that I was a danger.

I became quietly outraged. I had never talked to that counselor. I had told him every week I had a headache, and he let me take a nap. I didn't say more than five words to him at any one time. He didn't know me. Mom didn't know me. No one knew me.

The judge dismissed what Mom was saying and ordered I go into counseling because of what had happened. I was worried the counselor would think I was crazy. I was worried that I *was* crazy. Mom spent a long time trying to convince me I was crazy most of my life. After a while, I questioned what she was saying. Maybe I *was* mentally ill. Maybe I was like Ralph. How could I tell? Crazy people always say they aren't crazy—that was a part of being crazy.

I was careful what I talked to my counselor about. I really liked her, but I didn't trust her. She was a student therapist, so our sessions were videotaped so her teacher, Dawn, could watch them and give her feedback. I hated the idea that I was on videotape at my most vulnerable time. I made up stuff to talk about. I rarely told her the truth. I said what I thought she wanted to hear. I hated going. I purposely missed my rides to my appointment. I hid in the woods until I saw the taxi pull away. After missing a handful of appointments, Joan started picking me up from school. She was on to me.

One day at school, I went to the pay phone and called Mom. I missed her and wanted to talk. Peter answered. I missed him too. I missed everyone. I asked if I could talk to Mom. I heard him tell her I was on the phone. She hesitantly picked up. "You aren't supposed to be calling here. You'll get me in trouble."

"I know, Mom, but I miss you." I started to cry. "I wanna come home."

"You know what you need to do to return." She started to yell and then calmed down. "You need to tell the truth."

"I am telling the truth, Mom. You *know* what happened. You were there. You know I am telling the truth." The anger stopped my tears. "I just want to see you."

"Well, you'll see me at DCF next week." She was frustrated. I heard Peter and his girlfriend talking in the background.

"No, Mom—*now*. I want to see you now. I can skip school, and you can pick me up. I just want to see you. I want to come home."

"No, we can't do that. Not today anyway. Call me back tomorrow." *Click.* She hung up the phone, and I returned to class.

I couldn't wait to call her. It was all I could think about. I hoped she would change her mind and let me come back, at least for a little while. When I called her the following day, she told me she would pick me up, but I had to promise not to tell anyone. I made the promise, snuck out of school, and met Peter nearby. I was so excited to be home again and so nervous I was going to get into trouble. I had never skipped school like that before. Getting into trouble was worth it for me to be able to go home. Bill was at work and Kate was at school. Mom, Peter, and his girlfriend were the only ones there. I hoped returning home would feel like being home, but it didn't. I felt like a stranger. Mom was not thrilled to see me. She may have been nervous that we were going to get in trouble or she may have been angry. I couldn't tell.

After the initial awkwardness of being home again after months of being away, I went into my room to find a few things. It wasn't how I had left it. People had gone through my stuff. They read my journal, used my pillows, and took my blankets. I was furious.

No one cared that I wasn't home. No one had lost what I had lost. At that moment, it became apparent to me again that all they cared about was Bill not getting into trouble. They didn't care I spent Thanksgiving with people I didn't know or that all I had wished for Christmas that year was to be able to go home. They didn't care about me at all. I was a thorn in their sides.

Even so, my desire to be home with my family overpowered my rage. I wanted to go home more desperately than I had wanted anything else before. The fact that no one wanted me hurt. I was used to rejection. I had been rejected my whole life. I longed for the normalcy of their rejection as much as I longed for their love. It was home, and it was all I knew.

When my visit was up, I gathered up my journal and my Tom Petty CD, and Peter brought me back to school. No one had noticed I was missing. That was the beauty of being quiet. No one knew when I was there, and no one knew when I wasn't. I finished out my day and told no one of the visit. Hannah noticed I had some of my stuff and she asked me how I got it. I couldn't lie to her, but I didn't know how to get out of the mess I had created. I eventually told her about my visit and skipping school. She didn't care—she just told me to be careful.

The visits continued, sometimes more than once a week. We always planned it when Bill was at work. I was okay seeing Mom, Peter, and Kate, but I didn't want to see Bill. I resented him. I was angry he destroyed my world and turned my whole family against me. I was scared he would hurt me again if he knew I was there. I worried he would tell Mom I couldn't come home. When Mom said she let Bill know about our visits, I didn't know what to say. I stared at her. *Why?* He was winning again. We couldn't even have this secret.

Mom said Bill wanted me to think about what I was telling the authorities. She said all I had to do was take it back, and I could go home. "Bill's not mad at you. He knows you were just mad and said things you didn't mean."

I still didn't know what to say. "He shouldn't be mad at me. I didn't do anything to him. I should be the one who's mad." I didn't want to fight with her, but I was angry. I was hurt.

"Listen, Jessica. He wants to be friends." She spoke in a stern voice. "You want to come home, right? Then just hear me out."

"I *do* want to come home." I began to cry as I imagined life before all this happened. "I want to come home more than anything."

"Then listen to me." Her voice changed as she said, *"We think you should recant your story."*

"What does *recant* mean?"

"It means to take it back. We think you should tell them you were angry and everything blurred together. Tell them it was Ralph who did those things to you, and you only *thought* it was Bill who did it."

"Ralph's dead. I don't want to say he did that stuff to me. You know he didn't. You *know* what happened." I became angrier. They wanted me to blame my dead father for touching me. He never did that. Ever. He abused me in other ways, but not like that. My stomach churned.

"That's right, he is dead. He won't get in trouble." She looked at me. "No one gets in trouble this way."

"I can't do that. I *won't* do that."

"Fine!" she yelled. "I guess you really don't want to come home that bad after all. Maybe you should stop coming over too." She turned her back to me.

"Mom, *no*! Mom, please. I don't want to stop coming over. I do want to come home. I do!"

She turned back around to face me. "Then you know what to do."

Her plan sounded simple but blaming Ralph who couldn't defend himself made me sick. He *didn't* touch me in those ways. He often asked me if Bill had, and I always lied to him, saying no. This lie could be my ticket home, but I didn't know if I could live with myself if I told it. I was a fourteen-year-old girl. All I wanted was to go home. I wanted my mom to love me. I didn't know what to do.

Freshman year came to an end, and Joan allowed me to move in with Gram. I was sad to leave Hannah and her family, but I was so glad to be able to see Gram every day. She agreed to keep me away from Bill. Once I moved in with Gram, I was allowed to visit Mom,

Peter, and Kate at their house. I didn't have to sneak around anymore.

Since I was allowed to go to Mom's now, she had to work even harder to convince me to change my story. She didn't talk about it all the time, but she continued to bring it up. "Wouldn't it be nice to be able to come home?"

"I'm happy at Gram's."

"Well, wouldn't you like to do things with your family?"

"Gram is my family."

"Don't be a smartass. You know what I mean." She was annoyed that my desire to be home had lessened. "You know if you don't change your story, they will take Kate. You know Gram doesn't have room for both of you. Do you really want to be responsible for her growing up without *her* family?"

I could not believe the burden she had put on my shoulders. *I would be responsible for Kate growing up without a family? Me? Did she really blame this all on me?*

"What do you mean?"

She went on, "They told us if Bill is found guilty, Kate will be taken away."

"You didn't care when *I* was taken away. Why should I care if she's taken away? Why is that my fault?" I asked the questions, but I didn't want to be responsible for Kate growing up without her family. I knew how scary that was, and I didn't want my sister to have to go through what I had. I was lucky too. I had Hannah's family and Gram. Who would Kate have? The more I thought about it, the more the guilt grew. I really had messed things up. I really should have kept my secrets. I should have listened.

"I care," Mom said.

"Yeah...um—" I stopped. "Gram told me she needed me to help her today." I left and went to my bedroom at Gram's house. I thought about what Mom had said and about Kate and how scared she might be. I thought about the lie Mom asked me to tell. I thought about getting in trouble for lying to the judge. I didn't want to do it, but I had no other choice. I could protect Ralph's honor or save Kate.

Kate was seven. She couldn't lose her family. I couldn't be held responsible for that. She would hate me. Everyone would hate me. They already did, but maybe this could fix it. I knew what I had to do.

I walked back to Mom's house and found her on the porch smoking a Newport. "I'll do it."

She was so happy that she had won. "I knew you would do it for Kate!"

"I'm scared, Mom."

"Don't be silly. You can come home. You said that was what you wanted."

"I don't want to go to jail for lying. What if they find out I'm lying?"

"You're just a kid. You won't get in trouble. You are doing the right thing, you know?" She began explaining what I had to do next. "When you go to your counselor, you need to tell her you made a mistake. You need to tell her you were so angry and scared, you mixed up your memories. You tell her you remember who really touched you. You tell her it was Ralph that did it to you."

"But I was ten when he died. He couldn't have pinched my boobs. I didn't have any yet."

"Don't be difficult. Just tell them you made that part up."

"No. I didn't make that up. I'm not going to say I lied when I didn't."

"What do you think you'll be doing? *Lying.* What's one more lie?"

"I'm not comfortable with this. I'll say the parts that could be him were Ralph, but I won't say I lied. I don't want to get in trouble." I paused. "I don't want to go to jail for lying to the judge. Are you sure I won't get in trouble? Are you sure they won't know I am lying?"

"If you do it right, they won't."

The next time I saw my counselor, I began to tell her this made up story. "I remembered something." I didn't know if I could continue. I started to cry.

"What did you remember?" she asked me handing me a box of tissues.

"I remembered it was my dad. It wasn't Bill."

"What was your dad?"

"He was the one who touched me in bad ways. He was the one that…molested me." I couldn't keep the tears in any longer. I sobbed as I heard the words leave my mouth. *No!* I screamed in my head. I wanted to tell her I was lying. I wanted to tell her Mom's plan, but I couldn't. I couldn't risk it now. I had to do this for Kate.

I continued to tell her more of my new "memories" and told her I wanted to let the judge know I had made a mistake. She said she would tell Joan, and they would go from there. I know she questioned my new discovery. I know the timing of my being able to visit Mom without supervision had people questioning this. I waited for someone to fight me on it so I could tell them I had made it up, but no one ever did.

There was no turning back now. This was my "new story." I had to go with it now. My guilt grew. What would Ralph think? He was going to be so angry with me. He would hate me. I knew he would know what I had done. The guilt began to eat at me. It ate my joy. It ate my pleasure. It ate my happiness. I was empty inside. I felt alone. The only person who knew what I had done was Mom, and after I lied, she stopped being nice. She had what she wanted.

I had to go to court and tell the judge of my changed memories. He asked me if I understood what happened to people who lie under oath. He said it was a big deal to make up stories, and he asked me if anyone had told me to say the things I said to him. "No...no...Your Honor. I just...just remembered it was my dad and not Bill."

Then he asked me if Bill was the one who touched my breasts.

"Yes. He did." I couldn't lie about that.

He asked me if I was sure I wanted to change my initial story. I agreed. He ruled to allow the testimony that I had given previously be modified in the record, taking the blame from Bill and placing it on my dead father.

I waited to hear what the findings were. I waited and waited and finally, after what felt like forever, we learned that I couldn't go home because Bill had still acted inappropriately when he touched my breasts. The only way they would allow me to return home was if Mom was willing to have Bill leave. She was not. At least my lies helped Kate—the court ruled that Kate was not at risk and could stay at home.

Mom was still angry. She told me if I had changed my whole story, the judge would have let me go home. She didn't thank me for the parts of the story I did change. She didn't care about the amount of pain that lie caused me. They hadn't completely cleared Bill, so she was still angry. Again, I saw I wasn't on Mom's list of priorities. Nothing I could do would make her love me.

That was a lesson I continued to forget.

CHAPTER 14

The only thing that could change my situation was time. I had to "age out" of the system. I was happy to be able to live with Gram, but I was going to be a ward of the state until my eighteenth birthday. I was so sick of being judged for being a foster kid. When people heard I was in foster care, they treated me differently. They assumed I was a troublemaker. They figured all teenagers in state's custody had done something to be removed from their family.

Freshman year was over. Hannah and I spent most of our free time together. Hannah had begun dating Abigail's brother, Tim. He was a nice guy and soon became a close friend. The three of us spent a lot of time together.

Ethan and I dated for a few weeks, but it was too weird. He was my best friend, and I was worried dating was going to change our friendship. Turned out, breaking up changed it more. Since I told Ethan I wanted to stay friends, we had barely talked. It seemed the more I tried to do the right thing, the more of a mess I created.

I told Hannah and Tim I wanted a boyfriend for my fifteenth

birthday. I didn't want to be alone anymore, but mostly, I wanted someone to love me. Tim was five years older than Hannah was, so his friends were older too. He asked a couple guys, but they said no because I was only fifteen. Sixteen was the age of consent, the magic number older guys waited for in order to date a younger girl in hopes to take her virginity. I was bummed. I didn't want to be the third wheel anymore.

After a few weeks, Tim found one more guy to ask. He was four years older than Tim was. I didn't care. His name was Mark. Mark was almost twenty-four years old. He was an alcoholic who lived with his mom next door to Hannah. He only left the house to buy Michelob Light and Marlboros. He didn't have a job, and Tim said he thought he might be "a little crazy." Nothing about Mark sounded right, but when he said yes, I figured he couldn't be *that* bad.

Tim arranged our first date. He brought Hannah and me to the park in town, and we waited for Mark to arrive. As we waited in Tim's Cavalier, Tim gave me some more information about Mark. "Whatever you do, don't stare at his hand." Tim made eye contact with me in his rear view mirror.

"Why? That's my favorite part of a guy, the first thing I notice."

Tim chuckled a nervous laugh. "Because the dumb fuck lost a couple fingers at the mill."

"Oh, my God. Wait...how?

"I don't know... guess he was drunk and his fingers didn't leave the wood he was cuttin'...until they flew off his hand." He paused to laugh. "I heard there was blood everywhere."

"Stop! I'm going to be sick." I clutched my stomach as Tim laughed harder. "So you mean...he's missing fingers?"

"Yeah...is that a problem?"

"No. No...how many?"

"I don't know, I haven't seen him since it happened. He really hasn't left the house since then. He just sits home and drinks. I told you he's crazy." Tim turned around to face me. "Back in high school, he was obsessed with this girl he went to the prom with."

Jealousy rushed through my body as I imagined this man I hadn't even met yet being in love with someone else. I needed him to love *me*.

Tim continued, "Mark picked me up in his shitbox truck, and we spent hours driving past her house, waiting to see her."

"That's nuts."

"I know, Jess. He's fucking crazy. Just be careful, okay?"

"What if he does that to me?"

"I don't know. I don't think he will. That was years ago."

Mark pulled into the parking lot next to us in his loud, rusty, Chevy pickup. It was painted two different colors of brown and made a "bang" sound when he shut it off. We got out of the car to meet him. When he got out of his truck, a Marlboro hung out of his mouth, one hand shoved into the pocket of his faded Levi jeans, and his button down, blue striped, short sleeve shirt was only half tucked in. The slight breeze blew his brown hair out of place.

Tim walked over to him as he shut his truck door. "Hey, Mark. This is Jess," he said as he pointed to me. Hannah was behind me pushing me forward. My hair covered my eyes as I made my way over to him.

"Hi," I almost whispered.

Mark looked at me and nodded his head, the cigarette still dangling from his lips. Tim made small talk, and Mark just listened and kept nodding his head. I felt like I was going to throw up. I wasn't sure I was ready to date someone nine years older than me, not someone who might be *crazy*, but I wanted to be loved. I quickly played the pros and cons in my mind. Pros: He will love me, I won't be alone, and I won't be the third wheel. Cons: Everything else. With a hard blink of my eyes, I decided.

At the end of our meeting, Mark gave me his phone number. I waited a few days and called him. His mother answered the phone, and the first question she asked was, "How old are you?"

"Eighteen." I knew she didn't believe me. When Mark got on the phone, he didn't say much but agreed to go to the street festival held in town every summer. After I hung up, I wondered if I was doing the right thing. *Should I see him again?* I was uneasy about our age difference. He seemed to like me, and my desire to be loved overpowered all my common sense.

On our date, we were quiet. We sat at a table full of strangers and listened to the music. Finally, a slow song played, and I asked Mark if he wanted to dance. He shook his head, and we made our way toward the crowd of people dancing in the street. He held me close as we danced in circles. There was no turning back. I needed his attention. I needed to be loved. The night ended, and he drove me home. Gram didn't question who I had been with or how I got home. She trusted me to make smart choices, but all my logic was lost when my emotions took over.

Mark and I began spending more time together. He agreed to stop drinking when I told him I wouldn't date someone who drank. He stayed sober throughout our whole relationship. Somehow, Mom found out how old Mark was. She told my new social worker, Ben, and we had to have a meeting. Gram said she wanted to meet Mark before our meeting. Gram liked him, but she liked everyone. She asked me if I was happy, and I told her I was.

Ben and Mom arrived at Gram's where we gathered in the living room. At the meeting, Gram told Ben she had met Mark and that he was a nice boy.

Mom interrupted, "You mean man."

"Stop it, Wendy. Just let Jessie be happy."

"He's a grown man. All he wants her for is sex."

"Wendy, that's enough. It's not always about sex. Just because you slept around doesn't…"

"Jesus, Mom, this isn't about me…"

Ben interrupted them to stop the bickering. "What we have to think about is Jessica's well-being. I personally don't think she should be dating someone that much older than her."

Gram shook her head. "What you don't understand is Mark is more of a boy than a man. He's slow, not quite retarded, but not all there, either. He's a nice boy, and Jessie is a smart girl. I trust her, and him."

"Well, if you are willing to promise me, Jessica, that you and Mark will not have sex, and that you, Theresa, are willing to watch them when they are together, I say they can be friends." Ben looked over at Mom who had her arms folded across her chest.

"This is unbelievable. She's got you fooled. She has you all fooled."

Gram ignored Mom and looked at me. "Well, Jessie, can you promise us you won't have sex?"

My face grew hot as Gram talked. I let my hair fall over my face so I didn't have to see any of them and then nodded my head up and down. "I promise."

"It's settled. Now can we leave the poor girl alone? Unless you have something else you want to bitch about, Wendy?"

Mom stormed out of the living room and left the meeting. Ben soon followed, and Gram and I were left to laugh about what was said. "Why don't you have Mark over to watch movies this weekend? Just make sure there's no sex." She threw her head back and laughed.

"Funny, Gram!"

After about six months, I changed my mind. I wanted to find a boy my own age. I told Gram I wanted to end the relationship. She told me I would break Mark's heart and said all boys were the same. She reminded me Mark drove us places. He was helpful, and we needed someone who could help us like he did, so I stayed with him. I tried to find the good in him as Gram asked me to.

About this time, Mom let Cliff, a friend of a friend of Peter, move into her basement. He was twenty-one years old. When I visited Mom's house while Bill was at work, I saw Cliff. There was something about him I liked. He talked to me and listened. I felt like I had all of his attention. When I was with Cliff, he made me feel special. I felt like he understood me. Mom noticed my interest in Cliff and encouraged me to go with him when he went on errands.

I told Cliff how unhappy I was with Mark. "If you're not happy, you should dump him."

"I don't know if I can. I mean, I don't know how."

"Hell, if you break up with him, I may even date you." His hand went to my knee as he looked in my eyes.

Butterflies danced in my stomach as the warmth from his hand rushed through me. I couldn't stop thinking about being his girl-friend. I was falling in love with him, and I wanted him to love me too. One night, after Mark went home for the night, I saw Cliff outside by his car. I got his attention and asked him to come over. I snuck him into my room after Gram went to sleep. We talked for hours. I told him I didn't want to lose my virginity to Mark because he had already had sex with at least one girl. I wanted my first time to be with someone I loved and someone who loved me. I wanted it to be special. Cliff was intrigued to learn I was a virgin, and his interest in me grew.

The next weekend after Mark left, Cliff snuck over again. We talked more and then he kissed me. I felt so many things with that kiss—euphoria followed by a rush of guilt. I didn't want to be with Mark, but I didn't want to cheat on him either. Cliff continued to kiss me. He was chewing blue winter-mint gum, and it was all I could taste. He was wearing a leather jacket with the American flag on the back. The smell of leather was intoxicating. He shut off my lights and pushed me onto the bed. He continued to kiss me. He took off his coat, unbuckled his belt, and slid off his pants. He unbuttoned my pants and pulled them off me, pulling my underwear off at the same time.

"Cliff, I don't want to do this." He quieted me with a kiss. "No, Cliff."

"*Hush…*" he whispered as he pushed his erect penis inside of me.

"Cliff, no. I can't do this." Tears welled. "Please stop."

He didn't stop. Each time he thrust inside me, it hurt a little more. I closed my eyes tight, but tears still escaped. Gram woke up and was in the kitchen. She was only steps from my bedroom door. I wanted her to save me, but I was ashamed. I didn't want her to know what had happened. I felt dirty. I wanted Cliff off me. He lay perfectly still on top of me, his penis still inside me. He put his hand over my mouth to quiet my sobs.

When it sounded like Gram had gone back to bed, he finished. And then he left. I wanted to take a shower, but I couldn't move from my bed. I couldn't move at all. I cried all night long. I couldn't help but feel responsible for what had happened. I felt like I had asked for it as if I were a bad person because I let him do it to me.

Hannah called me the next morning, and I wanted to tell her what happened, but I was embarrassed. "Cliff came over last night and guess what?" I asked her trying to sound excited.

"You did it, didn't you? I'm so excited for you, Jess!"

"Yeah…it was great," I said the words I should have been saying after my first time. I didn't want her to know what actually happened. I didn't want her to know I was dirty or easy.

The next night, Cliff came to my bedroom window. He tapped on the glass until I moved the curtain back. He asked me to let him in. I didn't know what to do, but I didn't want him to wake up Gram. I let him in and sat on my bed with my arms crossed and my eyes to the floor. He tried to kiss me, but I just sat there.

"What's the matter with you?" he asked as he came closer.

"I just don't feel good," I said without making eye contact.

"You know you wanted it as much as I did last night."

"Yeah..." My tears returned.

"We were interrupted—I want to do it again."

"I don't feel good. I don't want to, not tonight."

"You know I can have any girl I want, right? You know you're lucky I fucked you? Most girls have to beg me for it. But you, you're special. Don't make me regret fucking you. I'm so glad your mom told me to fuck you."

"What?"

"Your mom asked me to make you fall in love with me so you'd do what you could to get back home," he said as he started taking off his pants. "I don't have long tonight—I have an appointment."

I gave in.

I let him do what he wanted to. I wilted as I realized it was Mom who put him up to this. I realized it was all a lie—our whole friendship was a ploy at getting me to fall in love with him. He never liked me. He was doing Mom a favor, and I was the pawn *again*. I laid there and found a place in my mind to go to take the pain away.

"You need to do something to keep me hard," he whispered loudly in my ear.

"I don't know what to do."

"You really are worthless. I don't know why I bothered with you." He put his pants back on and left.

I was thankful he was gone but felt devastated by what he'd

divulged. Did Mom really make him pretend to like me? I really *was* worthless. I really wasn't worth loving. I should be thankful Mark liked me. *Mark*. I had let him down. He wasn't going to like me now. I had ruined my life in those few short moments.

Blackness took over my world. Suicide seemed like the only option. I would be better off dead than to continue to live when no one wanted me. I didn't know how I wanted to die or how I was going to do it, but I knew I wanted to. I *needed* to. It was the only way to make the pain stop.

A few days later, when I was at Mom's house, I used her word processor to write my obituary. I figured I needed to write it myself because no one else knew me. I didn't intend for anyone to find what I had written until it was too late—until there was no turning back. I screwed that up too. The copy of my obituary I printed fell from my notebook onto the floor in Mom's living room.

The school pulled me out of class and told me Ben was there to pick me up. I didn't know what was going on. Ben told me I had to go talk to my counselor. I asked him why.

"Your mom found something you wrote."

My heart jumped into my throat. "What did she find?"

"You know what she found. Why did you write it? Why would you write such a thing?"

I closed my eyes as I tried to escape the situation I was in. I couldn't do it now. They would always be watching me. I really messed this up. I couldn't do anything right. I sat in his car in silence until we reached my counselor's office. She met me at the door with a concerned look on her face and walked me back to her office. "Your mom found the obituary you wrote."

I jumped in. "Yeah, we were talking about that stuff at school. I wanted to see what mine would say."

"So, you mean you don't want to hurt yourself?" Her eyes met mine. "I don't want anything to happen to you, Jessica."

As I heard her speak my name, I began to cry.

"Honey, what's the matter? I want to help you. I don't want you to hurt yourself."

"I figured if I wrote my obituary no one would wonder what to say about me after I die."

"Why do you want to die? What's the matter?"

"I had sex."

"With who?" she asked as she leaned forward toward me.

"With Cliff. I told him no, but he didn't listen. He just kept doing it. And now...and now I messed everything up." Tears took over my words.

"Honey, he *raped* you. You didn't do anything wrong. *He* did. He is the bad guy here, not you." She put her hand on my knee.

Her concern radiated throughout my body. She really did care about me. I would be letting her down if I killed myself. In my darkness, I had forgotten the people who actually loved me. The list was short, but it was my list. I would be letting them down if I hurt myself. I could not let anyone else down.

"I have to report what happened. You will have to talk to the police and a judge, to let them know what happened."

The more she spoke, the more afraid I became. I didn't want to talk to the judge again. I didn't want another court case to deal with. I wanted it to be over. I began to cry as she made the phone calls. Dawn, the lady behind the camera, came in to sit with me while the counselor made the phone calls. She told me she had seen me on the tapes and knew I was brave. After talking with her, the idea of being videotaped didn't seem so bad. I didn't mind if she was the one watching me. After the phone calls, Dawn left the room.

My counselor told me I had to go to the police station to file a police report.

"What if I had wanted it and I wasn't *raped*?"

She knew what I was doing. "He would still get in trouble, and you would still have to file a police report because you are under age, but if it were consensual, you wouldn't have to testify."

I tapped my left foot on the floor and watched it go up and down.

"It's up to you to say what happened. No one else was there. You are the only one who knows the truth. But I beg you to tell the truth. I beg you to let him pay for what he did."

When the officer interviewed me, I told him it was consensual. I told him I was scared because it was my first time, and I didn't want him to get into trouble. I couldn't tell the truth. I couldn't go to court or be the victim again. I wanted this over with as quickly as it had happened.

Because a law had been broken, Ben had to be told what happened. On the ride home, Ben said he was disappointed in me, and he needed to have a meeting with Gram, Mom, and me, to talk about birth control options. I was so sick to think Gram would have to know I had sex. Or that Mom would know. Or that anyone would know. I couldn't even tell them I didn't want it. I had to act like it was something I agreed to or I had to go to court.

When Ben and I arrived home, Mom and Gram were waiting for me. Ben sat in the living room with us and told them, "Jessica has something she needs to say to you."

All eyes were on me. "No. I don't have anything to say." I looked down at my hands and hid my face behind my hair.

He went on. "Well, if you aren't going to tell them, I will." I closed my eyes tight as he went on. "Jessica told her counselor today that she had sex. I feel that she needs to be on some type of birth control."

Gram sat quietly listening. Mom chimed in, "I told you if you let her date that old man, she'd be having sex."

"It wasn't Mark! It was Cliff! He told me what you did."

My mom's face dropped. "I-I-I told him I'd kill him if he touched her."

Ben said, "In light of what has happened, I am going to ask that Cliff move out."

If Cliff moved out, Mom lost $100 a month in rent. She would hold that against me, but I didn't care. I didn't care about anything anymore. I didn't care that Mom didn't love me. I didn't care that I would never get to go home again. I stopped caring.

After our meeting, Cliff moved out, and Mom was angry at me. She told me, "Your own brother doesn't want anything to do with you because he's afraid you'll get him in trouble too. You're really good at getting people in trouble, aren't you? You're a dirty little whore. You should learn to keep your legs shut." Her words were filled with anger, but I didn't care. I couldn't care. I was dead inside.

CHAPTER 15

en drove me to Planned Parenthood the following
week. We sat in the waiting room where pregnant
women of all ages were reading magazines and babies cried as their
mom's rocked them. As I scanned the room, it hit me. *What if I'm
pregnant?* I hadn't even considered that as a possibility. Cliff hadn't
used protection either time. I wasn't ready to have a baby, but
there was no way I could have an abortion. And adoption... I
couldn't bear the thought of not knowing where my baby was.

I imagined holding my baby and rocking it in my arms. I
thought about school. What would the kids say if I had a big pregnant belly? I couldn't hide it. I might not want to. Mom had told
me I was conceived in rape, but my baby wouldn't know the
circumstances. But what would I tell it? It? Was it a he or she?
Each thought took me deeper away from the crowded waiting
room I sat in. The nurse called my name and broke me out of the
trance I was in.

She handed me a cup and told me to leave a urine sample. As I
shut the door behind me, the thoughts about the possible life

inside me came back. As I set the sample on the shelf, I took a deep breath and decided I was ready for whatever happened next.

The nurse walked me into an exam room and handed me a folded white sheet and a green hospital gown. She asked me to undress and wait for the doctor. Shame came rolling in as she shut the door behind her. I carefully took my clothes off as I used the sheet to hide my body. After I put the folded clothes on the chair, I sat on the exam table and waited. My mind kept wandering back to the baby and the changes it would bring.

When the doctor opened the door, I was pulled out of my thoughts and back into the office. "Good news... you're not pregnant."

Well... that solved all the problems I had created but left me mourning the baby I had imagined the past twenty minutes. The doctor asked me a few questions, told me the importance of safe sex, talked about birth control options and explained a little of what she was going to do next. She asked me to put my head on the pillow and spread my legs as far apart as possible. I let the sheet drape over my legs as I opened them enough to make my knees stop touching.

"Drop your knees all the way...as far as you can." Her cold hands pressed my legs apart. "Scoot forward a little more."

I closed my eyes tight, pushed myself down the table, and dropped my knees open. I felt violated as I exposed myself to her in the daylight. The violation mimicked the time with Cliff, except he couldn't see me. She stuck her gloved fingers inside me and pressed as she talked to me. "Looks like a nice day out there."

Please stop talking. I managed to get a squeak out. "Mhm."

She inserted the cold, metal speculum into my vagina. It stung as she opened it wider inside of me. The real pain came when she inserted the long swab that felt like she was scraping my insides out. She explained she was looking to see if everything looked normal and to make sure I didn't have any sexually transmitted diseases. *Shit.* I hadn't thought about that, either.

When she was done, she took the speculum out and took my hand to help me sit up. She said the results from the exam would come in the mail in a few weeks but said everything looked good. My humiliation was louder than she was, and I missed most of what she said as I sat almost naked on top of the exam table. I felt just as dirty as I had after Cliff left me crying in bed. He had taken so much from me and still caused me pain, even now. I *hated* him and was grateful we were not creating a life together. I didn't have enough in me to sustain someone else. I could barely survive myself.

When the doctor left, I put my clothes on as quickly as possible. I made sure the sheet covered my skin until my clothes did. I left the appointment with birth control pills—a year's supply. The receptionist told me to call next year when I needed more pills and to schedule another exam. I was glad I didn't have to go back there anytime soon.

After the appointment, Mark and I talked. "We need to talk."

Mark stared blankly at me.

"Cliff and I had sex…"

"What the fuck?" He lit a cigarette as his hand shook. "I'm going to kill the sonofabitch."

"Please don't." I paused as I watched him. "It's over. I didn't want it, but it's over. I just want to go on with life."

"So, you didn't like it?"

"No. You can be mad at me, you can hate me, but please don't talk to him."

As he inhaled hard, ashes built on the cigarette between his lips.

"You can dump me if you want. I know I messed up."

"Is that what you want?" He jabbed the butt into the ashtray and lit another.

Yes. "No." I wanted to tell him yes, but I didn't want to hurt him. "But if you do, I understand." *Please, please say you want to.*

"Nah. I love you, hun. It's okay."

I forced a smile as we hugged. "I love you too."

I had been certain when Mark found out he was going to dump me. When he didn't, part of me fell back in love with him. I told Mark I was on birth control, and we could have sex now. I was still fifteen, and Mark was wary of having sex with me since we both promised we wouldn't until I at least turned sixteen. We fooled around a little in the past but never had sex. Gram gave us more freedom the more she got to know him. She trusted us, and we had plenty of time alone.

After Gram went to sleep, Mark and I went into my bedroom. We sat in the dark on my bed and kissed. I unbuttoned his jeans and put my hand on top of his boxers. I felt his penis harden under my hand as I kissed him. "I wanna make love to you," I whispered between kisses.

"Not yet, hun."

"Come on. No one will know." I put my hand under his boxers and stroked his penis. "Please. I really wanna."

"I don't know." He looked around the room. "I don't want to get in trouble."

"No one will know." I took off my pants and put his hand between my legs. "I want you." I pushed him back on the bed and took off his pants. I kissed his erect penis. "Please."

"Okay. But don't tell anyone." We kissed as he rolled on top of me and guided his penis inside me.

This was my first time. I was not giving it to Cliff. Sex felt good when I was in control. I was careful to make sure I took my birth control pill because I didn't want to get Mark in trouble. I didn't want anyone to find out because I didn't want to stop. I was falling in love with how I felt when I was with him.

Mark and I didn't go on dates. We stayed at Gram's house and watched movies. Day after day, it was the same thing. The kids at school talked about what they did over the weekend, and I listened. Our relationship was boring. There was no fun involved, only sex. I was fifteen, and we lived like an old married couple. I hated it. I loved the idea that I wasn't alone, but I hated who I *wasn't* alone with.

CHAPTER 16

*H*annah and I still spent a lot of time together. We walked miles around town—talking and laughing. I went to her house as often as I could. It was like going home. We spent hours trying to contact the dead, listening to music, and watching movies.

We went to the cemetery next to our high school. We spent many hours there walking around reading gravestones and imagining who these people beneath our feet were. We tried to imagine how they died and wondered about the family they had left behind. Since I was unsure if Ralph was really dead or just waiting for me to turn eighteen, I didn't visit his grave. I found a headstone on the lower level of the cemetery. I sat next to where a stranger's body was buried, and I talked to him. I asked him if I could visit him instead of Ralph, and if Ralph really was dead, if he could pass my messages along to him. I found comfort in visiting with a man I had never met. He was my makeshift father. It felt like a crazy thing to do. I didn't even tell Hannah.

In the cemetery, I felt peaceful. It was the only place to really bring me peace. The living gave me too many problems. I couldn't trust many people who walked the Earth, but these people who rested six feet under the ground I could trust. They needed respect, as did I. I felt at home on the grounds of the cemetery. When school got overwhelming, I escaped to the cemetery and sat with the man who replaced Ralph and told him my troubles. A quick walk around the headstones quieted my mind and made me feel reconnected. I was grateful for the life I still had. No matter how unsettled it was, I was still alive.

That fall, I received word Ralph's mom was sick. They told me she was in the hospital and wanted to see me. When Ralph first died, I visited my grandmother every few weekends. I was all she had left, so I tried to make a point to visit her. As I got older and had more things going on during the weekends, the visits began to dwindle down. It had been months since I had last seen her.

I was upset to hear she was sick and thought about going to see her, as it was her only wish. The hospital was two hours away, and the only person who offered me a ride was Ann. I hated her, and the idea of having to be in a car with her that long made me sick. I tried to forget about what was happening and tried to put it out of my mind. I figured my grandmother would get better, and I could see her once she returned home.

On Thanksgiving Day, the call came—my grandmother had passed away. There was nothing they could do to save her, and she went peacefully in her sleep. Guilt flooded me as I hung up the phone. All she had wanted was to see her granddaughter, but I couldn't do it. I let her down. I was her whole world, and I had failed her. There was no way to change what had happened. My head hung low as it all sunk in.

I had never been close to my grandmother. I knew she loved me, but she was different from Gram. I heard stories about how she spent time in a psychiatric hospital after she "went crazy" when her husband died, and she had tried to kill Ralph. She took a butcher knife and chased him around the house threatening to kill him. I had heard this wasn't the only time she had been hospitalized. I knew she loved me, but I was afraid of her. She had never been mean to me or done anything to hurt me. She treated me with love, and I never saw her have any outburst, but the thoughts never left my head. When I stayed with her, I slept so I faced the door. When I heard a noise, I woke up fearing she had a mental break and was coming to kill me.

I felt bad I had never been close to her and hadn't spent more time with her. She had a hard life, and I only added to her pain. Gram went with me to her funeral. I picked some daffodils from Mom's yard, wrapped the stems with wet paper towels, and placed the ends into a plastic bag to keep them alive for the trip to the cemetery. Her service was held at the same venue Ralph's had been five years before. I was older and now able to shrink away from the feelings that flooded me before.

The priest told us to place our flowers on top of her casket at the end of the service so they could go with her into the ground. Ann's daughter placed a single rose on top and then I placed the daffodils next to it. A slight breeze came through and blew the daffodils off. The single rose stayed put. I picked the flowers up and placed them back on top of the casket. They fell off again. Ann snickered as I picked them back up from the ground and held them. Gram saw my face and put her arm around me.

I didn't know if they were being blown off because my grandmother was mad at me or because they were flowers Mom had grown. The not knowing made the guilt return. *She really was upset with me.* I hurt her when all she wanted to do was love me. After we returned home, I shared my thoughts with Gram. She tried to reassure me that my grandmother wasn't mad at me and knew I loved her. Gram told me my flowers were blown off because they were lighter. I looked at her, knowing she was trying to put me at ease. "Lighter than a single rose?"

"You know she didn't like your mother. You were everything to her. She understood life was busy. Don't beat yourself up."

I tried to take comfort in her words. I tried to believe I had not let my grandmother down. The guilt didn't leave. It haunted me.

CHAPTER 17

Three years passed with Mark, and the same thing continued. Nothing. Nothing ever happened. Mark didn't have a job or any money. My part-time job sorting returnables at the redemption center and the social security benefit from Ralph's death went to buy cigarettes and food for Mark. Everything we bought I paid for.

My senior year of high school, I required special permission to bring Mark to the prom since he was so much older. After a lot of consideration, the school agreed he could come as my date. I bought the tickets and rented his tux. I didn't have extra money to purchase a dress. I looked at dresses, but there was nothing I was able to afford.

I didn't even want to go to prom after this, but I had already paid for the tickets and the tux rental. I came up with the idea of getting a dress at JC Penny. They didn't have any dresses I liked and none fancy enough for prom. I found a simple, long pink chiffon dress. There was no frill or flare, but it matched my disappointment.

All the other girls got their hair done and wore fancy, frilly dresses. I did my own hair, wore simple shoes, and the pink dress. Others gathered at local restaurants and arrived in Limos. I met up with Hannah and Tim at the cemetery next to the high school where we posed for pictures.

When we arrived at the Country Club for prom, I was embarrassed. Embarrassed by my dress, by my date, and by my life. I felt so different from the other girls. There were parents taking pictures of their children. No one came to take my picture. It was just Mark and me—a man too old to be there. He was twenty-six years old and probably as old as most of the chaperones. I was so sick of being different.

I was trapped in a dead-end relationship at seventeen years old. All the other kids in my class were talking about where they were going to college and their future plans. I couldn't join the conversation. My future was not something I wanted to think about. I couldn't stomach the thought of one more mundane day.

The guidance counselor wasn't helpful. He asked what I wanted to do but never offered help. After a while, I decided it was easier to say I didn't want to go to college. I didn't know how to fill out the forms to the colleges, and I didn't have the money to send in with the applications. I also needed help from Mom to fill out the student aid forms, but she refused to complete the required paperwork.

I was on high honors for most of my time in high school, but those accomplishments faded from my memory as I focused on my failure. The whole world was against me. I sank into myself as negative thoughts took over.

At graduation, the feelings of failure and uncertainty lingered. Throughout the ceremony, I looked around at my classmates and fidgeted in my seat under the hot June sun. What made them better than me? Why were their lives perfect? I didn't need perfection. I just needed a break from the constant struggle.

A month after graduation was my eighteenth birthday. Not only was I stepping over the threshold into adulthood, but I was also expecting Ralph to walk back into my life. Since his death, I believed Ralph had not died but was just hiding out to escape his responsibilities. At ten, I wasn't able to comprehend his departure was forever, so I developed an elaborate story that he would return on my eighteenth birthday.

Part of me knew how ridiculous this was, but part of me held on to hope. I began to wonder what I would say to him or if I'd forgive him for leaving me. Would feeling his arms around me in a loving embrace as he wished me—his only child—a happy birthday as I entered adulthood take away all the pain?

The night before my birthday, I couldn't sleep. I imagined Ralph walking toward me and smiled as I thought about having him in my life again. I would tell him the truth about Bill and say I was sorry for the lie Mom made me tell. I was nervous he'd be mad but figured he'd forgive me since he had disappeared. We were going to start over.

It was almost showtime. The past seven years of raw emotion were coming to a head. *A few more hours, and he'll be here…*

After falling asleep, I woke up to a rainy morning in July with my heart full of hope. I walked into Gram's living room and sat with her as she watched the morning news. I hadn't told anyone about the story I believed. Deep down, I knew it was crazy.

The hours passed, and Ralph didn't show up. There was no magical knock on the door or a special delivery of flowers from him to let me in on his secret. The afternoon turned to night, and there was still no sign of him. I hung onto anything I could to keep my story going. *Maybe he forgot when my birthday was. Maybe he was too far away to get back on time. Maybe he will come tomorrow.* My maybes turned to the reality that he wasn't coming back. He wasn't hiding. He really was dead. My dad died seven years before, and I had yet to process the loss.

My heart felt empty as the day ended. My eighteenth birthday was filled with pain. I had lost my father again. *Again.* How could I have done this to myself? Nothing in my life ever went the way I wanted it to. Why did I expect this to be different? Why?

My eyes bled tears the rest of the night. My heart was open and raw. A lump in my throat made it hard to breathe. All my hope was lost, and my world turned black. I finally told Gram what I held on to for all those years. She didn't think I was crazy. She was sad for me.

She knew I didn't have the right tools to grieve his loss at the time, and she was sorry I had to lose him all over again. A day I anticipated would be filled with joy was a day forever marked with sadness. I had no choice but to accept his death. I had to learn to live with the fact I would spend the rest of my life without a dad. I would get married and not have my dad walk me down the aisle. I would have kids without a grandfather. I would have to learn how to do all the things parents teach their daughters on my own. I would have to let go of him. I would have to let him travel on his journey.

I had only been to his gravesite since his funeral when I went for my grandmother's funeral. At first, Ann's scolding me for standing on him had scared me from ever wanting to go back. Later, I convinced myself he wasn't really there anyway. After my birthday, I told Gram and Mark I wanted to go to the cemetery to visit Ralph.

We arrived at the cemetery, and it all hit me. This was where my dad was going to spend eternity. This was the only place I could visit him. *This was it.* Gram and Mark got out of the car with me at first and then gave me some privacy. I talked to him in my head and was very careful not to step on him. My eyes went to the dates on the stone. Ralph was there with his dad and his mom. He was their only child, and I was his. I was the missing piece to this family. I was the only one still alive. I looked at their birth years: 1924, 1932, and 1954. I wanted 1981 to be there as well. I needed to be represented somehow. I looked through the change in the car and found a 1981 dime. I placed it on the stone under Ralph's birth year and said my goodbyes.

A short while later, I started getting phone calls every night at about the same time. I'd answer, and the other end of the line was dead. Days went by, and the calls kept coming. After a while, the call became expected.

A few weeks later, I returned to visit Ralph. I sat on the ground and looked for the dime. It was gone. I searched the ground around the stone, looked through the grass, still nothing. Where could it have gone? It was unlikely that someone had taken ten cents from a grave.

As I sat on top of the grave, the song, "I Just Called to Say I Love You" started to play in my head. Tears flooded my eyes. *It was him! He had been calling me!* It all connected—the calls, the dime, and the song. I sat there with him and smiled through my tears. He came back to say he loved me. He gave me signs he was okay. He was dead, but he was not gone. After that visit, the calls stopped.

CHAPTER 18

*S*oon after my birthday, I applied for a job in the cafeteria at the local college. They hired me on the spot, and I started working full-time. I didn't have my driver's license, and the college was about three miles from my house. I walked to work the first few days, and Mark brought me home. After walking and then standing in the hot kitchen for eight hours, I contacted a taxi, and we came up with a weekly deal. He brought me to work five days a week for ten dollars. It was more than worth it to arrive on time and not be tired before the start of my shift.

I loved my job. It was fun, and I worked with a great group of people. But when the summer ended, and college began, I started to dread my job. All the incoming students were my age. It was painful to watch the kids go to college while I worked as a "lunch lady." That could have been me. I could have been on the other side of the counter. I was angry at life for letting me down. I was disappointed in myself for not being good enough, for not being smart enough.

Dread turned to hate. I hated my job. I hated how everyone else seemed to be good at life. I hated that everyone else had a loving family behind them. I hated how every day of my life was a struggle. I began to look for another job.

Hannah was also looking for a new job. We applied to the same places so we could work together. We filled out applications at the local machine shops. A few days into the search, I received a call and a job offer at a factory specializing in precision machining. Hannah also received the same offer. Hannah and I hadn't seen each other every day since we graduated. It was like being back in school.

Hannah and I picked the same start date. We arrived at work together and filled out our new-hire paperwork. We were the first women to work on the shop floor. Others worked in the shipping department, but we were the first girls to be working with the guys. We made nine dollars an hour. That was over two dollars more than I made at the college. We also had to work a mandatory forty-four-hour workweek, which gave us four hours of overtime each week. Finally, life started to look up.

The guys at the shop were accommodating and friendly. We were not just the only women working on the shop floor, we were eighteen and nineteen years old—so we had their complete attention. With their attention and desire to "help" us, we learned the job fast. Within three months, they gave us a raise, and we were running and setting up CNC mill machines on our own. The computerized machines held tools to cut the metal used to make aircraft parts for the Defense Department. I felt like this was a career I could do for the rest of my life. I was always learning and enjoyed the attention.

Mark and I had been together for four years with no excitement or connection. He didn't like to hear about how much I liked my job, and he was jealous of the time I spent with Hannah and the men at work. The more I enjoyed life, the more I wanted to leave

Mark. I tried to find a way to tell him I wasn't happy. I was unsure how to break free. We were engaged the Christmas before. I said yes thinking it was my only option. We had been together for three years and figured that was my life. There was no way out of it, so I may as well move forward. I wasn't excited about the engagement and didn't even think about the wedding. It was a symbol of his ownership of me.

One afternoon, after Mark and I were out riding around in his truck, we parked in a parking lot and began to talk. "What do you want out of life?"

"What do you mean, hun?"

"I mean, don't you want a job? Don't you want to move out of your mom's house? Don't you want anything?"

"You know I have been looking for—"

"You've been looking for the last four years. You don't want to work. You expect me to buy everything. I want more out of life." I paused and looked out the window at the people walking into the store. "I'm not happy anymore. I think we should break up."

He lit a cigarette and looked straight ahead out the windshield. "You leave me, and I'll kill you." He turned and smiled at me. "And then I'll kill myself."

The smile on his face told me he was serious. *I was trapped.* Mark had never scared me before. He was boring, but always kind. I had never seen this side of him. "I'm tired. Can we go home?"

He turned the key in the ignition and put the truck in drive. I looked out the window all the way back. When he parked the truck, I got out and walked into the house alone. Mark followed and sat in the rocking chair in Gram's living room. I went to my room and went to bed. A few hours later, Gram went to bed, and Mark stood in the doorway of my room. I pretended to be asleep, and he finally left. A few minutes after, I heard his truck pull out of the driveway, so I got up and locked the front and back doors.

The following day, Mark came over after I got out of work and asked me to go for a ride with him. I got into his truck, and we rode in silence until he pulled into the parking lot we were in the day before. He put the truck in park, opened the center console between us, and uncovered a pistol. He picked up the gun and looked at me. "This is what I'll use if you ever leave me." He returned the gun and closed the console.

I didn't speak. I couldn't. The fear I had as a child when Ralph made threats he was going to kill Mom, Peter, and me returned. I was that same little girl, terrified the wrong move, the wrong word, would cost me my life.

Each time I got into Mark's truck, I was cautious, my eyes always went to the console. I didn't know what might make him snap. I didn't know what might get him to decide today was the day he took my life. I stayed with him because I didn't want to die. I wanted to live… but not like this.

CHAPTER 19

There was one man at the shop who caught my attention. He was more than just eye-catching—I was drawn to him. John, the manager of the tool crib, a room that housed all of the tools and supplies needed on the shop floor. The room was caged in and had rows of drawers full of tools. John worked alone in the tool crib, away from the machines.

When John looked at me, a spark ignited inside me, one I had never felt before. We exchanged a few words and smiles. The other guys warned me John was a jerk and said Hannah and I should stay away from him. I didn't see what they saw.

Our first conversation was in the tool crib, where it was just the two of us. I asked him for a carbide tool for the job I was working on. My face flushed when he looked at me. My hair was up in a messy ponytail, and my plastic safety glasses put distance between us. He found the tool I needed and held it in his hand. "How bad do you want it?"

My eyes locked with his as a smile pushed the glasses up on my face. "I need it." I reached for the tool, my hand brushing against his as he pulled it away.

"Need it? But how bad?"

"Real bad."

He laughed as he leaned against the door. "You need *my* tool real bad?"

"I do."

He put the tool in my hand and asked, "How old do you think I am?"

"I don't know? Thirty something?"

"I love you! Not quite, but thanks for thinking so!"

"Well, how old are you then?"

"How old are *you*?"

"I'm eighteen...almost nineteen."

"Jesus, eighteen? I'm way too old for you."

"Why? How old *are* you?"

"Way too old."

"My boyfriend is twenty-seven. Age is just a number. It doesn't matter to me at all."

"Boyfriend? Oh, man!"

"I don't want to be with him... but it's complicated."

"I'm forty-three. Still think age is just a number?"

"That's not too old."

"*Really*? You want to fool around with me? You're eighteen. You're just a kid. It wouldn't freak you out to be with me?"

"Not at all." I stood staring into his hazel eyes through our safety glasses.

When my hand closed around the tool, he noticed my engagement ring. "You're engaged? That's more than complicated."

"It's a long story. Maybe I can tell you some night." I turned and walked away to return to my machine. *He liked me too.*

At the end the day, John came out of the tool crib to watch me leave with Hannah. He yelled over the buzz of the machines, "I want to hear that story." Hannah looked at me confused as a smile lit up my face. I couldn't wipe it off, even if I wanted to. I was going to fall hard for John, and I couldn't wait.

As Hannah and I walked our usual two-mile walk around town after work, I told her what had happened.

"Jess, you're crazy! He's too old. *Way* too old. And he's a jerk. Nobody at the shop likes him." She looked at me and laughed. "What about Mark?"

"I'm so sick of him! I just wish he'd leave me alone."

"Tell him. Dump him. Go have fun with grandpa." She laughed harder.

"I wish it were that easy."

"You know he won't actually kill you if you dump him. He just wants to scare you."

"I *don't* know. Enough of him! Do you think I should do it? Do you think I should hook up with John? He's so hot!" As I finished my sentence, John drove by in his white Corvette, and my smile returned.

Hannah smiled too. "Looks like you already know what you're gonna do."

"It'll be the closest I'll ever get to getting it on with Tom Petty!"

"You're twisted!"

"What? He's the hottest!" I said through my laughter.

"You and your old men! Just do it, I know you want to! Do it!" she said as we both continued to laugh.

The next day at work, John and I talked again. "I'm going to lock you in here, and you'll be my sex kitten," he said as he grabbed the door of the tool crib.

I smiled. "Okay, whatever you want."

"Whoa…really? *Anything?*"

"Yup, anything. Want to meet after work tonight?"

"I don't know." He hesitated. "What about your boyfriend? Where would we meet?"

"Forget about him. He's a jerk."

"Okay, so where do you want to meet?"

"You could come pick me up near my house. I don't drive."

"Holy shit…you don't drive yet? You *are* just a kid! Holy shit."

"It's fine. I'll learn, but I don't want to wait that long."

"Okay, okay, I'll pick you up. Just tell me where and when. Give me a call when you figure it out." He handed me a folded piece of paper with his number written on it.

The rest of the day went by so slowly. The anticipation was killing me. I couldn't wait to be with John. I wanted so badly to kiss him, to smell him, to feel him—to love him. I wanted to prove to the other guys John was worthy of love. The more they talked about their dislike of him, the more I wanted to love him. I knew all too well what it was like to be without love.

When Mark came over that night, I told him I didn't feel well and wanted to go to sleep. After he left, I called John and told him to meet me at the soccer field near the elementary school. He said he would be right there—he only lived two miles from my house.

I started walking down the road past Mom's house, and I saw John's big, green Ford pickup truck. He pulled over next to me and told me to get in and duck down. "I brought the truck tonight, so no one will recognize me." I got into the truck and crouched down next to him. "Make sure you stay down so your boyfriend doesn't see you."

"Okay."

"This is crazy. I can't believe we're doing this. Are you sure you want to?"

"Absolutely."

"Just so you know, we're just fuck buddies, okay? You're engaged, and I'm not looking for anything serious."

Fuck buddies? The words pierced my heart as they left his lips, but I wanted him more than the pain his words had caused. "Yeah... I get it."

We pulled into his driveway, and he said it was safe to sit up. The long driveway brought us past an old shack and under maple trees to an old, white trailer and an open field. "Don't mind this place, it's temporary, I'm going to build a house here someday."

"It's nice and private here." We got out of the truck and walked up the three wooden stairs that led to the door. Once we were inside, he grabbed me and pulled me close. "I can't believe we're doing this!" he said as he put my hand on his pants over his penis. "Feel that—that's for you."

We started to kiss. My mind raced. *What if he didn't like me? What if I wasn't good enough? What if Mark found out? What if...?* I tried to let go of all of the thoughts and enjoy the moment.

John took me by the hand and led me down a short hall to his bedroom. He unbuttoned my shirt and pushed it off my shoulders as he kissed me. He pulled his t-shirt over his head as I unhooked my bra and dropped it on the floor. His hand cupped my breasts as he stood back to look at me. "I can't believe we're doing this."

He unbuttoned my jeans and pushed them off my hips. I stepped out of them and took my underwear off. My hands traced a scar on his stomach as he unbuttoned his Levi's and they fell to the floor. He pulled me close and kissed me more as the warmth of his hands covered my body. He lowered me onto his neatly made king-size bed and got on top of me.

His penis entered me as his lips found mine. Pure ecstasy. I watched his face as he made love to me. I didn't want it to end. With every thrust inside, I fell deeper. I was in love. John owned my heart, whether he wanted it or not.

When we were done, we held each other in bed. It was perfect. I wanted it to last forever. I wanted to be with him for the rest of my life. With each passing second, my love grew. I loved him, and I was sure I could make him see he loved me too.

Reality crashed down when he told me he had to take me home so he could get to bed since we both had to get to work in the morning. I stayed awake thinking about how perfect it felt being with John. *How would I tell Mark I wanted to leave him?*

The following day at work, John smiled at me as I walked by, but he didn't pay as much attention to me as he had before. When I made my usual trip to the tool crib, he was quiet. I kept a smile on my face, but it didn't keep the pain away. I feared he had not fallen for me as I had for him.

On my next trip to the tool crib, John took me aside. "We need to be careful and not let anyone know about us. Maybe you ought a get what you need in one trip."

I felt tears start to well in my eyes. "Okay." The familiar taste of rejection filled my mouth as the need to vomit came over me. I rushed out of the tool crib and into the bathroom where I locked myself in a stall and let the pain fall from my eyes.

That night, when Mark came over, I couldn't look at him. I told him I wasn't feeling well again and wanted to go to bed. When he left, I went to my room and cried. I cried because I didn't understand my feelings, and I cried because I wanted love from a man who wasn't looking for love. The next day was my four-year anniversary with Mark, but I didn't want to spend it with him. After he left, I called John and asked him if he wanted to meet again. To my surprise, he did.

At John's house, I tried to do everything I could to make him fall for me. I paid full attention to him. I let him do what he wanted to me. After we were finished, I held him tight. I thought if he felt the love I had for him, he would love me back.

"You're not falling in love with me, are you?"

His words caught me off guard. "No, of course not."

"Good, because this is just about sex, remember? Nothing more. I don't want you to think anything is going to come of this." He got out of bed and started to get dressed.

He wasn't going to love me. I had fallen in love with a man who would never love me. I was embarrassed for thinking I was worthy of his love. I wanted to get home and go to bed so I could cry myself to sleep. I was destined to be unhappy—Mom was right, I was unlovable.

As I sat on my bed in my room, my eyes were drawn to my bookcase to a book Hannah and I used to read. *This could do it. This could make John love me.* The book I had put away years ago was filled with spells. The apprehension I had with the idea of witchcraft escaped me. I was desperate.

I picked up the book and flipped through the pages. *Make someone fall in love with you spell.* I found it! I read the instructions over and over again. I had to do this. I had to make him love me. Maybe this was the only way.

I told Hannah what I had decided to do. "Be careful. Witchcraft isn't something to mess around with."

"I know…but I need help."

She sighed. "I don't know, Jess. It can get pretty intense. Are you sure?"

"Yes. I need John to love me."

She shook her head. "I don't know…"

I read and reread what I needed in order to cast the spell. A picture of John and a red candle. I had the red candle, but I didn't have a picture. How was I going to get one? Without the picture, I wouldn't be able to cast the spell.

As I walked to the vending machine at work past the bulletin board, my eyes focused on the wall of photos someone had hung. There in the collage was a picture of John. I knew then I had to cast the spell. *This was my sign.* I walked past the wall of photos multiple times to figure out how I was going to get it without anyone noticing. I made Hannah come with me, and I pointed out his picture. Our eyes met. She knew what my plan was. She told me at lunch that when everyone was outside, I could get it. She convinced me no one would notice it missing, and if they did, why would they suspect me?

At lunchtime, when everyone left, I stayed inside and walked back past the bulletin board. Hannah met me there. I hesitated. "I can't do it!" I walked away. When we got outside, Hannah pulled something out of her pocket. *The picture.* She had taken it down as I walked away. This was going to happen. John was going to fall in love with me. He had to. We were meant to be. I knew it.

When I got home, I put the picture in a safe place, found the red candle, and a lighter. I ate dinner with Mark and Gram and waited for Mark to go home. I sat and watched more TV with Gram. When she got up to go to bed, I went into my room and pulled out the picture. My eyes stared into John's eyes, and my heart filled with love. I had to cast the spell. I lit the red candle, continued to stare into his eyes, and recited the words to the spell. I chanted the words as the wax from the candle melted onto the photo. My eyes went to the flame. I imagined the two of us living a happy life, getting married and having children. I imagined the two of us growing old together. I imagined the feeling of being loved. I wished. I hoped. And I believed my desire would come true. Life had to gift me this wish.

It was time for me to feel love and happiness.

CHAPTER 20

*N*othing changed. I wanted to leave Mark, but I didn't know how. My desire to be with John grew with each passing day. My body ached for him. I wanted to feel his skin next to mine. I couldn't look Mark in the eyes any longer. I hated every minute we were together. I was his prisoner. My only escape was work. I could go there and dream about the life I wanted. I could see John and hope he saw me.

I needed to learn how to drive. Since Abigail's accident, I was afraid of the responsibility behind the wheel and wasn't confident enough to try. There was no other form of transportation in northern Vermont. Everything was at least two miles away from my house. If I didn't learn how to drive, I would have to depend on others to get around for the rest of my life. I needed the freedom that driving offered.

Hannah offered to give me lessons when she heard I was ready. I found a rusty, spray painted white Subaru wagon for four hundred dollars that I bought on the spot. I began studying for my learner's permit, and within a few weeks, I passed and was able to start learning. Hannah made me drive us to work and then around town after. Within a couple of months, I had an appointment to get my license.

This was the only way to make my escape from Mark. If I wanted to have a chance with John, I had to get it. There was so much at stake. I had to pass the test. I had to.

Mom drove me to the DMV an hour from our house to take the road test. I only had eight weeks of practice. I had to make them count and had to forget how nervous I was. My heart bounced around in my chest as I waited for the instructor to call my name. Butterflies from my stomach swam up to my throat as I waited. My foot bounced on the white tile floor as the minutes on the clock ticked by.

A short, round man with slicked back thinning hair wore a blue zip-up jacket and held a clipboard. He used his middle finger to push his glasses up, and with a nasal voice, he called my name. *This was it.* We walked to my car and got in. He didn't say a word to me. My hand shook as I fastened my seat belt. I looked in my rearview and side mirrors, swallowed hard, and looked at the man for instruction. He pointed out the window and told me to go right.

I followed his directions as he navigated me through the unfamiliar town...with traffic lights. We didn't have them in Johnsville, and they were not something I had expected to encounter. When it turned red, I pulled too far ahead and stopped. My hands at ten and two slipped around the steering wheel as I tried to calm my nerves. *I can do this. I will do this.*

He directed me to a steep hill, and halfway up, he asked me to do a hill start. I was a master at these. This was foolproof. With my foot on the brake, I looked out the windows and in the mirrors. I put my foot back on the gas—*screech*. "Whoops." My face grew hot as I continued up the hill.

Next on the list—parallel parking. This was the one thing I struggled with each time with Hannah. Any confidence I had talked myself into was lost, but I had to try. I pulled up next to a Toyota Camry and turned the wheel, inching my way into the open space. A little off, but I was in. *I did it!*

The instructor guided me back to the DMV where I parked the car. Sweat rolled down my forehead. "Did I... did I pass?"

Silent, his eyes scanned the notes on his clipboard. With his red pen in hand, he scribbled on the top of the paper. *Oh no...I really screwed this up.*

"You just barely made it," he said as he looked up from his papers. "By one point."

"I passed? Really? I get my license? Today?"

"Yes. Take this inside, and they will get your photo and your new license ready for you." He handed me the yellow paper.

I did it. I was free! I needed this more than I had needed anything ever before. I couldn't wait to get to work and tell Hannah and the guys—and John—I had passed. I was in control of my own destiny. Literally, now. After I returned Mom home, I put *Tom Petty and the Heartbreakers Greatest Hits* into the CD player, turned to song fourteen, cranked the volume, and headed to work. Alone. For the first time ever, I was alone in the car. The windows down, my hair blew all over the place as I drove on the dirt road to work, singing, "Free Fallin'."

When I got to work, my smile said it all. Everyone who knew where I had been that morning knew I passed my test. All the guys congratulated me as I made it to my machine. John came over and told me he was happy for me and asked if I wanted to celebrate. I smiled and said I did. I was right—having my license was going to change my life.

When Mark came over after work, I knew he was upset I had passed. I think he knew what was coming too. I had my freedom now. I could go where I wanted to go, and I didn't have to ask anyone for help. I grew distant. I needed him to fall out of love with me and see I wasn't who he wanted. I didn't kiss him back when he kissed me. I didn't hug him. I just stood there.

After Mark left that night, I waited a little while and then drove to John's house. When I got there, we talked a little. "Why did you want to see me *now*?"

"I always want to see you."

I looked at him, unsure what to say. *What was he talking about?*

"I was afraid to get my heart broken...again." He looked away. "Haven't you heard?"

"Heard what?"

"The assholes at the shop didn't tell you?"

I shook my head no. "Tell me what?"

"That I have a thing for young blondes?" He rubbed his forehead. "I left my wife a few years ago after I fell in love with a girl in the office. She was just out of high school...like you...and she wanted to be a model."

Great...he's been with a model? No wonder he doesn't want me. The self-hating thoughts swam around my head as he continued.

"We moved to Vegas, I paid her tuition to modeling school... and she dumped me. I had to come back home with my tail between my legs. Everyone thought it was funny...karma, they said, for cheating on my wife."

I put my hand on his leg, "I'm sorry. I didn't know."

"She broke my heart, and I have been gun shy since. I haven't dated anyone, haven't really been looking...until you." He took my hand. "I'm afraid to get hurt again, and then you're a young blonde too, so everyone will be an asshole about it if they find out...they'll say I didn't learn my lesson."

"I won't hurt you."

"Leave your boyfriend then, prove it."

"I'm scared...he bought a gun and said he'd kill me if I left him...that's what makes it complicated."

"He's all talk. He just wants to scare you. Trust me...you'll be fine."

I wasn't sure he was right, but I had to find out. The information he gave me about the girl who broke his heart only made me love him more. He needed my love, even if he didn't know it. He needed to know he was worth loving. I had to leave Mark.

I had to do something. I couldn't stay forced into a relationship because of fear. John and I kept seeing each other, more often than before. Each time I was with him, my love for him grew stronger. I decided breaking free was worth the risk of dying. I wasn't happy with Mark, and if my only way out was death, I decided then so be it.

The next time Mark came over, I didn't let him come inside. We stood on the lawn in front of Gram's house as I broke the news. "I don't love you anymore." I waited as I watched him. He stared at me as though he hadn't heard me, so I kept talking. "I don't want to be with you anymore. I want to stop seeing each other." I took off my engagement ring and handed it to him.

"No! *No!* No!" He yelled as he pushed the ring back at me. "We're getting married. We're going to move in together. *No!*"

"No. I don't want that. I don't want any of that. Please, just leave. I don't want to see you anymore."

"I'm not going anywhere! You can't make me!" He stood on the lawn yelling at me.

I walked away, got into my car, and drove off. I didn't know where to go. I was scared he would follow me. I ended up at Hannah's house. "I just dumped Mark...I don't know what to do."

"I can't believe you did it!"

I tried to catch my breath. "He's pissed. I don't wanna die, Hannah."

"You should go to John's. He won't look for you there, but I bet you anything he's on his way here."

"Yeah..."

She hugged me. "I'm so happy for you Jess... just be safe... okay?"

I left her house and drove to John's. I told him how angry Mark had been. He assured me I was going to be okay. We went to bed where I spent the night with him for the first time. As we lay in bed together, we saw headlights pull into the yard. John grabbed his Smith and Wesson and looked out the window—nothing. He put the gun by the bed, and we fell asleep in each other's arms. This was what I had dreamed of since our first meeting almost a year before.

The next day, Hannah told me Mark went to her house the night before. He had been drinking and wouldn't leave. Tim called the police because Mark kept banging on their door. Mark left when he heard they had called the police. I told her about the headlights John and I had seen. She assured me it wasn't Mark because he didn't know I was seeing John. She had to be right. It must have been someone else.

Fear overshadowed me. Every time I went outside, I waited for the bullet. I looked over my shoulder at all times. I didn't know what Mark was capable of, and I was worried I was going to find out. The threat of the pistol loomed over me. I kept the information of the pistol away from Gram and Mom. I didn't want Gram to be afraid, and I didn't want Mom to know she was right about Mark.

When I arrived at work, there was a vase of red roses on my workbench. Excitement filled me—could they be from John? My heart beat fast as I pulled out the card: *I luv u, hun. Please come back.* Disgusted I threw them in the trash. Why wouldn't he just leave me alone?

As I drove through town, I saw Mark's truck in my rearview mirror. He inched closer to me, his truck right on my bumper. I stiffened up as my grip on the steering wheel tightened. I turned onto the main road in town and tried to lose him. A few cars separated us, but I could still see him. I pressed hard on the gas pedal and swerved onto a side road. He didn't follow. I circled back around and made my way back to the road. The town was too small to escape him for long. I didn't know which way he had gone.

I returned home and had dinner with Gram. She questioned where Mark had been. "We broke up."

"What? When?" Her fork dropped on the plate.

"Last week."

"Well, he was too old for you anyway."

"I know, Gram." *What? He wasn't too old for me five years ago.*

"He's a nice boy, but you're too smart for him, Jessie."

"Don't let him in if he comes by, okay?"

"I can still be nice to him. I'm sure he's sad."

"Gram... please... he...has a gun."

"Oh, stop it..."

"No, Gram, I'm serious. He *showed* it to me."

"Oh, dear. Well, I'm glad you're rid of him."

I hadn't seen Mark behind me in a few days, so I pulled into the car wash to vacuum my car. As I stood up from the back seat, Mark's truck was parked behind my car, blocking me in so I couldn't leave.

He staggered toward me. "What are you doing with that guy?"

"What guy?" I hoped someone would notice what was happening.

"You know. Don't play stupid. I know you're fucking him. I know you were at his house the other night."

I swallowed my heart. "How do you know?"

He moved closer to me. "I followed you there. I know you've been at this house a lot."

"It doesn't matter what I do. We are *not* together." I started to walk backward toward the front of my car as I took my keys out of my jeans pocket.

"You're a whore!" he yelled. "Don't leave! I am talking to you!"

"You're scaring me. I don't wanna talk. Stop following me." I got into my car and maneuvered around his truck. My heart raced. He *was* following me. Everywhere. I hadn't seen him follow me to John's. My fear grew as my mind brought me to the possibilities of what he had seen. I drove straight to John's house and told him what had happened. He said I needed to go to the police and get a restraining order.

The following day, I left work early, then went to the domestic violence advocacy center, and asked for their help getting a restraining order. I felt so alone, not able to bring myself to tell Peter, Mom, or Gram what was going on.

The advocate went with me to the courthouse, and we waited while the judge looked at the order. It was denied. The judge said since Mark had never put his hands on me there weren't enough grounds to grant the order. They sent me to the state police to ask for a no trespass order. When I explained to the officer what had been happening, he agreed to deliver the notice. He told me it might scare him enough into leaving me alone. Thankfully, it worked. Mark stopped following me.

CHAPTER 21

"Gram, I think it's time I get my own place. I'll be twenty in a couple of weeks."

"I think that's a good idea. You deserve some freedom."

"I'm worried about leaving you, though."

"Don't be, I'll be fine. Besides…maybe I want some freedom too." She laughed as she reclined back into her La-Z-Boy.

"Really? You'll be okay?"

"Of course, I will, Jessie."

Her approval filled me with excitement and washed away the doubt I held. She would be okay and so would I. I opened up the newspaper to the classified section and circled a few apartments I could afford. I dialed the phone and spoke to the first landlord. *Not excepting renters without references.* The next apartment had already been rented. *Maybe it's just not meant to be.*

The third call was it. I had an appointment to look at an apartment in the next town, fifteen minutes away. I followed the directions the landlord had given me and pulled up in front of an old, white farmhouse. A tall, slender man stepped out of his rusty Volvo and shook my hand. "Nice to meet you. Let's take a look inside."

He led me to the front door that enclosed a porch. We walked past two doors to get to a worn, white door with a black number "3" nailed into the center. He pulled out a key ring and tried several before it opened. We stepped inside a tiny kitchen with bright orange Formica countertops and rough, wood cupboards. He flipped a switch and showed me a large bathroom with a claw-foot tub. A few steps further there was a small living room with bay windows overlooking the farm next door.

"Up there is where the bedroom is." He pointed past the stairs covered in orange shag carpet to the loft. I followed him up to a large open room that had a view of the living room.

"This is the bedroom?"

"No, no, it's in there." I followed him into a smaller room with the same view of the farm.

"I'll take it. When can I move in?"

"Well...usually, I have tenants fill out an application, but you seem like a nice girl." He scratched his head. "Are you sure you can afford it? I'm going to need first, last and the security deposit before you can move in."

I pulled out a wad of money from my jacket pocket. "I have it right here."

"Ok, you can move in as soon as you'd like."

I went straight to Gram's to tell her about the apartment, and we worked on a plan to get me moved in. Within a couple of weeks, I was sleeping at my apartment...alone. After paying rent and utilities, I didn't have extra money for cable. Peter came by and helped me build some of the furniture I bought and hooked up a DVD player in the living room. He said having background noise was better than silence. He was right because the silence was deafening.

With the few extra dollars I had each month, I was able to pay for dial-up internet. The internet offered me a connection to the outside world. I spent my free time in chat rooms, where I made friends with three Canadians. Two men and one girl about my age. When the thought of sleeping alone was too much to bear, I chatted with my new friends until morning. They were friends who I told all my secrets to and seemed closer to me than some of the people I saw every day.

After a few weeks of being alone, John offered to have me stay with him. After work, I went to my apartment, showered, ate dinner, which most nights consisted of leftover tuna pea wiggle (the only thing I knew how to cook) and waited for John to let me know he was ready for me. For six months, I spent every night with John but never had dinner with him or brought any of my things there. As much as I loved him and wanted him to feel the same, I was reluctant to get too comfortable.

After I left Mark, John still didn't want to get serious. We were a step above "fuck buddies." We dated but could see other people. I hated the idea but was content to be with him in any capacity. As with Mom, the more he pushed me away, the stronger my desire to have the unattainable grew.

John knew I wanted a family, but he said he was happy living the life of a bachelor. With time, I was sure he'd change his mind. When he didn't, I began dating other guys. I was open with John about it and wanted him to see what he was missing. He didn't want me to stop sleeping with him, but he said he understood if I found someone who could give me what I wanted. *I wanted John to love me.*

Rejection made me dread going to the shop. I didn't want to spend the rest of my life chasing a man and pressing buttons on a machine. I needed something to change. My heart ached for John's love—my mind knew it would never be mine. Seeing John every day at work made it hard to say no to his nightly invitations. I needed a new job, but leaving the shop would mean a lower paying job, and I was barely able to pay my bills as it was.

Mom had been going to Springfield College on the weekends to get her Bachelor's degree in human services. As I sat in the audience of her graduation, I was inspired to try college. If she could do it all these years after high school, I knew I could too.

"Mom, I think I want to go to college like you did."

"That's a good idea. You should. You're too smart to work in a factory."

"I hate it there. I need to get out but—"

"There's no room for *buts*. You need to find a new job."

"But...I mean...I need the money."

"For what? That apartment you're never at?"

"How do you know that?"

"I'm not stupid. Just move in with John."

"No...it's not like that—"

"You either make excuses, or you make a life..." Her eyes darted to the window. "I've fucked things up in my past, but I have a chance to start over. You're young, you have time."

"I don't know what to do."

"Why don't you move out of that apartment and move into the basement?"

"You're out of your mind. I can't live with Bill...I hate him."

"You make excuses or..."

"Whatever, Mom."

Mom's offer came lurking back. The room in the basement was perfect. I'd have privacy and extra money. Bill was the only thing in the way, but that was a wall I wasn't ready to climb. He had screwed things up for me in the past. I couldn't give him that power again.

Frustration grew when John declined to spend Thanksgiving with Gram and me. He chose to spend it with his friend's family. There was no more sugar coating it. I knew then he wasn't going to be who I needed him to be. Over dinner, I talked to Gram about Mom's offer. "Give it a try, Jessie."

"I hate him and what he did to me."

"I know, but you're letting him win."

My sister Kate came over while we were talking. "Bill wants to talk to you. Come over with me?"

"I don't know, I don't think so."

"Please...for me... It's Thanksgiving."

"I don't—"

"I want to be able to see you more. Pretty please, Jess?"

Gram giggled. "How can you say no, Jessie?"

Kate took my hand and started to pull me towards the door. "I'll be back, Gram." I shook Kate off me and followed behind her. My body tensed as I remembered all I had lost over the last six years.

Kate slid the sliding glass patio door open. Bill sat at the kitchen table, his left leg crossed over his right knee. "Hi, stranger. I wanna talk to you," he said as he stood up.

"Okay." My emotions ran out of control. My cheeks blushed, and my heart echoed in my ears.

"Come with me." He started walking to the basement. "Let's go down here so we can talk alone."

"No, I want to talk up here."

"What are you scared of? I'm not a bad person. Come with me, or we don't talk," he said, anger tinging his words.

I followed him downstairs to the bedroom in the basement

where he sat down. He patted a spot on the bed next to him for me to sit. I continued to stand. "Sit," he said.

I made my way to the edge of the bed furthest from him.

"You know, you really fucked my life up, Jess."

"I fucked *your* life up?" I stood up. "You fucked *my* life up!"

"Jess, you know I never did those things to you. It was all a misunderstanding. You know… I love you."

"If you loved me, you wouldn't have let them take me away. You wouldn't have kept me from Mom."

"Jess, your mom says you want to move in. If you want to live here, you have to get along with me." He stopped and pointed around the room, "This could be your room for just a hundred bucks a month."

"Fuck off." I started to leave.

"You need to say you're sorry, or you won't be able to see your mom or Kate again. You need me. You need to live here. You can't afford to live on your own. If you ever want to go to college and be more than a factory whore, you need to go to school." He waited for me to respond. "Sit," he pointed to the spot on the bed next to him again.

I sat back down. He was right. I needed to go to college, and I needed a place to live.

"You know I'm right. Just tell me you're sorry, and I'll fix this room up any way you want."

The words were like poison as they left my mouth.

"I'm sorry."

I hated myself for giving in. I hated myself for letting him think I was in the wrong. My world grew dark as I thought about the prison I had created for myself with those two words.

CHAPTER 22

I moved out of my apartment into Mom's basement. I started taking classes at the community college and found a job at a local daycare. I was going to make something of myself. I had to. Friends came easy at college, and I craved more attention. I wanted to be someone's girlfriend with the possibility of being a wife. The clock was ticking, and I needed something to happen.

Living at home again erased my memory of the past. After six years, I was with my family, and I wanted to belong. Mom said she knew of a good boy she wanted me to meet. Desperation outweighed my hesitation to trust her. I was sick of wasting my time with relationships that weren't going anywhere. I agreed Mom could give my number to his mother. *What could it hurt?* A month passed, and the phone rang. It was Chuck, the "good boy." We set a date for later in the week.

I waited by the window and saw Chuck pull into the driveway in his new, silver Oldsmobile sedan. I met him outside, so he didn't have to meet my family. The drive to dinner was awkward.

He talked a lot, and I was quiet. Something about him made me uncomfortable. I couldn't put my finger on it.

We arrived at the Italian restaurant where Chuck opened the door for me and then greeted the hostess by name. He rubbed his round belly. "I come here a lot. It's good food." The hostess seated us at a table for two by a window and menus were presented to us. Chuck pushed his aside. I held mine up to cover my face. *I need to get out of here.*

My feet curled around the chair legs behind me to keep from tapping them. Chuck grabbed the menu and pulled it away from my face. "Chicken Parmigiana is my favorite. You should try it."

I took a sip of my water. "Okay."

"You don't talk much, huh?" Nervous laughter followed.

I shook my head. "Not really."

The waitress came to take our orders. Chuck picked up both menus and handed them to her. "We'll both have the chicken parm and two Bud Lights."

"Make that one. I don't drink."

"You can still bring two. I drink!"

The more he spoke, the more an uneasy feeling grew inside of me. Why did I think listening to Mom was a good idea? Chuck's ear lobes were attached to his round head, his double chin lightly shadowed by facial hair. Crumbs hung off his face as he shoved bread into his mouth. There was not a hint of attraction—he made my stomach churn.

"So do you remember me from high school? I was a star basketball player."

"No, sorry. I don't like sports."

"Oh...so you never saw me play? I'm a helluva player. You shoulda seen me. All the ladies wanted me."

"That's good."

"I remember you. You were so hot, with your short skirt. I used to watch you."

"That's creepy."

"No, no... not like a stalker. I just thought you were pretty."

"Thanks."

Our food came out, and Chuck piled spaghetti onto his fork and jammed it into his mouth. "Mmmmm."

I cut my food with a knife and took little bites, using caution not to drop anything. Chuck made sounds as he devoured his dinner while I pushed mine around my plate. A few bites were all I could stomach after watching him eat. "Are you gonna eat that?"

"Nah, I'm full."

He took my plate and stacked it on top of his. "It's too good to let it go to waste." I took my napkin and wiped my mouth. I hoped he'd do the same. He was vile, but he paid attention to me and seemed to like me. Maybe I needed to be open-minded and give him a shot.

After Chuck finished both meals, we got back in his car and went to the movies. He picked *Hannibal Lecter*. He bought popcorn and a soda and found seats in the back. We watched the movie without talking. At the end of the night, Chuck brought me home. I thanked him for the evening, and he leaned over to kiss me. I turned my head, so the kiss planted on my cheek. "Can I see you again?"

Think of an excuse... "Sure."

After Chuck left, I called John and went to his house for the night. I told him I didn't like Chuck, and I wasn't sure I would see him again. I waited for John to tell me not to see him, but instead, he said, "Why don't you try it again, maybe it'll go better next time." Disappointment flooded me—Chuck might be my only option.

Chuck called a couple of days later and invited me to dinner again. Although I wanted to decline, I didn't know how to tell him no. One of his friends was at the restaurant having dinner with his wife, and Chuck invited them to eat with us. At dinner, Chuck and his friend joked about farting, masturbation, and porn. I hated pornography since Bill used to make Peter watch it with him. It forced me to think about the things from my childhood I wanted to forget. After the night ended, I told Chuck I didn't have fun, and I didn't want to hang out with his friends anymore.

"Oh, my God. You need to lighten up. You don't know how to have fun. Stop taking things so seriously!" Maybe he was right. Maybe I didn't know how to have fun.

The more I hung out with Chuck, the more I disliked him. I was looking for a way to stop seeing him, but for some reason, I couldn't do it. I didn't know how to say no when he asked me out on a date, and John encouraged me to keep trying. Everything inside me said *no*, but the words I spoke didn't match.

One night, as Chuck left my house, he told me he loved me. I couldn't say it back. Instead, I said, "Thank you." I couldn't tell him I loved him when I didn't even like him, but if he did love me, this was what I had been searching for.

My friend Jill from Canada was pregnant. I wanted to see her before the baby was born. I looked for bus tickets to try to find a way up there. Chuck found out what I was doing and offered to drive me. I told him I'd rather take the bus, but he insisted. Again, I didn't know how to tell him no, and I agreed to his offer.

We planned the trip for the weekend of the New Year. We left very early because it was a fourteen-hour drive. The drive was fun since there were so many new things to see. By the end of the ride, Chuck became angry and mean. I figured he was tired from the drive and tried to look past it.

When we arrived at Jill's house, Chuck told me I needed to have sex with him to repay him for driving. I was tired and wanted to go to bed but did what he wanted. The next few days were awful. Chuck drank a lot, and so did the guy Jill was dating. Chuck made fun of me and called me a bitch and a whore. I wanted to go home. Chuck was treating me the way Ralph used to treat me.

The drive home was more of the same. Chuck was mean to me, and we didn't talk much the entire fourteen-hour drive home. I made up my mind I needed to break things off with him as soon as we got home. I wanted to wait a few days so it didn't look like I had only used him for the ride.

When I got home, I called John and went over to his house for the night. I was so happy to be with him again. He was where my heart was, where I was supposed to be. A few days passed, and I ignored Chuck's calls. He showed up at my house and asked me to go out with him. I told him I didn't feel up to it, but he insisted. He was acting nice again, but I was still upset. He acted as if nothing had happened. I didn't understand how he could forget about it...I couldn't.

The weeks passed, and it was time I told Chuck I didn't want to see him anymore. Something was wrong. Something felt different. My period was a week late, and my breasts were tender.

I had wanted a baby for years. I wanted a family. I wanted someone I could love who would love me back. But not like this, not with him. I had a few pregnancy scares when I was with John, so I had an extra test in my room. I found it, went into the bathroom, and took the pregnancy test. I waited for the two minutes to pass. The clock was barely moving. *Please be negative.*

Two minutes were up. I picked up the test to check. It was positive.

Positive.

My world became dark with fear. I would never be able to leave him now. I was destined to be with him for the rest of my life.

Panic multiplied. My fear grew. A moment I had longed for was tarnished—just like all the other moments in my life. This baby was going to change my life. I had no idea what to do. I needed to talk to Hannah, but it was late. I had to go to bed.

I called John and went to his house for the night. I didn't tell him. I couldn't. I lay in bed next to him and cried while he slept. All I wanted was to be with him, to have a family with him. He had made it clear he didn't want the same thing. I wanted more than anything to have a family. I wanted what I never had growing up. I wanted love. I didn't like Chuck. I loved John. *What had I done?*

CHAPTER 23

On my break at work, I called Chuck. "Can you come have lunch with me today?"

"Thought you'd never ask. You miss me, don't ya?"

My nose scrunched up as nausea hit me. "I just have something to tell you."

"You're pregnant, aren't ya? I fuckin' hope you're pregnant!"

"Just please come. Meet me by my car."

As I walked back into work, I tried to be excited he was happy. If he wanted a baby, he would be a good dad. I owed my baby that much. Maybe I could learn to love Chuck—I'd have the rest of my life to try.

Chuck had parked next to my car and was there when I went out for lunch. He rolled down the window. "Get in, I'm starving."

Nausea struck again as I opened the door. He drove to McDonald's drive-through. "What do you want?"

"I'm not hungry."

"All right, give me your credit card then."

"For what?"

"You invited me to lunch, so you pay."

I dug my credit card out of my pocket and handed it to him. After he got his food, he pulled into a parking spot and devoured the fish sandwich, tartar sauce smeared all over his face. "So what do ya wanna tell me?" He reached his hand over to my stomach and rubbed the remains of his lunch on my jacket. "You're pregnant, ain't ya?"

"Yeah..."

"Thank God! I hoped that'd happen. I knew that was the only way to keep you from leaving."

"Really? You wanted this to happen?"

"Yup...I know you ain't been happy, and you have your pick of men, so it was the only way to keep you."

I looked out the window, nausea swept over me, sweat formed on my forehead, and tears welled in my eyes. *What have I done?*

"Aww, don't be sad. I own ya now. I'll take care of you and the baby."

"Like making me buy you lunch?"

He laughed. "I guess we'll take care of each other. We're a family now."

A family. I waited my whole life for a family. I had to make it work. If not for me, for the baby.

After Chuck found out I was pregnant, he wouldn't leave Mom's house. He asked her if he could spend the night with me— she said yes. The familiar feeling of being trapped returned. I needed space from him, but he refused to give it to me. With him as my shadow, there was no way to see John. John didn't even know I was pregnant. I had to find a way to talk to him, but I was Chuck's prisoner now.

Opportunity struck when Chuck needed me to bring him to

pick up his car. Alone for the first time in days, I opened my cell phone and dialed John's number. I didn't want to do it this way, but I didn't know when another chance might come. My heartbeat echoed in my ears as the phone rang on the other end.

"Hello?"

The sound of his voice broke me. "Hi...it's me..."

"It's been a while."

"I know... I've just been thinking...and..."

Silence on the other end of the phone turned my words into tears. With a deep breath, I continued. "And I need more... I need to find someone who wants what I do... I can't... I can't see you any—"

"I'm sorry, Jess. Please don't cry."

"I'm sorry too. I've gotta go...bye." That was the end of a relationship with a man I loved more than anything.

I pulled into the driveway behind Chuck, still in the grip of the pain of losing John. I needed Chuck to leave, but he refused. He wanted to know why I was so upset, but I couldn't tell him. I curled up on my bed and cried until I fell asleep.

I told Mom I was pregnant. She was happy to know Chuck wasn't going anywhere. "Aren't you glad I found him?"

"I guess."

"You guess? Too late now!" She laughed and went back to washing the dishes.

I had to tell Gram, but I was ashamed. I had only been dating Chuck for three months, and she hadn't even met him yet. I didn't want Mom to tell her before I did and knew it would be the first thing out of Mom's mouth the next time she saw her.

I walked over to Gram's and sat in the rocking chair in the living room. "Gram...I've gotta tell you something." My eyes found my feet as I struggled to find the words.

She turned off the TV. "What is it dear?"

"Ahh...umm...well...I...I'm pregnant."

"Well...okay...that's exciting...right?"

"Hmmm...I guess."

"Sure it is dear. A baby is lovely. You'll be a great mom."

My nose scrunched as I tried to stop the tears. A mom. I was going to be someone's mom. "You think so?"

"I know so. It'd be better if you were married...but I guess it's not 1950 anymore and not like your mother showed you how to do it right."

"I don't really like Chuck..."

"Well, you better try, honey."

"Yeah...I will."

Chuck proposed on Valentine's Day. As with Mark, I said yes because I didn't know what else to say. He was the father of this baby. We were going to be a family, like it or not. I made my choices, and I had to pay for them.

Then Chuck and I got into a fight when I found out he used my computer to look at porn. He denied it, but I had proof. His lie took my trust. When he knew I had caught him in the lie, he left. He finally left.

After hours of him not returning or calling, I thought he was gone for good. Hopeful he wasn't going to return, I called John. I had to see him. John was hesitant to have me visit because Hannah had told him about the baby and Chuck.

John agreed to have me over. As I drove up his driveway, I took off my engagement ring and put in the cup holder. I never wanted it on my finger again.

John was outside on his porch steps when I arrived. As soon as I saw him, I started to cry. I missed him so much. All of the feelings I had been trying to forget came pouring out. I sat next to him on the stairs and put my head in his lap. "I miss you."

He stroked my hair as I cried. "I miss you too."

Surprised by his response, I picked my head up and looked at him. "I don't want to be with Chuck, but I'm scared to have this baby alone."

"I'll help." He took my hand. "I'll even go to the hospital with you."

"Really? You'd want to see that?" Laughter replaced some sadness.

"Well, I won't look." He smiled and then looked down. "I woulda had a baby with you if I knew you didn't need to be married."

Frozen by his words, I stared ahead, a weight settled on my heart. *What did that even mean?* He wanted a baby, but not marriage? Why did he wait until now to tell me? The only reason I dated other people was that he said he didn't want a family. The pain of this new discovery shredded my insides. I was angry with John, and then myself. A million emotions swirled inside of me and around this baby. I cried harder. *Why was I rushing things? Why couldn't I have waited? Why? Why? Why?*

I spent the night with John. I didn't want anyone to find me. I wanted to pretend, if only for a few hours, my life was how I wanted it. As he held me, I imagined us as a family. My heart was hollow as reality drifted in. I tried to push those thoughts out and savor the moment. This was how it was supposed to be. This was home. This was perfect.

But this was my life, and my life wasn't perfect.

The next morning, John had to go to work, and I had to get ready to go to my ultrasound. John didn't know I had this appointment. I didn't want him to feel obligated to come. Besides, Chuck knew about it, and I didn't want anything to happen if Chuck decided to go. As I pulled out of John's driveway, emptiness overpowered me. I was leaving the man I loved. Again. I wanted to take

John up on his offer to help me with this baby, but guilt wouldn't let me accept. I needed to let Chuck have a chance to be a father.

I wanted to bring this baby into love. I didn't want to make this baby suffer. I wanted to give this baby a happy life and not be in the middle of a war. I thought being with Chuck would keep the peace. *I* wouldn't have peace with Chuck, but this baby might. I grew up without a father. I wanted to give this baby all that I didn't have.

The ringing phone greeted me as I walked into my room. It was Chuck. He was angry I hadn't answered before. He said he had come earlier, and I wasn't home. He wanted to know where I'd been, who I had been with, and what I'd been doing. I said nothing. I swallowed the tears and listened as he yelled at me. *This.* This was my life. This chaos was what I knew. This was what I deserved.

Chuck arrived at my house in time to drive me to the hospital for the ultrasound. On the drive there, my thoughts kept going back to the night before. The feeling of pure ecstasy filled my body. That was what I longed for. Chuck broke me out of my concentration with his rude comments. I stayed quiet as he continued. "You think you're perfect? You were probably a whore last night. You're a stupid whore. You think I'm a bad guy? Well, take a look in the fuckin' mirror." Pain leaked out of my eyes. I couldn't hold it in any longer. He won. He always won.

When he saw my tears, he stopped and said he was sorry. My heart filled with hunger pains. I was hungry for love, for pure, genuine love. My desire to feed the ache intensified, but I couldn't feed it—so it continued to starve.

When we arrived at the hospital, I wiped the tears from my cheeks and got out of the car. Chuck walked over to take my hand, but I wouldn't let him. He grabbed me and hugged me, my arms at my sides. I stood still and said nothing, wishing he'd get off me.

Wishing he'd disappear. Wishing we'd never met. "Come on. You know I love you," he said as he kissed my cheek.

I pushed him away and started to walk. "We have to get in there. We're going to be late."

When it was time for the ultrasound, they called me back to go into a room and asked me to get on the exam table. They covered my belly with gel and pressed the wand onto my skin. This little baby growing inside of me was right before my eyes. I had to find a way to make this work. I had to make life good for this baby.

The technician asked if we wanted to know the sex of the baby. As I tried to swallow my sadness, I nodded. Tears left my eyes as I watched the tiny life on the screen. I'd always wanted to be a mom. I wanted to do this right. My heart ached as I thought about the life I was now responsible for.

"That right there," the technician said as he pointed to the screen, "that's a boy." This little person inside of me was a boy. I was going to have a baby boy in my arms in a few short months. I began to cry. This baby needed a name. There were so many things to do to get ready. So many things to work out. It was overwhelming. I couldn't mess this up—he depended on me.

When Chuck heard I was having a boy, he was elated. He had said he wanted a son so he could carry on the name. He was the fourth Charles in the family, and he said this baby would be the fifth. *Over my dead body.*

When we left the appointment, Chuck drove to tell his mother and then his father the news. I liked Chuck's family as much as I liked him. I got out of the car at each stop and quietly stood in the background. He had highjacked this baby. I was just the incubator. He was going to take all credit for this little life. There was no turning back. This was *Chuck's* baby now. There was no way I could be with John. I was stuck.

Chuck and I began looking for an apartment so this baby could have a home. He was due to arrive in September, and it was already May. Time was passing quickly. There was so much to do and things we needed to get for the baby. We found a place and had moved in by July. I started collecting things the baby would need. Chuck didn't buy anything, even though he worked full time.

I was unable to enroll for the fall semester at college. My job at the daycare ended for the summer, and I was unable to return since the baby was due soon after the start of the new school year. I received a small unemployment check, so I had to put most of the purchases on my credit card. The balance grew and grew, and still, Chuck didn't help pay for anything.

Instead, he was buying pornography—magazines, videos, and phone sex. While cleaning, I found his collection under the bed. This baby that he was taking all the credit for meant nothing to him. He was too busy taking care of himself.

I confronted him when he got home from work. He denied everything. I pulled out the collection of magazines and videos, and he said they weren't his. I told him if he was going to lie to me and not help support this baby, I was leaving. I had my bag packed and my hand on the door.

When Chuck saw I was serious, he became enraged. He pushed my hand off the door handle and pulled my bag from me, throwing it across the room. "You are *not* going anywhere!" he yelled as he put himself between the door and me. "If you leave, I will take that baby. You're unfit! You won't get that baby! That is *my* baby!"

My chest tightened with fear as the baby kicked. We had fought before, but this was the first time I felt afraid. I couldn't say anything. The words he spoke wouldn't leave my head. What if he *could* take my baby? What if he would? I couldn't stand the thought of losing my baby before I even held him in my arms. The fear worked. It kept me from leaving.

When Chuck saw he won, he told me he was sorry. "You know I love you."

I said nothing. I quietly receded into my body. This was my life now. I had to find a way to make it viable. I still had not told Chuck I loved him. I couldn't speak those words because they were not true. I didn't love him. I never would.

CHAPTER 24

hen I was seven months pregnant, Kate was fourteen years old. She had been dating her boyfriend for a few months, and they were sexually active. She told her boyfriend a secret she carried with her for the past seven years, and he made her tell Mom. She told Mom Bill had been molesting her since she was seven—the year I was taken out of the home.

Kate told Mom all of the horrible, gruesome things he had been doing to her. They called the police and then me. Mom told me I needed to meet her down at the domestic violence center so they could fill out a restraining order.

As I heard the words Mom spoke on the other end of the phone, I was inundated with a mix of emotions. I was sad for what had happened to Kate and sickened to hear some of the things Bill had done. A rush of guilt came over me as I thought back to those lies I had told on the witness stand to try to protect Kate. It had backfired. If I hadn't let Mom talk me into it, Kate would have been safe.

I was angry with Mom for pushing me into those lies. I was

mad at her for protecting Kate, for standing by her side when she hadn't helped me at all. *I was jealous.* Kate's father had violated her, but Mom loved her. That was all I wanted. I was torn between rage and sadness.

When I arrived at the center, I found Mom and Kate filling out papers in the back room with an advocate. I looked at Kate and yelled through my tears, "I told you to *never* let him touch you."

The advocate walked over to me and took me by the shoulder. "Kate needs you to be supportive right now. If you can't offer her support, I'm going to have to ask you to leave."

I shook her hand off my shoulder and left the room. Flames of anger shot through my body, and my pulse slammed against my neck. I paced the waiting room as Chuck sat drinking coffee. The advocate didn't know what I knew. She didn't have her family stolen from her. The more I thought about it, the more the anger boiled inside of me.

Mom knew. She came out to make sure I was okay. Her eyes looked sad as they met mine. "I'm sorry, Jess. If I had listened to you... this never would have happened." Her head dropped as she slid into the chair next to Chuck. Her body shook as she sobbed. For the first time, I saw Mom as damaged. She understood what it was like to be a failure—we had that in common. Knowing how much Mom hurt dulled some of my anger. I loved her and didn't want to see her in pain.

The police arrested Bill at work. He was released on bail while he waited for a trial. Mom fell into a deep depression. She slept away her days as she had done when I was younger and we had lived with Ralph. Kate stayed with her boyfriend's family, leaving Mom alone. I was scared Bill was going to kill her. I offered Mom to stay with Chuck and me, but she refused.

When I went to visit her, she was always in bed, dishes of food stacked on the floor around her. When I stood by her bed and talked to her, her head never came out from under her pillow. A darkness encased her now.

She had gained weight, and she was now close to four hundred pounds. With Bill out of the house and losing his income, she was behind on all of the bills. In the hours she was awake, she managed to adopt five more cats. They filled a void for her but also left the house smelling of ammonia. They didn't use a litter box, but instead, they took over the house. Piles of cat feces lined every room, and the floors were wet with urine.

Moldy food took over the refrigerator and piles of laundry grew in the bathroom. The lawn outside turned to a hayfield and spiders took up shop on the front porch. The smell from the house seeped outside as the days grew hotter. Mom didn't care about the mess or about anything.

The monster that ate my mommy had returned.

CHAPTER 25

I tried to help Mom, but she pushed me away. She told me she didn't deserve my love because of how she failed me. I wanted her love and hoped with Bill out of the picture, I could have the mom I had always wanted, but the grips of depression had Mom now, and it had a more powerful hold over her than Bill had.

My due date was fast approaching, and I wanted Mom to be part of my baby's life. I hoped she could love him as Gram had loved me. I wanted my baby to have a gram as special as mine. I asked Mom for advice on what kind of diapers to buy and what to expect during childbirth. My questions seemed to tug her out into the light a little. She spent less time in bed, and Kate and her boyfriend moved back in with her.

My due date came and went. My body was tired from carrying the baby, and I longed to have him in my arms. Eight days after the baby was due, I was admitted to the birthing center to be induced. Chuck came with me.

Twelve hours passed and nothing happened. Chuck's parents

were in the waiting room growing impatient. When I left my room to walk around the birthing loop, I saw Chuck's dad as he paced the hall. Chuck left me to calm his father.

As Chuck reached his dad, a contraction took over me. I grabbed onto the railing on the wall and let out a quiet scream. Chuck looked at me but stayed with his dad as they joked about how long I was taking. A nurse came over to me and placed her hands on my stomach as she waited for the next one to come. She shook her head as she looked at Chuck and his father and brushed the hair away from my face. Another contraction came, and after it passed, she told Chuck to come help me.

After two hours of contractions, the midwife said it was time to push. The pain was like nothing I had ever experienced before. I refused all pain medication because Mom said it was best for the baby. On my back in bed, Chuck had one of my legs in his arms, holding it back and a nurse had the other as I pushed. "I see his head! Give me another push."

Minutes later, crying filled the room. At 10:14 p.m. on September 29, 2003, Ian was born. My heart was full. I had loved him from the moment I knew he existed, but when I saw him, the love multiplied a million times. I didn't think it was possible to love someone so much. I held my reason for living in my arms. Ian needed me as much as I needed him. I had to shake all of the hurt and pain away. I had to be the best I could be for him.

The next morning, Mom brought Gram and Kate to meet Ian. As I handed Mom my son, I was excited for what the future held. Maybe Ian would be what it took to make Mom and me close, or at least she could give him the love she never gave me. She kissed his forehead and handed him to Gram as she sat in the chair next to my bed. "He's beautiful, Jessie. You did a good job, honey." She pulled down his blanket and kissed his face. "You're a lucky little boy. Your mommy is pretty special." Gram's words made me see how lucky *I* was to have her. If Mom couldn't give Ian or me what I needed, at least I knew he had his great-grammy.

The hospital released us to go home the following day. Ian cried the whole drive home, and Chuck yelled at me to shut him up. As I sat next to Ian in the backseat, I imagined what it would have been like if I had taken John up on his offer. I imagined bringing Ian home to a house of love. Instead, we were going to a house of horrors.

The only time Chuck was helpful with Ian was when people came to visit. He wanted them to think he was doing a great job and took all of the credit. I didn't care—at least in those moments I had a few minutes to rest. When Chuck went to work, and I was too exhausted to do it anymore, Mom came over to hold Ian while I tried to nap. I placed him on her chest as she sat in a chair next to the couch where I curled up under a blanket and listened to Ian coo. As Mom held Ian, I imagined what it would have been like to have her be so loving to me. I was grateful Ian would know what her love felt like.

CHAPTER 26

*I*an made me desire to be my best, so I decided to finish the degree I had started. I enrolled at Springfield College and began classes in Human Services in the spring semester. I loved going to class, but I hated leaving Ian. The only thing that got me through the day was to know I was doing this for him. I wanted to be able to get a good job so I could support Ian on my own if I ever needed to. I never wanted to have to depend on a man for money. I watched Mom do this my whole life, and I didn't want to be like that. I wanted to be self-sufficient.

After I started classes back up, Chuck and I began looking for a house. We felt Ian needed a home he could grow up in. After a lot of searching and work, we found a house we could afford. It was $47,000 and a very short walk from where Chuck's family lived. The house was built in 1852, and the inside looked like it had not been renovated since. It was a big house with a large shed connected to the back and a barn in the front yard. It sat on the main road and shook when trucks drove by. The only upside was Hannah, Tim, and their son were also close by.

I was excited for Ian to have a home, but I wished we were moving into the house John said he wanted to build. No matter how much time passed, I couldn't shake my desire to be with John. Living in Chuck's hometown gave him more power. Everyone knew who he pretended to be. I was the stranger in town.

Once we were settled into the house, I found out I was pregnant again. I always wanted to have my kids with one man, so they would be full siblings. I didn't want to be like Mom and have three babies with three fathers. Ian was a year old. I was going to have two babies to take care of. I wasn't sure how I was going to do it, but I had to. There was no turning back.

Days after I found out I was pregnant, Chuck quit his job. It was up to me to support the family on my own. I had received a small inheritance from my grandfather right before we bought the house. I dreamed of buying a laptop so I could write. Between covering the expenses for the house and Chuck's impulse purchases, the money went fast. It was gone before I could buy the laptop, and that dream was put on hold. I stayed at my job—I worked with a teenage boy with autism. He was violent and punched me in the stomach. I was scared he was going to hurt the baby, but I needed to work.

I told Chuck I was scared for the baby's safety. He told me to suck it up. I continued working until the boy's family moved away, leaving me unemployed. I didn't know how I was going to find a job when I was seven months pregnant. I was finishing up my bachelor's degree and was extremely tired taking care of Ian, doing my internship, homework, and worrying about this baby due to arrive in a few short weeks.

Chuck found a job at the high school where he worked second shift as a janitor. I was relieved we had an income coming in again. The pressure of being forced to work made Chuck lose his temper.

He called me a fat whore and a crazy bitch and lost his patience with Ian.

At my previous job, I had made friends with a coworker, Jamie. She was the first person I had confided in about Chuck. "Chuck scares me."

"What do you mean? Does he hit you or Ian?"

"No...but he's come close. He's pushed me...he mostly calls us names."

"Us? He calls Ian names? He's a baby, for Christ's sake."

"Yeah...I know...I don't know what to do."

"Leave him. You guys don't deserve that."

"I can't...I mean...where would we go?"

"My house. I mean it. If you need a safe place to go, you come to my house. Besides, I love babies."

Jamie and I came up with a plan. I would leave with Ian when Chuck was at work. I wouldn't let him know until I was gone. Chuck didn't know where Jamie lived. There was no way he would find us. She lived in a town an hour away from our house.

I packed a few things into my car. I found what I needed for the baby when it would come and put it aside. I had Ian's favorite teddy bear and our clothes packed in the trunk of my car. I was just waiting for Chuck to leave for work.

A neighbor saw me put the things in my car and had told Chuck. He went into the trunk and saw the things I had packed. He stormed into the house and yelled, "What do you think you're doing? Why is your trunk packed? Who do you think you are?"

I picked Ian up because the yelling had scared him. He started to cry. I held him close and told him it was okay as I swayed him back and forth. Chuck became more outraged as I ignored him. I didn't know how to respond—I just knew I didn't want to fight. I didn't want Ian to be scared. I softly said, "We just need to be safe."

As my words hit his ears, he charged at me. I was still holding Ian. Chuck put his hands around my neck and pushed us into a wall. He pushed harder and yelled louder. Ian screamed. I was so afraid Chuck was going to hurt Ian. I was afraid he was going to kill me, and that's when Chuck said, "I am going to kill you. I am going to kill you, and you won't have to worry about being safe. No one will miss you, no one will notice. I'm going to cut you up into small pieces and throw you into the river. No one will ever know, no one will ever look for you."

Through his threats, I managed to free myself from his grip. I stood up on my feet and hugged Ian tightly to try to stop his screams. He was terrified. His father was trying to murder his mother right before his eyes.

Chuck's rage filled the entire house. We couldn't escape now. We were trapped. He was going to kill me. I had no doubt that I was about to take my last breath. I kissed Ian and continued to try to quiet him, to ease his fear. He was my life. I might only have moments left. I wanted Ian to remember my love. I wanted him to know I loved him. I didn't want him to be afraid.

I don't know what stopped Chuck. My focus was on the fear that flowed through my veins. I didn't want Ian to know how afraid I was. I tried to distract myself, to distract him. Chuck's rage abruptly changed to love.

"You know I love you. I wouldn't hurt you." He came closer to me and moved my hair out of my face. My body tightened as he touched me. He tried to take Ian out of my arms, but Ian grabbed tightly around my neck.

"Don't you touch him." Those were the first words I had spoken since he found out about my plan.

"Come on, you know I wouldn't hurt him. I wouldn't hurt you. You're overreacting."

"Leave us alone. He's scared. Just go. Please, just go." Ian hugged me tighter. He didn't want me to let him go.

"Buddy. I love you. Come see Daddy," he said as he brushed his hand on Ian's cheek.

"I asked you to leave." My body shook as I held Ian close.

Chuck left the room, but he didn't leave the house. He was supposed to go to work, but he called out. He wouldn't leave. I went into my bedroom, sat on the bed, and rocked Ian. He was still crying. He was a baby, under two, and he knew what terror tasted like. This was not the life I wanted for my child.

I replayed the situation over and over in my head. I didn't know what to do. I didn't know how to get out of it. Another baby was coming in a few short weeks. Chuck told me if I ever told anyone what happened, he would take Ian, and I would never see him again. I believed him. I lived every day wondering what was going to happen next.

CHAPTER 27

*C*ontractions came on quick as I sat on the living room floor with Ian in my lap as we read together. I had just returned from the doctor's office, and they had told me there was no sign of the baby coming soon. I tried to brush off the pain and continued to read to Ian. The pain became too much to handle. I had to try to walk it off. Each step sent shockwaves of pain through my body as my belly tightened. "Chuck...I think it's time."

With a Bud Light in his hand, he walked into the living room. "It can't be. They said it wasn't coming anytime soon."

The pain sent a scream out of my mouth as my eyes closed. "I don't...don't care what they said."

Chuck called his mom to sit with Ian. "Jessica *thinks* she's in labor. I've gotta take her to the hospital...yeah...okay...no, take your time."

"I don't *think*...I *know!*" Another scream escaped from my lips.

Ian came to my side scared by the sounds I made. "Mama, you otay?"

"Yes, honey, Mama's okay. Your sister's coming."

Minutes that felt like hours passed before Chuck's mom arrived, a water bottle filled with vodka in her hand. Uneasy to leave Ian with her, my stress multiplied. *He'll be fine. Don't worry.* But I worried. I always worried when he was in her care. She was forgetful and drank more vodka than water.

On the drive to the hospital, Chuck became nervous we weren't going to make it. I braced myself on the dashboard of the minivan as the contractions came on faster and stronger. We arrived at the hospital as a contraction ended. "I got to get in there before another one comes."

Chuck rushed into the emergency room to tell them I was on my way. I waddled in behind him as another contraction hit. I braced myself on a chair in the waiting room as I tried to gather my composure. The woman at the desk ran to get a wheelchair and rushed me to the elevator. She delivered me to the birthing center where the nurses were with other patients. "We need help...quick!"

A nurse broke away from what she was doing and took me to a free room where she had me undress and assessed me. "Oh, my goodness...she's ready to push! Page the midwife."

I gripped the rails on the bed above my head as the pain shot through me. The same midwife that delivered Ian arrived. "You mean business...zero to sixty, huh?" She laughed as she gowned up. She sat between my legs and examined me. "Push, sweet-heart...you're having a baby tonight!"

Thirty minutes later, at 7:12 p.m., Emerson was born on July 19, 2005. She was a beautiful baby. I couldn't wait for Ian to meet her. I held her in my arms and felt my heart warm with love. A daughter. I wouldn't make her fight for my love—I couldn't imagine *not* loving her.

Chuck went home the next morning to get Ian so he could meet Emerson. Mom, Kate, and Gram arrived while he was gone. Gram stood above my bed, pulled the pink blanket from her face, and smiled. "She's perfect, Jessie."

"Do you want to hold her?" I sat up, let Gram sit on the bed next to us, and passed the bundle over to her. "Hi, sweet baby. You were in a hurry, weren't you?" She bounced her on her lap as she looked down at her. "That just means you're going to make things happen." Gram smiled and looked at me. "Just like your mommy." My heart was full as I watched Gram fall in love with her.

Chuck and Ian arrived while Mom held Emerson. Ian inched his way past all the guests and ran to me. "Mommy, you come home now?"

I patted the bed next to me and kissed Ian's forehead. "Soon, honey. Want to meet Emerson?"

Ian nodded, and Mom passed her to Chuck. Chuck motioned for me to get off the bed and sat down with her. Ian hid behind me. "She's little, isn't she, buddy?"

He nodded again as he peeked around me. Kate picked him up and hugged him. "You're a big brother now."

He grinned as he hid his head. "Mommy, you come home?"

"Tomorrow, buddy. I love you."

Chuck left with Ian to bring him home. Mom, Gram, and Kate left soon after. I rested with Emerson and cuddled her close. She was never going to question if she was loved.

Life became increasingly stressful as I finished my bachelor's degree, worked full-time, took care of Gram on the weekends, and raised two babies. Chuck was little help. He made sure he had time for himself but never let me have any time for me. I didn't mind though because I cherished the time I had with my babies. My children loved me unconditionally—just as Gram did. My wish for a family and someone to love had come true.

Work and life kept me busy. I liked it that way. It meant less time Chuck and I had to be together. Even though we'd bought a house and had two kids together, I wouldn't set a date to get married. I still held on to hope that John and I would be together someday. My plan was to stay with Chuck until the kids were eighteen and then leave. I would find John. We'd get married and live the rest of our lives together, happily, with love, respect, and safety.

That dream was shattered. "Did you hear? John's getting married." Tim talked as he flipped hamburgers on his grill.

"*Married*? To who?"

"I don't know her name, but she has a daughter. She even has John going to church with her!"

"Are you serious? They're getting married?"

"You don't care, do you? Jess...you have two kids and Chuck."

"No...I don't care...I just think it's strange. I mean...he said he *never* wanted to get married."

"It's probably all that bible thumping." He threw his head back and laughed.

John wouldn't marry me, but he was considering marriage with someone else? I *really* wasn't good enough. After I heard the news, I told Chuck he could pick a wedding date. John had thrown away my hopes and dreams. All I had left was garbage. Why bother? Why not just admit this *was* my life?

We picked a date and started to plan a simple wedding and reception. I didn't feel right about any of it. I had second thoughts. I asked Chuck if I could just change my last name, and skip the wedding. He said no. Everything inside me screamed, *"No!"* I didn't listen. The wedding went on despite my apprehension.

Nothing about the wedding was how I imagined. The pain of not having Ralph there was illuminated. I asked Chuck not to drink at the wedding or reception. I explained how uncomfortable his drinking made me. He promised he wouldn't even take a sip.

Before the ceremony began, Peter stood with me as he waited to walk me down the aisle. "You know Chuck is half in the bag?"

"He's not supposed to be drinking today."

"Well...it doesn't look like he can even stand up straight."

"He promised me..."

"Maybe he's just nervous."

"Peter...I don't want to do this. I don't want to get married."

"Oh, stop it. You're just nervous. It'll be fine. Besides...the church is full of people. What would you tell them?"

"I don't like him...I don't want to be his wife."

Peter looked at me in my wedding dress. "Well, Jess, it's a little too late for that. You'll be fine."

As the music played, Peter walked me down the aisle, my arm locked with his. Nausea swept over me as I took small, slow steps, trying to delay the inevitable. I looked around and saw Mom holding Emerson, Ian sitting with Gram, and Uncle Doug watching me. I saw Hannah and Kate waiting by the minister for me. And Chuck. *What am I doing? Run!*

I didn't run. We said our vows, and I cried. Not happy bride's tears, but tears of desperation. I hated myself for going through with something I shouldn't have. I hated I wasn't strong enough to listen to myself. The minister pronounced us "husband and wife," and I wanted to throw up. Chuck tried to kiss me, and I took a step back. I didn't want this.

We held the reception at the Town Hall just three houses up the road from ours. Chuck continued to drink. Every time I saw him, he had another Bud Light in his hand. The reception I had worked so hard to plan became a party for Chuck and his friends. After everyone had cake and the flowers were tossed, I gathered up Ian and Emerson and walked home with them.

We were home for over two hours before Chuck noticed we

were missing. He came home drunk and started a fight. "Where the fuck did you go? You think you're too good for them?"

"Why did you drink? You promised me..."

"Shut the fuck up! I only had one...maybe two."

"You're drunk! Get out of here."

"You're a fat bitch, you fuckin' whore. You're just jealous I have friends. You have to be in control of me all the fuckin' time."

"Get out of here. I *hate* you. I don't want to be your wife."

"It's too late now...I own you now."

"Like hell you do! I'm going to find the minister and rip up the marriage license!"

Chuck slammed the door behind him as he staggered back up the road to the party. I watched TV with Emerson and Ian as I tried to figure out how to contact the minister. I *had* to get out of this.

Night fell before Chuck arrived home. He apologized and said he wanted to start over. Too much had happened to forget. There was no starting over. The damage had been done. A marriage license would not make me love him—nothing would.

CHAPTER 28

a month after the wedding, I graduated from Springfield College with my bachelor's degree in Human Services. I graduated with a 4.0-grade point average. I took my unhappiness with life and worked extra hard at school. Like when I was a kid, school was the only thing I felt I was good at. I thought about staying to complete my master's degree, but I didn't think I had what it took to succeed. I figured it'd be too hard for me, so I decided to be happy with what I had.

Soon after graduation, I interviewed for my dream job as a case manager working with the elderly and disabled. At the interview, as I sat down at a table full of people, I saw Ben, one of my previous social workers. He was the director of the organization. He didn't want to hire me based on his past experience with me as a teenager in foster care. It was awkward and uncomfortable to have him back in my life, but I wasn't going to let his presence stop me.

A week after the interview, I was offered the job. Patty, the woman who was to become my supervisor, decided to go against

Ben's wishes and gave me a chance. I began earning much more than I ever had in the past. I was well on my way to being self-sufficient.

Patty was a free spirit and fun to work for, and she became a friend and invited me to a psychic party she was hosting at her home. Patty lived near the office, so I told Chuck I had to work late. I knew he wouldn't approve of my going, and I didn't want to risk missing it. No one else from the office went to the party because they didn't believe. I followed Patty to her house and waited for the other six guests to arrive. Amber, the psychic, arrived soon after we did.

Amber explained to the group she read tarot cards to predict our future and also said she was a medium. I wanted to talk to a medium since Hannah and I started trying to communicate with the dead. My heart skipped around in my chest as I listened to Amber talk. *She could talk to Ralph for me.* I was just moments away from talking to my dad...after fifteen years.

Patty knew I had to get home, so she let me get my reading first. I walked down the hall to a bedroom lit only by a lamp and sat across from Amber. She handed me the deck of cards. "Shuffle them until you feel comfortable."

I started shuffling the cards as my hands trembled. The cards were bigger than my hands and were hard to grasp. I gave the cards one more shuffle and handed them back to Amber.

"Don't be nervous. There's nothing to worry about." Amber spread the cards out on the table that separated us. She went through each card and told me what they meant for me. When she was finished reading the cards, she looked up at me. "I never do this...but the spirits are telling me I have to."

My eyes widened as I waited for her to continue.

"They're telling me you need to leave your husband. He's dangerous. Get out."

Tears fell from my eyes as I heard the warning. "What spirits?"

"The ones here with us." She motioned around the room.

"Is my dad here?"

She closed her eyes and waited. "Yes...he's here."

I wiped the tears from my eyes to look around the room. "Tell him I'm sorry...and I love him."

"You just did." She closed her eyes again. "He said you don't have to be sorry...he understands." She smiled and shook her head. "He said he's proud of you...and he loves you."

Ralph was back, or maybe he never left. I couldn't believe he was in the room with me. "I really miss him...he's been dead longer than I knew him."

"He's sorry he had to leave you. He knows what you went through...he said he was right about your mom."

I nodded my head.

"He wants you to leave your husband. He doesn't like him."

"Yeah...me neither." I chuckled as I wiped the tears from my cheek.

"Do you have any other questions?"

"What about my gram? Is she...I mean...what do you see about her?"

She drew a card from the deck and placed it on the table. "I see something with her heart."

"When?" I wished I hadn't mentioned Gram. I didn't want to think about it.

"Oh...not anytime soon."

I drove home after the reading with a new energy inside me. I was able to talk to Ralph, and he wasn't mad at me. That was a relief. And I wasn't the only one who knew I had to leave Chuck. I hoped the spirits watching were enough to protect me until I could make my escape. I pushed the information about Gram out of my mind. I didn't want to think about life without her.

CHAPTER 29

A couple of years into the job, I found out I was pregnant with baby number three. Chuck and I continued to fight, but that was the norm now. We couldn't have a conversation without calling each other names or yelling. Ian was four and Emerson was two. Chuck only occasionally put his hands on me now. Most of the abuse was emotional.

Until I was nine months pregnant. Chuck spent the day belittling me. "You're a fat whore. No one has ever loved you. Your own mother hates you. You're just a piece of shit."

After hours of listening, I couldn't take it anymore. I had the cordless phone in my hand from my daily call to Gram, and without thinking, I threw it at Chuck's bare back. I wanted him to stop talking. I was nine months pregnant, my husband was verbally abusing me, and my hormones were raging. I wanted him to leave me alone.

He spun around and yelled, "You're gonna pay for that, you stupid, fat whore!"

Ian and Emerson were in the living room, and they stopped playing as he ran to me. I ran past him into the living room to get the kids to a safe spot, but as I got into the living room, Chuck pushed me into the changing table. When I didn't fall, he pushed me again, harder. I stumbled and landed on the floor in the kids' playroom as Ian yelled, "Daddy, no! Stop, Daddy!"

On the floor, I held my stomach. Chuck came over and kicked me over and over again in the back. He kicked me harder each time his foot made contact. Ian ran over to try to make him stop. I fought back the tears because I didn't want Ian to be afraid. Emerson stood in the corner of the living room, crying as she watched her father continue to yell at me. I needed help. I managed to get to my feet and walked to the phone. When Chuck saw what I was doing, he ripped the phone out of the wall and threw it. "What the fuck do you think you are doing? You're not calling anyone." He pushed me into the doorway to the upstairs, pushing me so hard my body broke the door. The kids both watched and cried. We were all at his mercy.

Chuck pulled me up out from the broken door and dragged me into the kitchen by my hair. He tried to smash my head onto the hot wood stove. I couldn't let my face hit the stove. I somehow managed to brace myself in the doorframe of the bathroom that was in front of the wood stove. He took my head, bounced it off the door jam, and yelled, "I'm going to kill you!"

The kids followed us into the kitchen. Their screams filled the house. Ian yelled, "Let her go! Let Mommy go!"

Chuck didn't let me go. He grabbed me by the neck and pushed me into the wall as he yelled, "You're dead! I'm going to kill you and hide your body."

"Daddy! Please don't kill Mommy. Please, Daddy, please." Ian's pleas didn't stop him.

Chuck continued to yell, "You're dead, you fuckin' whore. You're dead! The kids won't care if you're dead. They don't even love you."

"Daddy, no! Daddy, we love Mommy. Daddy, no." Ian pleaded with him.

Chuck finally let go of me, and the kids ran over to me. Emerson hugged my legs, and Ian stood guard. Chuck was angry they were so upset. "Stop your fuckin' crying. God damn it...make the little fuckers stop."

I held them close to keep Chuck away from them. Chuck paced the kitchen as they continued to cry. "Get the fuck over it!"

My whole body hurt. The baby stopped moving. I was scared he had killed the baby inside of me. I sat in the living room with Ian and Emerson in my lap, and I cried with them. Chuck sat on the couch to watch us. "I need to go to the hospital...the baby isn't moving."

"You're not going anywhere. You just want to get me in trouble."

"No...I'm scared the baby's hurt."

"You're fine, the baby's fine."

My body was covered in bruises. It hurt to sit down. After a while, the baby did move, and Chuck reminded me he was right, there was nothing wrong. He told me again if I told anyone what happened he'd kill me and take the kids. He said he would cut the baby out of me and take it too. I couldn't leave them. I couldn't let him kill me and leave them with him.

At my doctor's appointment, a nurse asked about the bruises. I said I had fallen down the stairs. I hoped they wouldn't believe me, but they didn't ask again. She told me it was selfish of me not to come in right after the fall. I felt like I'd failed this baby too, just like I failed at everything.

After that day, my dislike for Chuck grew to hate. I hated him for all he had done to me. I hated him for all he did to my kids. I hated him for all he pretended to be. I hated him for all the hope he stole from me. I hated him for everything. We'd been together for six years, and I still hadn't told him I loved him. Now there was no way he'd ever hear me speak those words.

CHAPTER 30

April 21, 2008, my second daughter, Ruby was born. She was eleven pounds eleven ounces. Ruby was so large, her clavicle broke on her way out. Other than that, she was healthy. Chuck's brutality had not harmed her.

Chuck reminded me on a regular basis how I wasn't good enough. How I was too fat. Too stupid. Too lazy. Too ugly. He reiterated that no one would ever love me. He told me he was doing me a favor by being married to me. After a while, I started to believe the words he spoke to me. I felt like all those awful things and more. I was trapped. Living in a house in the town he grew up in was no place I wanted to be on my own. Our neighbors were all people he grew up with. They thought he was a nice person, but they didn't know who he was behind closed doors.

I wanted a divorce. I hated him. I hated my life with him. We owed more money on the house than it was worth. There was no way I could survive on my own. The house was too big and old for me to take care of alone. I didn't have money to pay for an apartment and the bills at the house. It was all too overwhelming for me. There really was no way out. Every day was a struggle. Depression became like the blood that ran through my veins. My body felt heavy, and my heart was sad.

Mom continued to struggle with depression too. Her collection of cats grew to fifteen, and the filth in the house stayed with you long after a visit. She married Mary, a woman she met online from England, but she still spent most of her time in bed. Soon after Mary arrived, Mom stopped driving, and her weight continued to rise. She was over six hundred pounds and now unable to walk.

Gram lived next to Mom still, but Mom's promise to take care of Gram wasn't fulfilled. Kate lived at home with Mom, but she didn't help Gram either. I became Gram's caretaker because she had always been mine. She was eighty-eight now and had a hard time walking. She used a wheelchair anytime she left the house. It was hard to watch her decline before my eyes, but I was grateful I was able to help.

I loved to watch Gram interact with Ian, Emerson, and Ruby. Every weekend, I brought the kids to her house, and we all had lunch together, and Gram read to them as I cleaned. The kids loved Gram as much as I did.

I didn't tell Gram or Mom about Chuck's abuse. It was another skeleton in the closet to add to the many from my childhood. If there was one thing I was good at, it was keeping secrets. I didn't want the kids to have to carry that burden, so I told them all the time "there are no secrets."

Secrets were poison.

CHAPTER 31

The summer after Ruby was born, Hannah took me aside at her son's birthday party and said, "I have wanted to find a way to tell you something for a while, but I didn't want to upset you while you were pregnant..."

The color left my face as I waited for her to continue. I rocked Ruby in my arms to keep her from fussing. Tears formed in my eyes as Hannah went on. "See, this is why I didn't want to tell you, but you need to know." She paused a moment longer as I tried to pull myself together. "John has been sick—"

"What do you mean? Is he okay? How long? Why didn't you tell me? I could've helped."

Hannah put her arm around me. "He begged me not to tell you. He said he didn't want to worry you, and I didn't want to get you upset while you were pregnant."

"He's okay now, but he had cancer. They just told him it's all gone."

I could feel the lump forming in my throat. "Cancer? Where, of what?"

"He said it was in his esophagus, but it's gone now. Don't worry. He's fine and back at work now."

"He was sick enough to miss work?" I stared blankly at her, still rocking Ruby.

"He was—but he's fine. Don't worry."

How could I not worry? I loved John from the day I met him, and the way I felt after hearing this news proved I never stopped.

"Here comes Chuck. Let's get out of here." She took me by the arm to look at the river. Chuck knew I didn't love him and was upset I still loved John so intensely. Hannah knew I couldn't handle hearing something negative from Chuck just yet so she shielded me from him.

I went home that afternoon and fell apart. John was no longer with the woman Tim had told me about. He was all alone now. My love for John was what got me through many unhappy days. That was all that made me believe love still existed. I was relieved to hear John was cancer free, but there was something inside me that knew he was not out of the woods.

Three weeks later, Gram received a call from Uncle Doug. He told her he had been diagnosed with pancreatic cancer but was confident he could beat it. He had been going to specialty clinics that used all the best technology to help fight cancer.

This news devastated Gram. Doug lived fourteen hours away in Detroit and only visited a handful of times since he moved out of state forty years before. Doug was her oldest and her pride and joy. He was the child that always made her proud. Mom could never compare.

Doug and his wife, Kelly, planned a trip to visit Gram. Gram knew it was his "goodbye trip," but she didn't let on. When Doug and Kelly arrived at Gram's trailer, I greeted them at the door. Doug was six foot three and had always been a large man. When he started up the driveway, I noticed how much weight he had lost.

Doug noticed I was looking at him and cracked a joke, "Cancer, it's the best diet I have ever been on!"

Nervous laughter erupted from my mouth. "I should try it."

Kelly snapped at us, "Cancer is not something to joke about!"

I was unsure how to act around Doug. I knew this was going to be our last time seeing each other, but I also wanted to hold onto hope he could fight it—that he could beat the odds and survive.

The last two trips Doug made to Vermont, he and his family stayed in a cabin on a pond twenty minutes from Gram's trailer. Doug spent a lot of his visit at the cabin because he was too tired to do much visiting. We planned a time Peter, his two boys, Gram, my kids, and I could all meet at the cabin they were staying at the night before they were leaving.

Doug and I sat on the front porch and talked as night fell around us. It was the first time we had time to talk alone. "You know I'm gonna beat this, right? I'm going to fight until there is no more fight left in me." He flexed a muscle on his arm.

"I know."

"I want to thank you for taking care of Mom. Wendy is good for nothin', but she had you, and that's good for something."

"Gram takes care of me too."

He laughed. "She's a good broad, ain't she."

"We're kind of lucky."

"Jess...if I can't beat this God forsaken shit, I want to be cremated." His eyes drifted off toward the water. "And I want my ashes scattered over there." He nodded his head to where his eyes had been looking.

I sat in the awkward silence with him as he faced the reality of his illness. I wanted to tell him he had nothing to worry about... but I knew I was wrong.

"I want to spend eternity in Vermont. This is my home." He

hung his head as he looked at his folded hands in his lap. "I don't know why I ever left."

"You were too big for this place. You're better than Vermont."

"Nah...Vermont's special."

"So are you...I love you, Uncle Doug."

"I love you too, kid."

We sat together in the glow of the porch light and listened to crickets in the background chirp until we were interrupted by the gang of noisy kids. When we said goodbye, it was forever. The only person I had to help me through losing Gram was leaving me before I had to face that loss. It was selfish to think that way, but he was all I had who I could depend on. I didn't know Doug well, but we had a special connection. My love for him was strong since he offered to save me so many years ago. It was hard to watch him leave knowing I wouldn't get to see him again, but it was more painful to watch the woman I loved lose her son.

CHAPTER 32

*G*ram began to need more of my time, and with work and the kids, I wasn't able to meet all of her needs. I talked to her about the possibility of her moving in with Chuck, the kids, and me. She didn't want to leave her house, but she knew she wasn't safe at home alone any longer. By the end of the summer, Gram and I were living together again.

With Gram at the house, Chuck stopped yelling and no longer hurt me. He didn't want Gram to know who he *really* was. Gram was still protecting me, whether she knew it or not. Gram brought peace to the house.

Summer turned to autumn, and I received a call from Hannah. "Jess…John's cancer is back. He's still fighting, but it doesn't look good."

I walked to the bathroom and shut the door behind me.

"Jess…are you there?"

"Yeah…how much time does he have?"

"I'm not sure. He's getting treatment still and comes to work some days."

"Who's helping him? Is he alone? I can help."

"His brother is helping, taking him to appointments and stuff."

"I've gotta see him…"

"I don't know, Jess. He may not want you to…he looks different."

I thought about how much weight I had gained since I saw him. *I looked different too.* "I don't care. I love him."

"I know Jess…I just wanted you to know."

"Thanks, Hannah. Tell him for me? That I love him?"

"I will, Jess. I love you."

"Love you too."

After the call from Hannah, I drove past the cancer center in town and saw John's car in the parking lot. Tears started flowing. Seeing his car there made it real for me. I pulled over up the road and called his house, partly because I wanted to hear his voice but also because I intended to leave him a message. It had been years since I called him, but his number was etched in my memory. I dialed the phone and waited as it rang. I heard his voice, and my body ached for him. I wasn't able to speak when it came time to leave the message. I called back and again, couldn't get the words out. I sat in the parking lot and cried heavy, deep sobs. I was going to lose John, and I wasn't going to be able to say goodbye.

I pulled out a notepad and wrote John a letter. I wrote everything I had always been too afraid to say, holding nothing back. I told him I loved him, and I had never stopped. I told him all the secrets my heart held for all those years. I couldn't find all the words I wanted to share. The magnitude of love I held for him was more than any words I could find. I cried as I tried to make it perfect. I cried as I thought about losing him. I cried because we never would be together again. I cried and cried and cried.

I mailed the letter and never heard back. I asked Hannah if he had said anything. She told me he was not coming to work anymore because he was too sick. I hoped he was strong enough to have read the letter. I wanted him to know how I felt about him before he left this Earth. The only thing left for me to do was to wait. Wait for the call that told me he was gone. Wait for his disease to take him. Just wait.

CHAPTER 33

T was scheduled to have my wisdom teeth extracted in December. I was nervous John would die during this time because I didn't want to miss his funeral. The night before I went in to have my oral surgery, I had a dream:

Three women came to me in a white room where I sat in a chair. They came over to me and told me, "John is better now. His cancer is gone." They walked out of the room, their white gowns flowing behind them.

I woke up relieved. Maybe he was going to be okay. Maybe he was going to be able to beat it. Maybe he wouldn't leave me.

As we drove past his house on the way to my surgery, I was at peace knowing he was okay. When I returned home, the pain controlled me. The Ibuprofen they gave me didn't touch it. Unable to fall asleep, I attempted to rest on the couch, my head propped up on a stack of pillows. The quietness of the night was interrupted by *Santa Claus is Coming to Town* sung by the motion-activated ornament that hung on the Christmas tree across the room. My eyes went to the tree as my heart made way to my throat.

No movement in the room, the tree stood still in the corner.

The silence was again stolen by the words of the song. Minutes later, the song played again...and again. Alone in the living room, I got the feeling there was someone there with me—but who?

Two days later, I opened the newspaper and knew. John. He died the night the ornament kept going off. He came to say good-bye. In his obituary, it thanked the three angels who helped care for him. It was the three angels who came to me in my dream. They told me he was cancer free, and now he was. I was overcome with sadness as I looked into John's eyes staring back at me from his obituary photo. He was gone—but he knew I loved him and he loved me. He made the trip to say goodbye and sent the angels to prepare me.

Chuck laughed when he picked up the paper. "So much for your fantasy man."

"I'm going."

"What...where?"

"To the funeral."

"Like hell you are...and leave me with these kids?"

"I don't care what you say, I'm going."

Hannah took me to the funeral. We walked up to his ashes—on a table lined with photographs—and I lost it. I fell apart as soon as the reality of what had happened hit me. John was really gone. All of my hopes and dreams about escaping my awful marriage and reuniting with the man I loved were gone. I was angry with myself for waiting. Disgusted with myself for gaining so much weight and hiding away from him so he wouldn't see what I had become. I felt guilty he was alone. Regrets of a lifetime flooded me.

When I pulled myself together, I looked around the room—these people didn't know me, and they didn't know how much I loved him. No one really knew we had even dated. I was just someone that worked with him years ago. I was a nobody in the sea of people. When I realized my insignificance, my heart boiled with rage. Why didn't I matter? Why was I not good enough for him to love me? Why would I spend the rest of my life without the love I so desperately longed for?

Hannah and I looked through the albums of pictures on the table. That's where I found the reason. In that book was the girl who had broken his heart. He still loved her, and he was afraid of being hurt again. I paid the price for what she did to him, and she wasn't even there to say goodbye. John didn't matter to her, but she was all that mattered to him. I was stuck loving a man that couldn't love me back. And now he was gone. I ran out of time to make him love me. There were no more chances. I was left with only a broken heart consumed by grief.

The pain of losing someone I never truly had was complicated. He was never really mine to lose, and at the same time, *I mourned the loss of what could have been*. My heart hurt—I lost so much and then nothing at all.

Like losing Ralph, I couldn't grieve John's death. Chuck was jealous and angry that I loved John and not him. When I started to cry, he'd yell, "He's dead! Get over it!" I wasn't over it. I'd never be over it. I learned to swallow the pain—and built a wall around my heart.

CHAPTER 34

While dinner cooked in the oven on February 2, 2009, the phone rang. The caller id displayed Uncle Doug's name. *Oh no…*

"Hello?"

"Jess?"

"Yeah…is everything all right?"

"No…everything is *not* all right. Doug is dead. He's…he's gone." Aunt Kelly sniffled into the other end of the phone. "I came home from work and found him."

"I'm sorry…I don't—"

"Sorry doesn't bring my best friend back. What am I going to do?"

"I don't know…do you want to talk to Gram?"

"No…I can't. You tell her…I just can't."

"Okay…I love—"

Click.

As I hung up the phone, shock hit. It couldn't be true. It had only been two short months since cancer stole John—and now

Doug? I had to tell Gram—but how? How do you tell a mother her son is dead? The longer I thought about what I had to do, waves of nausea washed over me.

I took a deep breath, wiped my eyes, and walked down the hall to Gram's room. She sat in her recliner and watched *Jeopardy*. I pulled her wheelchair in front of her and sat down. As I looked at her, I began to cry. "What's the matter, Jessie?"

"Uncle Doug died." *Not like that!* As I fought with myself for blurting out the news without care, Gram stared back at me.

"I'm sorry, Gram...I...I didn't mean to say that."

"He's dead? Doug...is dead? No...please...*no!*"

"I'm sorry, Gram...Aunt Kelly called and told me."

"Are you sure?" she looked at me with so much pain in her eyes. She sobbed, and all I could do was watch. I didn't know what to say or how to comfort her. I sat with her as we processed the news. I didn't know how to take the pain away. I sat helpless as the heart of the woman I loved so much broke. She was consumed with grief, and there was nothing I could do to fix it.

After Doug died, Gram started to talk about her death. Still stuck in the grief from losing John and Doug, I couldn't listen to her. When she would begin to talk about her death, I changed the subject with the hope ignoring the issue would prevent it from happening. I wasn't ready to lose her—I never would be.

"Jessie...will you go to the funeral home with me and help me prepare my funeral?"

"What for, Gram? You're not going to die...you have nothing to worry about."

"I'm almost ninety...I'm going to die someday. I just don't want you to worry about it after I'm gone."

"We've got time, Gram."

She sighed. "There's some stuff I want you to include in my obituary...do you want to write it down?"

"Gram…you're *not* going to die…we have time."

Every conversation Gram and I had circled back around to her wish to plan for her death. She started the conversation, and I ended it. I began spending less time with her. It was too painful to think about losing her. The hours we spent together turned to minutes as the pain became too much. I tried to detach from her, so when I did lose her, it wouldn't hurt so much. I hated not being with her every second I could, but the wall I built when John died continued to grow.

One night, as I helped Gram get ready for bed, she looked up at me and took my hand as I pulled the covers over her. "You have turned out so well, Jessie. You have a family, a good job, an education. You don't need me any—."

"You're wrong, Gram, I *need* you. I'll always need you. Please, I can't think of life without you."

"Oh honey, I'm ready. I have lived a full life. My son is gone. My work here is done."

"Please, Gram. No. I can't live without you. I just can't even think about it." I fought back tears. "Goodnight, Gram. I love you."

"I love you, Jessie." Those were the words I couldn't imagine *not* hearing again. After that night, she never talked to me about her death. She knew I would never be in a place where I'd be okay with it.

Since work kept me busy, Chuck took Gram to her doctor's appointment in Dartmouth. Gram said it was just a regular appointment. When they returned, Gram said she was scheduled for a procedure the following week. Chuck didn't have any information, and I didn't fully understand what was going to happen. I took the day off from work and rode to Dartmouth with Chuck and Gram to wait while they did the procedure.

On the drive there, I sat in the backseat behind Gram. I leaned forward and tapped her on the shoulder. "Gram...you know you're going to be ninety in just a few weeks?"

"Oh, geez...you had to remind me?" A deep belly laugh rumbled out of her.

"I think we should throw a party...what do you say, Gram?"

"No...don't you dare."

"Ahh, come on..."

"I had a lot of fun at my eighty-fifth you threw me, but I'm not up for another one...I'm too old."

"You're not too old! You're a spring chicken. I'm not making any promises... We'll just have to wait and see."

When we arrived at the hospital, the nurse explained what was going to happen. They were going to give her anesthesia to prepare for the surgery where they were going to open the arteries in her leg to help with circulation. "Anesthesia? Surgery? They said this was just a simple procedure. Why does she have to have anesthesia?"

The nurse explained this was an operation, and Gram likely would need to spend the night. The lightness of the day was lost as fear crept in. At her age, she might not recover from being put under anesthesia.

"Gram, you don't have to do this...we can go home right now."

"No, stop it. I'm here, and I trust these people." She took the nurse's hand. "Tell her I'll be fine."

The nurse shook her head.

"I don't know, Gram...this isn't what I expected."

"Honey, I'm in a lot of pain...I have to try to see if this helps." She took off her jade ring and held it out for me to take. "Keep this safe for me."

"Gram...no...that's your lucky ring...you need it."

"Take it, Jessie." She pushed the ring closer to me.

I took the ring and slid it onto my ring finger. Even though she was so much smaller than I was, our fingers were the same size. It fit perfectly. After the nurse took her in for surgery. I began to worry. I paced back and forth. Waiting.

Waiting.

Waiting.

Hours passed, and a doctor came out. He told us Gram was out of surgery, and I could go see her. In the recovery room, she didn't look or act like herself. She was still under anesthesia and in and out of sleep. "What's wrong with her?" I asked the nurse by her bedside.

"Nothing...it's normal for the medicine to still be affecting her. You can go home now if you'd like. She's staying with us for the night."

I didn't want to leave her there, but I had to get back to my babies. I was torn between the people who mattered most in my life.

The next morning, I called to check on Gram. She still wasn't ready to come home. Around two o'clock, the phone on my desk at work rang—it was time to get her. When I arrived, she was ready to leave. She hadn't slept the night before and wanted to go home to rest. The nurse gave me discharge instructions and handed me a couple of prescriptions to fill. As we started for home, Gram wiggled around in her seat. "What's wrong Gram...should I bring you back to the hospital?"

"I just can't get comfortable."

I helped her adjust her seat so she could lean back for the ride home. When we arrived in town, I turned my directional signal on and slowed in front of the pharmacy.

"Not tonight, Jessie. I just want to get home."

"The nurse said you need these."

"Fiddle faddle. I need to rest."

I tucked the prescriptions into my visor and continued home. Chuck had to help me get Gram into the house because she was too weak to walk. When she got through the door, Ian, Emerson, and Ruby met her with excitement. Since she had moved in, they hadn't been apart. The first smile I had seen since the previous day formed on her face. "I missed you kids...but Grammy's tired." She blew them kisses, and I wheeled her into her room where I helped her into bed. I handed her the jade ring back and made sure she put it back on her finger. *She needed the luck from this ring now more than ever.*

The following afternoon when I arrived home from work, she still wasn't feeling well. I asked if she wanted to go to the hospital, but she refused. I went to my weekly Weight Watchers meeting up the road. When I returned from the meeting, Chuck met me at the door. "The ambulance is on the way...Gram's not feeling well." I raced past him to Gram's room.

Gram's face was as white as the bed sheet behind her. "Gram... are you okay?"

"I'm fine, dear...just a little dizzy. Nothing to worry about."

The ambulance pulled in front of the house, and three men jumped out and unloaded their equipment. I hovered over them, sick to my stomach. One of the EMTs asked me to give them some space while they examined her. I left her room but paced the hall in front of it, waiting to hear she was fine.

She wasn't fine—she had a heart attack. They were unsure when it happened, so she needed to get to the hospital for more tests. The crew rolled her onto a stretcher and loaded her into the ambulance. The sirens blasted as they pulled into the road to head to the hospital. I followed in my car.

At the emergency room, the nurse asked Gram questions, but she was having a hard time answering them. The nurse turned the questions to me. I told the nurse about the operation and explained she came home the day before. "Did they send her home with any new prescriptions?"

My heart sank as I remembered the two folded above my visor out in my car. My face grew hot. "She had two, but...but they haven't been filled yet."

She looked down her glasses at me. "What two didn't *you* fill?"

"I...I'm not sure...I don't remember."

"Was one Plavix?"

I shook my head yes. "Yes, that sounds right."

She spun away from the computer. "Why wouldn't you fill that? If they sent her home with it, it was important. They give people prescriptions for a reason."

I could tell by the tone of her voice I had messed up. "I tried to get it for her on the way home, but she was in too much pain to stop and wait for it."

"And you still didn't get it filled? You had all day."

My head dropped. *I* did this to Gram. I should have made sure she had it.

"She had a heart attack, and it *could* have been prevented. They give that medication to prevent heart attacks, you know."

I didn't know. "No one told us that."

"It shouldn't matter. You have no excuse for not making sure she had that medication," she sternly said as she left the room.

Gram told me it was okay, that she was fine. She said, "I must be pretty stupid to have been having a heart attack and not know it."

"I'm sorry, Gram. I should've gotten you that medicine." Tears formed in my eyes.

"I told you to go home. It's not your fault."

The emergency room shifted the blame to Dartmouth. They should have never let her go—there was no way she was stable enough to go home. We waited as a bed became available at Dartmouth and for an ambulance to take her down. The same crew that brought her from home was ready to make the trip to Dartmouth.

"I'm coming with you."

"Don't be silly...the kids need you....I'm fine."

"I don't want you down there alone."

"It's late...go get some rest...besides..." She giggled. "I'm looking forward to the ride with these handsome fellas." She winked and pointed at the EMTs in the room.

The following day, Peter and Kate came with me to visit Gram. She was in the Cardiac Unit. When I entered her room, I noticed a purple Do Not Resuscitate (DNR) bracelet on her wrist. "Gram! Do you know what that thing means?" I pointed to her bracelet. "You have to take that off!" I looked around the room for scissors.

"I *know* what it means...and I want to keep it on."

"Gram...you gotta get that thing off." I went to the nurse's station and told them I was her healthcare power of attorney, and I wanted the bracelet off her. They had to listen to what Gram wanted. She was still capable of making her own decisions.

I returned to Gram's room and stood against the wall. I bit my bottom lip to keep myself from crying. I tried to hold back the tears, but I couldn't. When Gram saw me crying, she told me she was tired, and we left the room. After she had rested a little, we returned to her room. A social worker was in with her. "You must be Jessie. I've heard so much about you." Gram met her with a smile.

I nodded as I noticed how quiet the room had gotten.

"I want to talk to you about your gram returning home on hospice."

"You mean palliative care?"

"No, I mean hospice care. Hospice is for people who have six months or less to—."

"Then she doesn't qualify."

The social worker capped her pen and stood up. "Maybe now isn't the right time to talk." She wasn't going to get me on the same page, no matter how hard she tried.

"I'm ready, Jessie." She looked me in the eyes. "I've lived a good life. I am ready to go now."

"No! I'm not ready!"

"I'm tired. Maybe you should get going home." She held my hand and gave me her ring. "Take this for me. I can't wear it here."

Her jade ring...her good luck charm. That ring was *her*. I had always told her that was the one thing I wanted when she died. The hand that ring had lived on provided me with so much comfort and love. I knew what she was doing.

"No, Gram, please, you need this," I said as I handed it back to her. "It's your good luck charm, you need it now."

"I want you to keep this safe for me. Please," she said as she put it in my hand.

"I love you, Gram. I'll see you tomorrow. Kate and I will bring Ian, Emerson, and Ruby to visit tomorrow. Maybe we will know when they'll let you come home." I kissed her on the cheek as we left for the day.

She smiled as we left the room. She was ready, and she knew I never would be. She knew I'd fight her on this for as long as I could. She knew how much I loved her, and I knew how much she loved me. I couldn't stand the thought that she wouldn't always be in my life. I couldn't imagine my life without her.

CHAPTER 35

$\mathcal{T}$oo nervous to sleep, I stared at the ceiling while the house hummed in the morning hours. Thoughts about the visit with Gram later in the day kept coming back to me. The kids missed their Grammy, but the idea of keeping a one, four, and six-year-old quiet at the hospital made me rethink the day's plan. When Gram saw Ian, Emerson, and Ruby, she'd want to get better for them...I had to figure out how to make it work.

Ring...ring...ring...

Paralyzed by the sound of the phone, my eyes widened to look at the clock. Red, digital numbers broadcasted the time... 6:32 a.m. I blinked my eyes to be sure. *No...this can't be. If I don't answer it...I don't have to know.* The answering machine kicked on...*beep*...I placed the pillow over my head to block out the voice. *No...not today.*

Chuck shook me, "The doctor just left a message...go call him back."

"I don't want to."

"Jesus...just go call the fuckin' doctor."

Cold sweat formed on my forehead, and my stomach ached. I pushed the blankets off and went downstairs to the phone. My mouth dry, my heart pounding. My hand shook as my finger pressed the button. The doctor left his name and number and asked for a return call as soon as possible. I dialed the number and asked for the physician. "He isn't available," the voice on the other end of the phone responded in a cold tone.

"He just called...he asked me to call—"

The voice on the other end of the phone warmed up a bit. "Oh, yes, he's been trying to reach you. Hold, please."

I blinked my eyes to get out the blackness that took over the room. My heart raced, and the room began to spin as I waited for the doctor.

"Jessica, I have some news to tell you..." My tears began to fall before he got the words out. "Your grandmother..."

"Is she okay? I am coming down to see her, is she okay? I...I can come now."

"No, Jessica. I'm afraid she's not. Your grandmother passed away this morning."

"*No, no, no!*"

"I am very sorry for your loss. She was a great lady. Would you like to come say goodbye and get her things?"

"No...please no..."

"I'm very sorry...I'll be around when you get here...please bring someone with you...you should not be driving."

I dropped the phone as nausea crept up my body. Everything went black as the words from the conversation played back. *Your grandmother passed away.*

"*Chuck!* Gram is dead. I have to go see her."

"Quiet the fuck down! You're going to wake the kids."

My body trembled as I walked in circles. *What do I do?* It can't be true...she can't be *gone*. I needed to get to her, to fix this. But how?

Ian rushed down the stairs. "Mommy, what's wrong? What's the matter? Mommy, Mommy, Mommy...why are you crying? What's wrong?"

I was numb—full of pain yet feeling so empty. "Grammy died this morning, honey."

He hugged my legs and began to cry without fully understanding what I had said. I paced the house not knowing what to do or who to tell. I called my boss and started crying before I got the words out, "My gram died this morning. I won't be in today." She told me how sorry she was and not to worry about work. I called my Aunt Kelly and told her. I called Peter and Mom. No one seemed to understand how much this hurt. No one was acting like their world was crashing in on them. *No one got it.*

When Ruby woke up, she crawled down the hall to Gram's room. She pushed the curtain back, looked at Gram's chair, and started to babble. It broke my heart to see her looking for her Grammy. *How would I explain to her, to any of them, that Grammy was gone?* Ruby saw something, and when I noticed, I smiled knowing Gram was around. I scooped Ruby up and gave her a kiss. I couldn't be in Gram's room knowing she wasn't coming home. The thought was too unbelievably painful to grasp.

Chuck drove me to the hospital. I was in such a rush to see Gram, but I was so afraid. When we arrived, I walked in feeling as if I were outside of my body, disconnected from who I had been. At the nurse's station, I saw the door to Gram's room. It was closed with a sign: *Please see the nurse before entering.* When the nurse saw my tears, she knew who I was and why I was there. She brought Chuck and me to the room and asked us to wait for the doctor. When I entered the room, I saw Gram in the bed. She looked at peace. She had a smirk on her face, which brought a quick smile to mine.

The smell in the room was indescribable. The comforting smell of the woman I loved mixed with the smell of death, fear, and despair. This was my first time being present with a dead body. And it was hers. Alone, that was overwhelming, but coupled together, it was crippling.

I was unsure what to do, what not to do, how to react, how to breathe, how to do anything. She was where she wanted to be since she had lost her son. She was gone. She was so peaceful, and I was so distraught. The one person who helped me through everything wasn't here to help me through the hardest thing I ever had to face. All I wanted was to have her comfort me and say just the right words to make me know it was all going to be okay. I wanted her back.

I was angry with her for leaving me, and then I felt guilty for thinking that way. I was angry with her for thinking I could survive without her because she knew I would be broken without her. I was angry at life for setting me up for so much pain. Then I was sad for being angry, and then I was numb. Completely numb. I couldn't feel anything. I couldn't see past the pain—crippling grief overpowered me.

The doctor came in and sat on the windowsill across from me, Gram's body behind us. He took my hand. "I'm very sorry for your loss." He sat with me as I cried, my hand still between his. "Your gram was a special lady...all the nurses fought over who got to take care of her." A quiet laugh escaped from him. "To be honest, I was looking forward to working with her today. She was funny...such a great sense of humor."

I nodded and smiled. *Everyone* loved Gram.

"She loved you and your children very much. She spoke highly of you. And I can see how much you loved her."

"She...she was my best friend." I turned my head to look at her body. *Come back to me, Gram...please.*

"Do you have any questions for me?"

"Was she in any pain? Was she scared? Was she alone when she...died?"

"No...to all three. She rang her bell for a nurse to help her go to the bathroom, and when the nurse came in, she noticed your gram looked off, so she called me in. When I arrived, I took her hand." He squeezed my hand between his. "She started telling me a joke, and she just went. Mid-sentence, her heart stopped...and she was gone."

She died with a smile on her face and laughter in her heart. She died how she lived, and that gave me comfort despite the pain.

"Could you have saved her?"

"Well, we could have tried...but it was not what she wanted. She was very clear she did not want any lifesaving measures. And...she was lucky to have such a peaceful death. If we had tried to resuscitate her, it might not have saved her, but if it had, it would have been painful for her. Please know your gram was at peace when she died." He gave my hand one last squeeze.

He was holding my hand with the same hand that had held Gram's as she took her last breath—that in itself gave me great comfort.

After he left, a million thoughts raced through my mind. This was going to be my last time seeing Gram again. *Ever.* I was never again going to be able to touch her skin with mine. I would never again be able to smell her skin or hold her hand. My time with her was limited, and the clock was ticking. As it all became too real for me to handle, I began to shatter.

As I stood above her lifeless body, my tears hit her face. I watched helplessly as the salty river of grief seeped into her skin. I frantically hoped for a miracle, for what was true to be a mistake, for her breath to return to her body, for anything to take me out of the pain where I was so deeply stuck. I picked up her hand, caressed her skin, and tried to wish her back to life. I used everything inside of myself to try to get her to come back to her body. I held her hand, knowing this would be the last time I would ever be able to feel the hands that had brought me so much comfort all my years before. This was going to be the last time for many things.

I bent down, kissed her forehead, and whispered *I love you* into her ear as I inhaled her smell. I ran my fingers through her hair and caressed her body. I leaned down next to her again and inhaled the fragrance of her hair one last time. I kissed her forehead as she had done to mine so many times as a child. My love for her was strong, so strong I thought for sure it was enough to bring her back to life. I needed a few more minutes with her. A few more days. A few more weeks. A few more years. In all honesty, I needed her to live forever so I would never have to live without her. How could life be so cruel that I was born into this world to have a best friend who was sixty-two-years older than I was? The fate was inevitable, but I had never wanted to believe it would actually happen. The fear of this loss was something I thought about every day for as long as I could remember. As soon as I knew it to be a possibility, I dreaded this day with every ounce of my being. I thought so much about it happening I became overwhelmed with grief. So I would just stop and push it out of my mind. I could no longer stop. I was out of control of the only thing that had ever made sense in my life.

My insides hollowed as the minutes passed by. The gnawing, raw pain took over where my blood had once flowed. My heart was broken. I could feel it ripping apart inside my chest. I could feel everything and nothing. The moments passed by so slowly and so quickly. My time was running out, but how could I leave her behind? How could I leave her there? Why couldn't I bring her home with me? The more I thought, the angrier I became. I wanted to wake up from this nightmare and have my life back. I wanted to be the person I had been hours ago when she was still alive. I wanted my safety net back. I wanted to change the unchangeable.

Arrangements were made with the funeral home. They would be there in a few hours to bring her to the crematorium. I panicked as I thought about her last ride. How could I let strangers take her? What was she going to wear? I hadn't brought any of her clothes with me. Where was her dignity? What had I been thinking? What was I going to do? The funeral director said they would ask the hospital to let her keep her hospital gown if that would make me feel better. I couldn't fathom the thought of her in the back of a hearse in a body bag, naked except a hospital gown. She was more than that to me, and I was not showing her the love she had shown me. The funeral director reminded me this was not her. She was no longer in there, and this was merely her vessel. When I was able to trust him, I knew I needed to leave.

The pain of knowing this was it, this was the last time my eyes would ever see Gram's body again, was unbearable. I wanted to stay with her until they came, but I had to get to the funeral home before they closed to get the arrangements settled since it was Good Friday and they were closed on Easter. Easter. How could I forget Easter was two days away? I had planned for her to be home for Easter and having dinner with us like she always did. I hadn't even made the kids their Easter baskets yet. How could I be the Easter Bunny when I couldn't even be myself?

I took Gram's hand one last time and held it as I kissed her, begging her silently to come back to me, to give me another chance. She was still. The smirk remained on her face, but she was gone. She was really gone. *Goodbye forever*, I said in my head as I kissed her for the last time.

As Chuck and I made our way to the funeral home to start the arrangements, everything seemed to be happening in slow motion. The funeral director was upset we were cutting into his time on Good Friday. He said he had a lot to do and wanted this done as soon as possible. He gave me paperwork to fill out and took me to look at urns. Upstairs in a large room, there were shelves of urns. Some had smaller ones that matched. I pointed to a small urn and asked what it was for, he said it was a keepsake urn to keep a small piece of the ashes after the rest are scattered or buried.

I spotted an elegant, baby blue urn with gold trim. The minute I saw it, I knew it was the one for her. It also had a keepsake urn next to it. I needed to keep some of her ashes. I couldn't stand the thought of losing all of her, forever. After we picked out the urn, he started asking me questions so he could get the obituary written. I sat with him as he typed the obituary. He was rushed and annoyed he was still there with me.

I didn't feel good about the obituary. There were questions that I didn't know the answers to, and I didn't have time to ask anyone. When he was finished writing it, he saved the document and then closed it so he could email it to the newspaper. When he looked for the attachment, it was gone. I felt like that was a sign from Gram, telling me she was unhappy with it. The funeral director became very upset and started retyping what he had just written. This time he made sure it saved before he closed the file. I didn't feel right about the words in the obituary, but he was impatiently waiting for me to leave. The way he had written it, my grandfather's name was written multiple times. She wouldn't have wanted that, but I didn't know how to fix it.

Once I returned home, I went into Gram's room. I felt so alone, so sad. I was lost. Completely, utterly lost. I felt overwhelmingly hopeless. Consumed by pain and darkness, I walked into her room and sat in her chair. I reached down beside the chair and pulled up a piece of paper. I began to cry as I saw her handwriting on a piece of notepad paper. *For my obituary* was written at the top. All those times she tried to tell me what she wanted in her obituary, and I couldn't listen. She knew. She knew she had to write it down, and she left it right where I could find it. I scanned the paper and ran out to Chuck.

"We have to stop them before they put that obituary in the paper! I was wrong about so much. Look!" I said as I handed him the paper. "We have to change it. We just have to!"

He told me to call the funeral home and tell them what I wanted changed. I spoke to a different funeral director and gave him the changes. He said we still had time to make the corrections. Now I knew for sure it was her who made the original disappear. He sent me a copy of the new obituary before he submitted it. This time it was perfect.

Seven days after her death, we had her funeral, on April 17 at two p.m. A very small crowd of people came. It was a pretty service filled with love. All the people who mattered were there. Peter, Kate, and I had made two picture collages that were displayed. Next to her urn were two framed photos—one of her with a big gold bow on her head and the other was of the two of us at my wedding. In front of her urn was an angel holding a small gold sign that read, "Thank you." It was as perfect as we could make such a solemn day.

I felt so alone in that room full of people. No one else there seemed to understand my pain. No one else had lost so much. They were sad, but they didn't understand. When Gram died, so did I. My life became forever changed. Without her, I didn't know how I'd survive. If it had not been for my children, I know I would have committed suicide. Life was a scary place, and my safety net was gone. I needed Gram more now than ever before. How was I going to make it? I had no idea.

CHAPTER 36

*D*arkness surrounded me for the first year after Gram died. Unable to feel a connection with Ian, Emerson, Ruby—or anyone, I knew it was time to find a counselor. My fear of being labeled, or worse...confirmation I *was* crazy, was no longer enough to keep me away. Gram would have wanted me to live. I had to do this for her.

I made an appointment with the employee assistance program offered by work. Pieces of my past spewed out my mouth. As the room filled with years of pain, the therapist suggested I find a counselor I could work with on a regular basis. I left with an appointment with the recommended counselor for the following week. My plan to be *cured* had failed. I was too messed up for a quick fix.

A big white sign covered in names and titles sat in front of an old blue, Victorian house. As my foot hit the stone walkway, I paused. *Was I ready to let go of the pain?* The image of Gram's face flashed in my mind. I twisted her jade ring on my finger and knew

I had to try. My hand turned the round, brass doorknob as tears formed behind my eyes. *This is for you, Gram.*

When the door opened, empty wooden chairs lined the room, and one small table covered in magazines was pushed against the window. A dirty, braided rug met my feet as I walked to the chair closest to the table. The echo of my heartbeat filled the room as I waited. The tick of the clock reminded me I was minutes away from digging into the pain.

A couple from my town turned the corner, tissues in the wife's hand. I picked up a *Sports Illustrated* and forced my attention to the pictures on the pages hoping they wouldn't notice me. The door closed behind them, and a short woman with brown hair and round glasses called my name. She reached out her hand. "Hi, I'm Fern. Follow me."

I followed Fern down the stairs to her office and sat in the yellowed, floral chair. She picked up her notepad and sat in front of me. "Tell me what brings you here."

"My gram died...and I'm still having a hard time."

"When?"

"About a year ago. She was—"

"Oh, yes, that's much too long to be upset."

The rest of the session continued the same way. She asked a question, waited for an answer, and then responded before I finished. At the end of the hour, she told me, "You should have come to see me before you had children. They don't deserve a broken mother." *A broken mother?*

I didn't return. Maybe I was broken, but I couldn't fix what was already done. She was a professional? If the bar was low enough for her to be a counselor, I figured I had a shot at it too. I made an appointment at Springfield College with the admissions director. My undergraduate file was on her desk when I arrived.

"I see you graduated with a 4.0 from here back in 2006. There should be no problem getting accepted, but you still have to follow the process." She handed me the application and a brochure on the program. Mental Health Counseling: A Sixty Credit Track. It would take two years to complete.

"I don't know if I have what it takes." I passed the application back to her.

"Are you serious?" She pushed it back at me. "Jessica, you had a 4.0. You have what it takes."

"I don't know..."

"How about you complete the application, wait to hear if you are accepted, and then decide?"

Two years was a lot of time, and all I wanted was to heal myself. I didn't want to depend on a stranger to *fix* me. This might be my only chance. Little did I know then how true that was. I completed the application and waited for the answer. Two days before Christmas, I received a letter in the mail from Springfield College. My hands shook as I opened the envelope. I pulled out the ivory paper, unfolded it and read *Congratulations*. Blinded by tears, I couldn't read the rest. I was accepted to start the graduate program in January.

When I walked through the door at orientation, my heart skipped a beat when I saw Dawn. It had been years since I had seen her. I hoped she didn't remember me, but also hoped that she did. Transported back to my teenage self, I knew I had a lot to work on and found comfort in the familiarly of Dawn.

At the end of orientation, I stayed after everyone else left. "I don't know if you remember—"

"I remember, Jess. How have you been?"

"That's a good question." My eyes drifted from hers. "It's been hard."

"I'm proud of you, Jess. You've come a long way."

I ached for approval, and the taste of hers made me know I made the right choice. As classes started, I made friends with the others in my cohort. We were a group of nine people from many different backgrounds. The one thing we shared was the struggle that brought us there. The path to self-discovery awaited me.

CHAPTER 37

*I*an was having troubles of his own. He was being bullied by a neighbor. When school started, the bullying continued because the boy was in Ian's class. At home, Ian was afraid to go outside. Chuck refused to do anything about it— the boy was the son of one of Chuck's childhood friends. He told Ian to be a man and get over it. *Ian was five years old.*

For the next two years, the bullying continued. Sometimes the boy left Ian alone, but the majority of the time, Ian was afraid. Because we were neighbors, and Chuck was friends with the parents, Ian had no peace.

While I was at work, Chuck took Ian to the boy's house to play, to teach the boys to be friends. When I arrived home, Ian cried as Chuck yelled at him to stop being a baby. Chuck left the room, and Ian ran to me.

Ian told me, "Daddy made me play with Duke." He wrapped his arms around my legs. "He had a gun... We were in his playhouse, and he pointed it at me."

I stroked his dirty blonde hair away from his face. "A toy gun?"

"No… a real one. He pointed it at me, and I ran away and told Daddy."

"That was a brave thing you did, honey. That must have been scary."

"Daddy told me to shut up and stop tattling." Ian began to cry again. "He called me a faggot and made me go back out and play."

"What happened next?"

"I told him no…and he pushed me…I fell down."

Anger boiled inside me as I imagined what *could* have happened. "I'm so glad you're safe, baby." I picked Ian up, hugged him tight, and kissed his cheek.

When I confronted Chuck about what happened, he said he thought it was a toy. It was only after Duke's dad went to check his gun collection and noticed one missing they realized it was real. Duke stole the gun from his father's room and had it in the play-house. "Ian did the right thing—he could've been killed! Don't you *ever* take him over there again."

"Jesus Christ. Shut the fuck up…he's not dead…get the fuck over it."

"You shut the fuck up… That's my son you almost killed. You better tell him you're sorry."

"Fuck you." He threw his empty Bud Light can at my feet.

Duke's family was just as scary. They were heavy into drugs and drank into the early hours of the morning.

Near the end of the school year, Ian reported the bullying at school had increased. We had meeting after meeting with the principal, who said, "Boys will be boys." Nothing was done. The last week of school, Ian came home in tears. The principal had left him in a dark room all day after Duke slammed his body into Ian's head while he sat reading his book. Duke wasn't removed from class, and even though Ian asked to call me, he wasn't allowed to.

Ian had a severe headache and was having trouble seeing. I took him to the emergency room for them to check him. After the tests were run, it was determined he had suffered a head injury. The nurse told me I needed to call the police. I explained to them the boy who had done this was also seven years old. Still, she insisted I call.

When Ian and I returned home, I did call the police. Chuck was livid. He didn't want his friends to get in trouble. He didn't care Ian was hurt.

Chuck called Ian a *pussy* and told him he needed to learn to be a man and then left before the police arrived. Ian worried his dad was right. "I don't want to talk to the police, Mommy."

"Honey, what Duke did to you was wrong. You need to be safe." I wondered why he should listen to me when he watched me tolerate abuse from Chuck.

Ian did talk to the police and let the officer know he was afraid. After the police spoke to Ian, he went next door and interviewed Duke and his family. When the police officer was done, he returned and said Duke was sorry and promised to leave Ian alone. Nothing else happened.

The next day, I went to the school and told them Ian wouldn't be returning for the rest of the year. I asked why Ian was kept in a dark room alone and then wasn't allowed to call home when he was injured. I was told they wanted to keep him safe, and Ian was easier to manage than Duke was. When I told them about the head injury, all the principal said was, "We didn't think it was that bad." No one was helping Ian. No one cared.

I felt powerless as I struggled to keep Ian safe. I wanted to expose what had happened, so I sent an email to the newspaper and shared our story. I received an email back the next morning and Annie, a reporter, interviewed me. Annie understood what we were up against and knew how afraid Ian was. She had been through this before with her son and offered helpful advice. She went to the school board meeting with me, and her kindness helped get us through this trying time.

I presented the issue to the school board. The board members, like everyone else, did nothing. They said the principal handled the situation correctly and reminded me the boys were only seven years old. Annie spoke up when defeat took me over. "What she is saying is she knows they are only seven, and that's why something needs to be done."

The school board assured us bullying was not an issue until at least fifth grade. Nothing we said was going to change their minds. It was fruitless. I wanted nothing more than to make sure Ian was safe, but the odds were against me. If I couldn't figure something out, he would have to return in the fall.

Emerson finished out kindergarten, and it was officially summer vacation. To celebrate, Ian went outside to play with his sisters. They played with the hose to cool off from the hot June sun. While Ian was outside, he overheard the neighbors talking. Swears and threats loomed over the back yard. Ian ran in to find me as I made dinner. When I followed Ian outside, the voices continued to blast over the fence. "Let's make a bonfire with their fence!"

I turned the hose off and gathered the kids up. Chuck was sleeping in his recliner, Bud Light in his hand. "Chuck! Get up… Your friends just threatened to burn our fence. Go do something."

He opened his eyes enough to look at me. "I told you not to fuck with them. But you didn't listen. You always have to run your fuckin' mouth."

"They're your friends… Go do something."

"Nothing is going to happen. Jesus…get over yourself."

I called the police to let them know of the threat. There was nothing they could do because nothing had happened—yet. To try to take the kids' minds off the mayhem in our back yard, I packed them into the minivan and went to Peter's house. Chuck came with us. Maybe he was afraid too.

As we sat in Peter's back yard, we heard the sirens of fire engines. My stomach turned to knots. I had a feeling they were headed to our house. I tried to ignore the thoughts and hoped I was overreacting. We continued to sit outside as the kids played. A tan minivan pulled up next to Peter's house. The window rolled down, and a familiar faced popped out. "Guys...*your house*...it's on fire! You need to get home now!"

My stomach sank. I had been right. Those sirens were for our house. We left the kids at Peter's, and Chuck and I drove back home. When we arrived, our house was engulfed in flames. It seemed like the whole town was standing outside watching our house and all of our belongings burn.

I stood on the lawn across the street as I looked into the kitchen window and witnessed the flames dance where I kept Gram's prized possession cookbooks—the ones that held her handwriting and favorite recipes. I saw the flames circle all of her furniture I had grown up with. There was nothing I could do. Nothing. Except stand there and watch. Watch the fire take the memories, good and bad. Watch the flames as they took all I had worked so hard for. Watch as my children's home was destroyed. Watch as their favorite toys went up in flames. Just watch.

Chuck stood with Duke's family as the flames grew higher. He took their sympathy and their beer. They toasted to the flames as though it were a bonfire. Chuck's family came, drinks in hand, as they viewed the show together. The town was entertained at our expense.

As the fire department worked relentlessly to extinguish the flames, the night grew later and later. I couldn't watch any longer. I had to get to my kids. I had to get out of the heat of the flames. I had to get away as everything I once knew no longer existed.

The kids were already asleep when Chuck and I returned to Peter's. In bed, all I heard was the water from the fire hoses hitting the house. The sound overpowered my thoughts. I smelled of smoke and charred memories. We had lost everything. I had held on to so many things I wasn't able to get rid of because everything had a meaning. Everything held a memory that I couldn't let go.

The next day, we were allowed to walk into the house to see if there was anything we could salvage. It was like nothing I had ever seen before as I walked through the rubble that was once our home. Nothing looked the same. The inside of the house was covered with blackness, as it had been figuratively for years. Our secrets were exposed. The walls that had blocked the abuse were gone. Strangers could look into our life. It felt so raw and vulnerable.

We were able to salvage a few important items. Ian's favorite bear, Stuffy, was under a pile of toys, soaked in water and covered in plaster that had fallen from the ceiling. The only photo I had of Ralph was safe in a suitcase where I had packed it years before when we renovated the house. The kids' Christmas stockings that had been handmade by their great-aunt were in a tote flooded with water. The water had kept them safe. The baby's first Christmas ornaments were found safe in a plastic tote, where almost all of the other ornaments had been destroyed. The ceramic cornucopia Gram had made was under a pile of rubble from the falling ceiling, a plastic shopping bag had melted around it. It was untouched, no damage at all. A deck of Angel cards covered in soot on my computer desk, also safe even though the rest of the items that surrounded them were not salvageable.

It was with those discoveries I knew someone was protecting us. Gram had been there watching over us. The items we recovered were precious, but they were just things. We were safe. Our animals were safe. No one was hurt. I learned to let go of my attachment to things that day. Things no longer had a hold over me. Everything that mattered was safe and sound, and they were not things at all.

Three fire investigators conducted investigations to determine the cause of the fire. All three concluded the fire was started in the basement in the wiring. I asked them if the neighbors had done it and reminded them of the threats we heard only moments before the house burned. They all assured me it was accidental and a coincidence.

We spent the next couple of weeks living in motels until we were able to find a rental that would accept us temporarily as we searched for a new home. The insurance company told us we could rebuild on our land or use the money to find a house anywhere. Those words brought freedom with them. We could leave the town that caused Ian so much pain and anxiety. I knew we had to leave and find somewhere else to start our lives again.

The next six weeks, we camped in two rooms of a cabin as we searched for a new home. Our goal was to move in before the start of the new school year. We found the perfect home in the perfect town. It was empty and ready to move in. Everything was falling into place. I spent countless hours completing the inventory of the inside of the home so the insurance company could compensate us for the belongings we had lost.

The next two weeks we had to get the house set up and filled with new possessions so the kids could settle in before the new school year started. We quickly replaced a lifetime of things and settled into our new home. We had enough left over to pay off most of our debt, and for the first time, we were in a position to live comfortably. In losing it all, we gained freedom. I underestimated the magnitude of this newfound freedom.

CHAPTER 38

Seeing Tom Petty live in concert was a lifelong dream, but the timing was never right, and I never had enough extra money. A tour was announced in 2012 right after the land our house had been on sold. I knew I had to go. One of the closest shows was in Orlando, Florida—over twelve hundred miles away.

My fear of flying tried to talk me out of going. Reasons why I shouldn't go flooded me. The kids, school, homework, work—the list got longer each time I went over it. I logged onto a ticket site, added two tickets to my cart, dug out my credit card, and made the purchase. *I was going to see Tom Petty!* Tom Petty and his music helped me through so many rough spots. Tom Petty's music was the soundtrack to my life. There was a song for everything. Every time I needed to be strong, I listened to "I Won't Back Down," and when I started to miss Gram, I listened to "Don't Fade on Me." I could relate to his words. It was like he was singing to me, and now, after all these years, he would be.

Amy, a friend from work, said she would go with me. I booked our plane tickets and found a hotel for us. Amy traveled a lot and knew her way around, so she helped ease some of my fear, plus the excitement didn't leave much room for anything else. When the plane landed in Orlando, I was just hours away from being in the same building as the man who saved my life so many times.

We found our seats—two sections off the floor. My body jittered with excitement, and my hands shook as I held my camera and waited to immortalize the moment. The lights turned off, and Regina Spektor took the stage. My heart drummed in my chest. I couldn't hear her music as I sat on the edge of my seat anxiously awaiting Tom.

Regina left the stage, and the lights came back on as the crew set the stage for Tom Petty and the Heartbreakers. Amy snapped a picture of me and laughed. "Jesus, Jess. Your eyes are about to bug out of your head."

I smiled. I couldn't speak.

"Relax...just breathe and enjoy!" She took one more picture of me, and the lights went back off.

This was it. Tom and the band walked on stage playing "Listen to her Heart." Tears fell, and a smile took over my face when I saw him. His words surrounded me with a warm embrace. I had to listen to my heart—he was right. My feet danced to the music as my eyes captured the beauty of the night. *Anything is possible.*

The night ended after twenty-one songs, each speaking to a different part of me. Being in the room with Tom and his words fueled me and made me want to be better. I needed to live, and I hadn't been. Something good was coming, and I would not back down.

After the euphoria from the show and the twenty-four hours in Orlando, it was time to get home. Amy and I arrived home at two in the morning. I had class seven hours later. I was exhausted, with only adrenaline keeping me awake. A dream I held for years had come true. That experience gave me the strength to look for more moments that offered the same.

Springfield College also offered me strength. I met many friends who became my family through the process. Instead of being with people who tore me down, I was with people who built me up. I shared parts of my story and heard encouragement.

Betty, a lecturer at Springfield College, taught many of the required classes. From the first class with her, I knew we were kindred spirits. She was gentle yet sarcastic and offered a safe place to learn who I was. I looked forward to spending time with her in class. She listened without judgment as my classmates, and I shared our stories. Betty taught us the importance of happiness. She reminded us it isn't selfish to be happy. Most importantly, she urged us not to settle. Life is too short to stay somewhere you don't belong. In our sexual behavior class, she taught us we cannot love someone until we love ourselves. I ruminated on those words —I couldn't love Ian, Emerson, or Ruby unless I loved myself. I had withheld my true self from them their entire lives. Betty said, "Change is hard but worth it." I was ready to find out.

The community Springfield offered was what brought me back. People genuinely cared about each other. Friendships formed and compassion offered. For the first time in many years, I belonged. With belonging came courage. I had a tribe. I was not in the world alone any longer.

I learned I wasn't all the awful things Chuck had beat into me for so many years. I started to see I didn't have to settle. I didn't have to live with the abuse. There was a way out. For the first time, I saw the light. The light of hope. The light of freedom. With the freedom came growth. I held my head higher. I started to see my worth.

For years, I had been beaten down in every sense of the word. My self-worth at zero, my self-esteem nonexistent. Slowly this shifted. Slow enough I didn't notice the changes within myself. People noticed and reacted to the changes I was undergoing, though.

One afternoon, as I walked away from Chuck as he called me names, he said, "You've changed. I don't like who you're becoming."

I held my head high as a smile took over my face. He was right. I *was* changing. There was no turning back now. The fire inside me only fueled the next changes to come. I didn't allow him to treat me as he had. He called me names or tried to pick a fight, and I walked away. He couldn't control me any longer. His words held no power over me.

I brought home divorce papers and told Chuck I wanted to file. He refused to sign them and said he would never leave. We began to fight again. Fights became more violent. There were no moments of peace. I had to get out of this relationship somehow. We didn't speak, only yelled.

Chuck threw me into the wall in the hall and called me lazy and worthless. I pushed him off me, and he slapped my face. I called the police. After eleven years of physical and emotional abuse, for the very first time, I called the police.

While we waited for them to arrive, Chuck begged me to tell them nothing happened. He said he'd stop and do whatever I wanted. The police officer arrived and told me if I didn't press charges, the next time they came, they would arrest Chuck. I didn't want the kids to watch their father taken away in handcuffs, so I decided not to press charges, and they left.

Two days passed, and Chuck flew into a fit of rage. I found a chat he had with a seventeen-year-old girl about her moving into our basement and confronted him. "Let your girlfriend know she isn't moving into the basement."

"What the fuck are you talking about?"

"You left your Facebook chat open... You're sick... She's only a few years older than your kids."

"Shut the fuck up, you fat whore... Her mom is mean to her... She needs me."

"Needs you? What are *you* going to do for her?"

"She needs a father."

"Do you know how twisted that sounds? You're sick... You are *never* to be with our girls alone if you think that's appropriate."

"I said shut the fuck up!" He pushed me into the wall, put his hands around my throat, and lifted me off the floor. "I'm going to fuckin' kill you... and I'll get away with it because you're a whore."

Emerson asked him to stop, but he didn't let go of me. My daughter grabbed the phone and dialed 911. When Chuck saw Emerson with the phone, he dropped me, ripped the phone from her hand, and disconnected it. I went outside with my cell phone and ran up the driveway. Chuck followed and begged me not to call. I dialed 911 and asked for the police to come. The dispatcher said an officer would be there soon and hung up. I stayed outside as Chuck tried to talk me out of filing a report. I knew he would be arrested, but I knew I didn't have a choice. Things were only going to escalate. If he didn't leave, he would kill me. I had no doubt in my mind—the father of my children was capable of killing me. I had lived with that fear from the first threat. Things were getting worse because he was losing control of me.

Two state troopers arrived. One went inside to talk to Chuck, the other took me in his car, and I told him what had happened. He said they were going to arrest Chuck and asked me to keep the kids away from the windows, so they didn't have to watch. I went inside and gathered the kids up. I couldn't keep them away. Ian and Emerson broke free and ran to the window. Ian yelled, "No, Daddy. No!" I again tried to get them away, but it was too late, they had seen their dad handcuffed and placed in the cruiser.

Ian called Chuck's parents and told them what happened. They told Ian they would go get Chuck and not to worry. I was worried. He was going to be free, and I was terrified. I couldn't fall asleep that night as I listened for each sound. Panic took over my body as I remembered the fear I felt as a child waiting for Ralph to fulfill his promise to kill Mom, Peter, and me. It had been years since I felt that amount of fear.

When morning came, I went to the closest ATM machine and took all the money out of our bank account. Chuck would be after it as soon as he could, and I had to take care of the kids. When Chuck was arrested, the police told me to get a restraining order the following day "just in case." I never had a restraining order on him before and was unsure what a piece of paper was going to do to protect us. I went to the domestic violence center to get help with the paperwork. The advocate sat me in a room by myself and gave me the form, extra paper, a pen, and tissues.

The fear had not left my body. I shook as I picked up the pen and started to relive the past eleven years of abuse. As I wrote the "worst event of abuse," I couldn't believe I hadn't made a move sooner. Guilt flooded me as I thought about what my kids had grown up in. We had been prisoners. I was too afraid to make my escape. The two times I had tried to leave were when some of the worst abuse took place.

The more I wrote and remembered, the sicker I became. Chuck *really* could have killed me. I could have been one of the headlines in the local newspaper that shakes things up for a while and then forgotten. As memories flooded all my senses, I knew I still had a long road ahead. I knew my children and I had to get to safety. These were the first steps, but I was so used to being controlled and powered by the fear that it was going to be a struggle.

As I walked to the courthouse, I felt like I was a sole survivor of a plane crash. I looked around and realized no one knew what was happening to my kids and me. No one had carried the fear I carried. People were going on about their lives as though it was a typical day, but my world—our world had been disrupted. I feared for my life. On constant alert, I saw nothing but felt any second could be my last. Pure terror replaced every thought. My heart raced as I walked into the courthouse. I handed the clerk my paperwork and waited.

By the end of the day, they had granted the restraining order. The order didn't stop the fear. A piece of paper wouldn't stop Chuck from killing me. I closed all of the curtains in our house and locked all the doors. My kids and I stayed inside in case Chuck came by. Fear took over our lives.

Ian was angry with me for not letting Chuck come home. Since he had watched the abuse the past ten years, he didn't understand why this time was different. Emerson was eight and went between missing her dad and being afraid of him. She blamed herself for getting him in trouble since she had attempted to call 911. Five-year-old Ruby was glad to be safe, away from Chuck.

Just days before Chuck's arrest, I found handprints on Ruby's back and bottom. He hit her so hard, he left hand prints with the creases from his palms bruised into her skin. I took pictures of the injuries, but fear kept me from acting. I wanted to protect her, but I didn't want him to hurt her worse while I figured out what to do. That fear had held me hostage the past eleven years.

CHAPTER 39

$\mathcal{M}$y graduation from Springfield College was four days after Chuck's arrest. I had finished my master's degree in Mental Health Counseling. Fear and a sense of not belonging to the world around me were still present, but I wasn't going to let Chuck steal this moment from me.

Mom was not able to come to my graduation because she hadn't been able to leave the house for the past year due to her weight. Now over six hundred pounds, she required round the clock care that Mary provided. Kate wasn't able to attend either since she now lived in the Netherlands, and our relationship suffered because of it. My world felt so small.

When I arrived at the church where graduation was, Ruby and Emerson went to sit with friends as they waited for Peter to arrive. Ian chose not to come. I saw Dawn in the hallway, and she swooped me into a hug and asked me if I was okay. I told her I didn't know and began to cry. She reminded me this was my day and to forget that "asshole" for now. Betty was a few steps away. With tears in my eyes, I walked over to her and asked her if she knew what had happened. She told me she had heard and to hang in there because I had many people behind me.

As part of the ceremony, we were given a flower to give to the individual who helped and supported us the most along this journey. When I had graduated with my bachelor's degree five years before, I had given the carnation to Gram. This was a painful reminder she wasn't there. As I waited for my turn to walk across the stage, I thought about who I wanted to have the flower—both of my daughters were in the audience, but I only had one flower. I looked over and saw Betty, and I knew. She was who I needed to thank. It was her support and encouragement that gave me the courage to know what I needed to do to become happy. She was the one who had helped me see there was another way. Life could change. I had to be willing to feel uncomfortable through the changes.

When it was time, I took the red carnation, walked over to Betty, and handed her the flower. She hugged me, and I thanked her for believing in me. She knew how important Gram was to me, and she had become important as well. She helped me see although Gram wasn't there, others who cared about me and loved me were. After the ceremony was over, friends came in to congratulate me. Annie, the reporter who had helped us so much with Ian's bullying; Laura, an old coworker who had known my family for years; Judy, a close friend I made while at Springfield; Peter and his girlfriend, three of Chuck's aunts, and Emerson and Ruby. Seeing all those people who came to support me made me see my circle wasn't as small as I had thought. I did have people who cared about me—my world wasn't so small after all.

The Monday after graduation, I filed for divorce now that Chuck was unable to stop me. A weight of ten thousand pounds lifted off me as I handed the paperwork to the court clerk. From the moment I said, "I do," I had waited for this. No apprehension —for the first time in my life, I didn't second guess myself.

A desire for connection sent me online to look for friendship. I craved someone to talk to and share my day with, so I sent a message to a guy who looked familiar. His profile said he was looking for the same. A couple days passed, and I hadn't heard back from the message I sent. I figured it wasn't meant to be and chalked it up to never being good enough to find anyone to even be friends with.

Later in the day, he responded. He sent a simple message back, and we began to chat. As we talked, I felt he was the one I had been searching for. Greg was respectful and polite and shared the same dry sense of humor. It was like talking to an old friend. We chatted the next night as well, and then I told him the situation I was in. I explained I was still married but had filed for divorce days before. I shared information with himabout the abuse but left out the details. We continued to talk that night and talked about meeting.

The following day, Greg sent me a message, "I've thought it over, and I don't believe we should meet. You seem really nice, but I'm looking for a clean start. I don't want to get involved in a messy situation. I hope we can still chat."

The hope of Greg's friendship was ripped from me. I understood where Greg was coming from, but the pain of rejection opened wounds I tried to forget. *What if Chuck was right and no one would ever love me?* I may have been physically free from Chuck, but the years of psychological abuse still held me prisoner.

Despite Greg's message, we still talked. I looked forward to his kindness. Two days later, Greg suggested we accidentally meet at Walmart—because an accident was out of his control. The accidental meeting was scheduled. In two hours, I would meet the man that brightened my dark spots. *Two hours!* I pulled on jeans and a tie-dye shirt and called Mary to see if she could watch the kids while I "shopped in peace."

I drove the kids to Mom and Mary's house and then sped to Walmart. When I arrived, I sent Greg a text message to let him know I was there. He didn't respond. I got out of my car and walked toward the store searching the crowd for the face from his profile. I didn't see anyone that looked like him, but I kept walking. As I turned around, I saw Greg walking toward me. He was more handsome than the pictures.

Greg was shy like me, so we each said "hi," and then silence followed while we thought of things to talk about. Since I had on a tie-dye t-shirt, he asked me if I was into the Grateful Dead. I told him they were okay, but Tom Petty was my drug of choice. We talked a little about music and decided to walk around the building. As we made our way behind the building, I joked, "We're strangers going behind the building... I hope you don't murder me!"

"Or you don't murder me!"

"Hey, I wouldn't do that!"

"And you think I would?" A nervous laugh followed.

He was very easy to talk to and the feeling I knew him magnified. I felt safe with him. Safer with a stranger than I had felt with many people from my past. He was who I had been searching for my entire life. He was *the one*.

As Greg walked me back to my car to say goodbye, my eyes began to water. I looked into his eyes, and I knew I had seen them before. *It was him.* He was the one from my dream all those years before. I'd found him! He'd kept his promise to wait for me. My heart was full as I drove away to pick up the kids.

Greg and I continued to talk every day. The more we talked, the more I *knew*. We met again two weeks later and again the following week. Our relationship evolved slowly yet quickly, pulling back as soon as it moved ahead. Greg, like me, had been hurt before. He didn't want to rush things, and I was still in a mess with Chuck.

Things would work out for us. Greg would be my last love, the one I had been so unsure I was going to find. I found him, and I wasn't willing to let him go. I waited patiently for him to be grounded enough to see it as well.

As the months passed, Chuck was granted permission to see Ian, Emerson, and Ruby. Chuck bullied me into changing the restraining order to allow him contact with me too. Years of control and abuse were hard to shake free from, and intimidation and threats still worked. Chuck was soon allowed to visit the kids at the house since he didn't have a place of his own yet. For my safety, I left when he arrived.

I began to stay the weekends with Greg when Chuck had the kids. It was nice to fall asleep in Greg's arms and feel safe. It was such an unknown feeling. As Betty had said, change was hard, but it was worth it. Life was falling into place.

On May 30, 2014, my divorce was granted. It was one of the happiest days of my life. I was able to break free from the years of abuse. I was able to be me again. My first stop with the divorce papers was the Social Security office where I began the process of changing my name back. It was official. I was free.

CHAPTER 40

a year later, after the divorce became final, Greg and I were ready for the next step in our relationship. The kids and I moved into Greg's house in New Hampshire over the summer. We settled in just in time for the kids to start a new school year. I continued to work as a hospice social worker, now with a forty-minute commute. Being able to feel like a family for the first time was worth the drive.

Even though Chuck was legally out of my life, my hatred for him still consumed me. I hated him for what he did to us and hated he was still trying to control me. That autumn, a coworker, Bea, told me I needed to be healed. "Jess, I think it's time you see a healer. You need to get that asshole out of your head."

"He's not in my head."

"Oh, stop! I know you think about all the things he did to screw you over... You talk about it all the time."

I wasn't aware I allowed my hatred for him to monopolize my time. "I do?"

"Yeah… but it's normal to hate the bastard after everything he did, but when you think about him, you are giving him your energy. You need to find someone who can help you cut the invisible strings, and be rid of the asshole for good." She tapped the center of her forehead. "Your third eye is blocked too. Go get that cleansed."

Third eye? I had an idea what Bea was talking about, but what did my third eye have to do with anything? I trusted Bea knew what she was talking about and sent a message to Amber, the psychic medium I had been seeing on and off for the past ten years. Amber responded with an appointment for the following week.

I arrived at Amber's house during my lunch hour. She walked me to the healing room off her living room. In the room was a massage table draped with a pale green sheet. The window across from the table was lined with crystals, and below the window was an altar with more crystals and smudge sticks. I took my shoes off as I entered the room, and Amber motioned for me to sit on the table. "Have you ever had Reiki before?"

"A few times, but I don't know if anything actually happened."

"Okay, well, I do things a little different." She laughed as she closed the door behind her. "I tone while I do Reiki, and I let intuition guide me."

I didn't know what she meant by tone but trusted her enough to find out. "Okay…"

"So you need to be healed? Anything special you want to work on?"

"A friend of mine said my third eye needs to be cleansed…and I need to be free from Chuck."

"I don't want to say it…but I told you so! I was happy to hear you finally left him… What was it, like ten years ago I told you to leave him?"

I sighed. "Yeah, I guess I'm a slow learner."

"No, you just weren't ready, but the spirits were not going to rest until you listened. You should be proud of yourself. It's not easy. Okay, Jess, lay back and let's get to work."

I stretched out on the table, and Amber pulled a crocheted afghan over me. I closed my eyes as she lit the smudge stick. The smell of sage encased me as Amber began to chant. She placed her hands on the crown of my head as her voice vibrated through me. Heat from her hands filled my body replacing the stress that had been there before. Her hands made way to the spot on my forehead Bea had pointed to before, then to my throat and stopped at my heart.

The warmth from Amber's hands and the sound of her voice circulated through my body. Her energy filled me as peace replaced worry. The minutes passed as Amber made her way to my feet. Her hands tugged my body down the table, and then her hand moved back up my body as I heard the match strike the box. The flame lit the smudge stick, and the smell of sage covered me. Amber blew out the smudge stick, and said, "You can open your eyes when you're ready."

I opened my eyes, my body still warm and relaxed.

"How do you feel?"

"Good."

"Just so you know…Chuck is not the cause of your problems. Your mom is."

"I don't understand… Chuck is the one who has hurt me so badly."

Amber wrinkled her nose at me. "And your mom never hurt you? I saw some pretty fucked up shit when I was working on you."

"Yeah, I guess…but that was so long ago."

"Jess…I'm telling you the damage she did to you is tangled deep inside you, lifetimes of hurt. I'm not saying Chuck isn't in there, but his ties to you are easy to cut, but your mom, that's going to take a lot of work."

Unable to believe what Amber was telling me, I sat up and looked around the room.

"And your youngest… Ruby? She needs a lot of attention. Something is up with her. She needs to see someone, but I don't see kids. My sister, Amethyst does."

"Ruby does struggle with anger at times. Do you think that's it?"

"I don't know really. The spirits just showed me she needs a lot of work. I don't have details." She wrote her sister's information on a piece of paper as well as the homework she wanted me to complete. "So I need you to write a letter to Chuck about all the shit he did to you and the kids, and then I need you to burn it. Then I need you to write a letter to your parents, and call Amethyst."

I took the piece of paper and slipped on my shoes. "Okay, thank you."

"See you next week, same time, same place."

Was Mom really the cause of all of my problems? I had a hard time believing Chuck was not more to blame for my troubles. I wrote the letter to Chuck. It was more difficult than I expected because I had to relive so many painful and scary memories. I was angry with myself for allowing him to hurt me so much and for allowing my children to watch all the abuse and listen to all the fights. I was sad the life I had dreamt about hadn't happened. The family I so longed for wasn't something I had created. I was reliving my past patterns of abuse with him. I was allowing my children to live in a home with so many uncertainties. The fear and hurt I had experienced as a little girl had been happening in my home. That part of our life was over, and it was time to be rid of it for good.

Once I finished the letter, Greg went outside with me and stood next to me while I burned it in the flame of a candle. I watched the letter burn and imagined all ties being broken. I imagined all the hurt and pain being released with the letter. I felt lighter after the letter finished burning knowing I was one step closer to being free from the past.

I also began journaling to my parents as Amber had instructed. In those entries, I began to see the pain Amber said I had buried deep within myself. My first entry was to my mom.

September 11, 2015

All I ever wanted was to be loved. The more you pushed me away, the more I tried. I tried to make you love me. I did everything I knew how to do to make you love me, but it never worked. I wasn't good enough for your love —or at least that's how you made me feel. I was a child, and all I ever wanted was for my mommy to love me—to tell me she loved me and mean it. I want to know why. Did you ever love me? Will you ever? Will I ever have these answers or will you die and leave me left with questions unanswered?

Amber was right—the hurt from Mom was still affecting me. There was a lot of work to do to release all the years of pain. At my next session with Amber, we talked about how it felt to write the letter and journal. I told her it was hard to sit and write the things I had been working so hard to keep buried. She reminded me that was the point of the exercise. She asked me to continue with the journaling and write to Mom again to see what came this time.

September 15, 2015

I don't want our last conversation to be one where we fight. I want to be able to tell you how I feel and have you listen and hear me, but I know you won't. I know you'll get angry or fall into your depression that eats you.

Holding onto it only poisons me—not you. I feel it's not my job to hurt you, regardless of how much you've hurt me. I don't have it in me to tell you all the truths I hold. I'll let you die knowing you fucked up, but you will never really know how bad you hurt me or made me feel unloved or unwanted. I wasn't your trash to throw away. I had value—at least Gram saw that. Thank God for her. Without her, I would have been dead, lost in a world without love.

I noticed a pattern in the two journal entries, which made me see the depth of the hurt I had been holding onto. My whole life I'd wanted her to love me. I wanted to be good enough for her. I tried repeatedly to be lovable. I tried everything I knew. Nothing ever worked. I felt like a little kid again, desperately searching for recognition and feeling unworthy. Amber was right—there was a lot of pain I had buried. As I uncovered it, I knew why.

I slowly started to see why I was so hard on myself. I saw why I never felt good enough. After all, how could I be good enough for anyone else when my own mother didn't love me? A mother loves her children no matter what, but mine didn't. I was that special case where I was so messed up that even guaranteed love wasn't a guarantee. And that was how I had lived my life. I allowed people to mistreat me and abuse me because I felt I deserved it. I didn't feel I was worthy of love or respect.

This realization made me grieve Gram even more. It brought back memories of her love. Until Ian, Emerson, and Ruby were born, she was the only person in my life to love me unconditionally. That was a gift I had always been grateful for, but now more so than ever. I was grateful and angry. I wanted that love back. Why did the only person who loved me have to be taken from me? My grief returned. Although, to be honest, it never really left. Anger raged through my body.

This was not fair. My life was a series of events that were not fair. I felt like a child stomping my feet and pouting. What had I done to deserve this life? What had I done to be born to a mother incapable of loving me? Why was I put in this situation?

During one session with Amber, she answered some of my questions. "I think I know why you were born to your mom and why you've found so many wounded people."

I opened my eyes wide as I waited to hear her discovery.

"While I was working on you, I saw a glimpse of your past life. You were a nurse in a psychiatric hospital… you saw many fucked up things and watched people as they were mistreated. You wanted to save them, but you couldn't." She paused while her words sank in. "You were given this life, with all these fucked up people, to show you what happens when those people are on the outside, to show you the value of treatment. You fought hard to get them out, and this life is to show you why they belonged where they were."

What Amber said made sense, and I could see how that life shaped me into who I was. It helped me understand why I had the family I had. I understood why I worked helping people and how I ended up in the medical field after having no desire to do so.

It reminded me Mom struggled with mental illness, and it was the mental illness—not her—that was incapable of loving me.

The monster that had eaten my mommy was depression. It all clicked and made sense.

My anger subsided, and I saw the *why* of the life I had lived. I could understand the reasons behind the pain.

During the healing work with Amber, I took Ruby to see her sister, Amethyst, as Amber had suggested. The kids liked Amethyst right away. Although the session was scheduled for Ruby, Amethyst did Reiki and talked to all three of the kids. At the end of the visit, Amethyst took me outside where we could talk alone. Amethyst told me Ruby had a lot of anger inside of her, and she could tell there was something in her that needed to come out. She said Emerson was good at pretending to be okay, and Ian held onto a lot of sadness. I set up another appointment, and we left.

Soon after the visit, Greg and I saw the difference in Ruby. Her anger was tamer and not as easily triggered. All of the kids appeared to feel better. I told Chuck about the session and how good it seemed to go for them. He was upset the kids were seeing someone and said it was a waste of time and money. I said the visits would continue as long as the kids were showing they were benefitting from it.

The following weekend was the weekend the kids went to Chuck's house. Ruby came back angry. She wasn't the little seven-year-old girl I had dropped off for a visit. She said inappropriate things about her body. I talked with her to ask her why she was behaving this way, but she didn't answer. The following day, Emerson told me I needed to ask Ruby again why she was behaving the way she was. "I walked in on Ruby with her shirt off sitting on Dad's bed... She was rubbing cream on his back...and... it made me feel icky. Ruby looked like she was hiding something."

I went inside to talk to Ruby. I asked her if anyone had ever done anything to make her feel uncomfortable. She didn't answer. "You can tell me anything, and I won't be upset. I just want to make sure you're safe."

Her blue eyes met mine. "Sometimes."

"Who touches you?"

"Daddy."

I swallowed hard and gathered my thoughts. I didn't want her to know how angry I was. "What does he touch?"

Her eyes darted away from mine.

"Sometimes people say scary things to make people keep secrets. When Kate was your age, her dad touched her, and told her if she told, he would hurt Grammy... Kate didn't tell for seven years… and you know what? Bill never hurt her again once she told."

Ruby looked up at me. "He told me not to tell."

"Honey, I want to keep you safe. If you tell me, I can help you."

She pointed to her chest and then between her legs. "He touches himself too…and makes noises."

I wanted to throw up. I never wanted my kids to go through the things I had, and now, because of *him,* they were. I failed to protect her. I wanted it all to go away.

"When?"

"Three or four weeks ago."

"How did you feel?"

"Scared."

I knew how she felt. I was seven when Bill touched me. I wanted to take it from her. I wanted her to have her innocence back. I wanted to wake up and have this be over, but it was far from over.

The conversation with Ruby uncovered more abuse. The more she talked, the more I died inside. My poor baby. I didn't let her know how upset I was. I was afraid my emotions would stop her from talking. When she was done, I hugged her and told her I had to report what she said to me in order to keep her safe. Ruby began to sob. "I promised not to tell. Now he's going to be mad at me."

"You did nothing wrong, Ruby. No one is mad at you. You were very brave. I love you."

I fell apart the moment Ruby left my sight. Sadness and anger raged through me. Chuck was the worst parts of both Ralph and Bill.

My whole body trembled as I dialed the child abuse hotline and made my report. My voice shook as I spoke and tried to hold back the tears. I wrote notes as I talked so I could remember the details

Ruby had told me, details I didn't want to remember. I wanted to forget.

My world went black—it felt much like losing Gram. Even though no one had died, the world as I knew it had. I was scared Chuck would hurt me in order to protect himself. I was afraid he'd kill me as he had threatened to do so many times before. I was worried Ruby would never be able to be free from these memories.

The next day, after dropping the kids off at school, I went in to let their principal know what had happened and to make sure she did not let the children leave with anyone except me. I left and went to the domestic violence center and asked for their help in completing a protection order. As before, they were accommodating and guided me through the process. I spent two hours writing out the reasons why we needed protection from Chuck, going back through all he had done to us over the years. As I read what I wrote, I could see how much pain and hurt he had caused us, and I felt so stupid for allowing him to hurt my kids. Nothing ever really seemed "that bad" until Ruby disclosed her newest secret. Chuck was a predator that was capable of anything. *Anything.* The protection order was granted so my kids would not have to visit him. I could keep them safe—finally.

Greg came with us when Ruby had to meet with Joan, my former social worker. All three kids spoke to Joan alone. Ruby had talked to Joan before when Chuck left hand prints on her backside. Ruby liked her, but she was embarrassed. She was afraid Joan wouldn't like her if she heard what had happened, and Ruby was scared she'd get into trouble. Ruby was afraid of what Chuck might do to her and to us.

Ruby was seven. Seven years old. She was a baby. Why was he allowed to change how she thought forever? Why did he think he could hurt her? Sexual abuse changes you. It changes how you think about yourself and about others. It takes all of your trust away and makes you constantly question your safety.

When Ruby talked to Joan, she didn't disclose all the things she had told me. Joan felt there was enough to keep Chuck away from them. However, in order for them to charge him criminally, she needed more. Joan asked me to call if more information came out. I was proud of Ruby, but I was disappointed Chuck would probably get away with it. I wouldn't allow my kids to be in a situation where he would be able to hurt them again.

CHAPTER 41

*S*oon after this, I brought Ruby back to see Amethyst. She did a healing ritual with Ruby and helped release some of the toxins the experience had created inside of her. Amethyst said she felt Ruby would be okay and the biggest thing was that I believed Ruby and kept her away from Chuck. She said their earlier sessions had helped release Ruby's hold to the secret, and it helped give her the courage to tell.

After meeting with Amethyst and Joan, and knowing she wouldn't have to see Chuck, Ruby's behavior continued to improve. She stopped wetting her pants and was able to sleep more soundly. And she started playing with her toys again. She was a seven-year-old for the first time. The changes in her helped keep me going. The battle was long and hard, like fighting a villain. We were the good guys, and we were going to win this—we *were* winning this.

I slipped into a depression. It mimicked the loss of Gram. My world grew darker and blacker. I felt hopeless, and my body hurt. All I wanted to do was sleep. I had a tough time focusing at work. I didn't want to help other people when I had failed my daughter. I took the blame for the hurt and pain Ruby had suffered. It also brought me back to the time when I was seven and Bill molested me. I was that seven-year-old girl. The difference though—I had believed my daughter. I made the abuse stop as soon as I found out about it. I didn't blame her. I didn't yell at her for allowing it to happen to her. *I believed her.*

Knowing I did what was right for my daughter felt good. I couldn't imagine doing anything differently. The pain I lived with knowing Mom picked Bill over me was something I tried to get over on many occasions. I buried that pain as deep as I could. I was hurt, angry, sad, betrayed, and heartbroken. I was grieving the loss of my innocence and childhood. I saw myself as that seven-year-old little girl, and it was evident how much Mom had let me down more than ever before. I was just a little girl. I was her little girl. It was her job to protect me, not feed me to the wolves.

I was still working with Amber, and she helped me work through these thoughts. She told me I needed to love myself and give myself the love I never received from Mom. Loving myself was hard—harder than it should have been. Amber asked me to say one good thing about myself, and I couldn't come up with anything. I stared at her blankly. Every thought I came up with had reasons why it wasn't true. My homework that week was to look myself in the eyes in the mirror for fifteen minutes and tell myself good things about me. Then I was to also sit in the dark and go where my mind took me, listening to the voices about myself in my head.

I told Greg about my homework, and he agreed it was something I needed to do. I told him I didn't want to do it, that I couldn't do it. He told me I needed to think about it and say two good things about myself every night before bed. At bedtime, I had hoped he had forgotten, but he hadn't. He asked me to tell him my two things for the night. I couldn't. I stalled and asked him to say two good things about himself, and he did. He then asked me again for my two good things. I couldn't come up with anything. As I thought of something, I talked myself out of it just as fast. I couldn't do it. I couldn't come up with even one good thing. Not one. I fell asleep still unable to think of anything.

I stood in front of the mirror, and I couldn't even make eye contact. I glanced at myself and quickly looked away. When I saw my reflection, I saw so many awful things. I was too fat. I was too tall. My nose was too big. My eyebrows were too bushy. My face was too round. My hair was too frizzy. My breasts were too small. My stomach was covered in stretch marks. My arms were too fat. My eyes were too sad. I couldn't say one nice thing to myself. I said a lot of horrible, nasty things but not one good thing.

When I sat in the dark with a candle burning, I listened to my thoughts: *You're not good enough. You are not good enough to be loved. You are not good enough to keep love. There is too much wrong with you to be good enough.* It was fifteen minutes of these thoughts. They flooded me. At one point, I felt goose bumps on my right leg that traveled up my body, almost as though Gram was trying to tell me to stop it and to love myself. I was good enough for her love but not good enough for anyone else's. I couldn't stop it. Each time I tried to stop it, I was brought back to why I wasn't good enough. I felt unworthy of love.

My depression turned to grief as every loss I had ever encountered replayed in my mind. I could feel myself falling deeper and deeper into those feelings, giving them control over my thoughts and over me. I was sad for that little girl. I wanted to have *my* mom protect me. I wanted her to love me.

When life became too overwhelming, I started seeing a counselor. After a lifetime of not trusting counselors and being afraid I was going to be labeled "crazy," I took the leap and made an appointment. I liked Roxy right away. I told her my feelings about counselors and how I was fighting with myself to go and explained to her how I had been betrayed by counselors in the past. She listened and didn't cast judgment. She didn't ask for my history, just asked what I wanted to talk about and we went from there. We made an appointment for the following week, and she remembered things I had said. She talked about people by name and asked questions that related to the things we had talked about. I was impressed, and she was easy to talk to.

I told Roxy what had happened with Ruby and how it made me feel. I told her I was scared I wasn't handling it well and feared Roxy would think I was crazy. I told her it had been close to seven years since I lost Gram, and I still hadn't finished grieving. She told me I was normal. *Normal.* I spent my whole life trying to prove I wasn't crazy, that I wasn't like Mom or Ralph. And after two visits, she knew I was normal. That gave me hope in my sea of darkness.

There were other people who had been through similar things, and they handled them similarly. She did say I had been through a lot, much of which sounded like torture, and it was surprising I had been so resilient. I cried as her words reached my ears. *Torture* was a strong word, and I had never looked at it like that, but as she said it, I could see it. She asked me what I would think if the things that had happened to me had happened to anyone else. I had never thought about it in that perspective before, but she was right. If I had heard someone else telling my story, I would agree there was torture.

We talked about Mom and how badly I wanted her to love me. I talked about how sad it made me seeing myself as Ruby and how painful it was to relive those moments. I told Roxy how alone I felt after Gram died. I told her about *everything.* She listened and offered her thoughts, but she never judged. "People do their best. Sometimes their best isn't the right thing, but it's the best they are capable of."

Roxy was right. I tried my best. I might have failed, but I always tried.

"There are reasons behind all of your actions. Your past has helped shape you into who you are." She handed me a box of tissues as I listened. "You are strong... Say it with me."

"I am strong." Tears came before the words left my mouth. It was hard to say positive things about myself, but Roxy was right. *I was strong.*

"You could have given up, but you never did. You are brave, a warrior."

The tears continued to fall as I listened and tried to believe her words.

"You can't love yourself because your mom never showed you love. I want you to treat yourself like your fourth child. Give yourself the love you give your children. Be patient with yourself. Let that little girl inside you know she is worthy of love."

The little girl inside of me longed for love. The ache was deep. If I were my child, I would love me—I had to try. I couldn't keep it from her any longer. When negative thoughts came in, I pushed them away. I imagined that little girl inside of me hearing the thoughts, and I couldn't do it to her. I had to parent my child-self. No one else could heal her.

Between Roxy, Amber, and Greg, I slowly started to see myself in a different light. I gave myself permission to like myself. It felt foreign, and I often began to revert back to the old way of thinking and believing. It was so hard to talk myself out of all of the negative thoughts. It was easy for me to nurture others, but I had a hard time thinking I deserved the same kindness and compassion.

My sessions with Amber slowed down, and she suggested that I train in Reiki so I could use it for my kids and myself. I attended the class and had my first Reiki attunement. I had a difficult time thinking about healing myself, but I gave into it and allowed myself to receive the healing as well. A few more sessions with Amber and she told me I was no longer "fucked up." She told me I was open now to the process. I later had my Reiki II attunement and wanted to start working towards becoming a Reiki Master.

During the Reiki II attunement, Amber said the process would bring out emotions. She said if there is anything I needed to work through, it will come out. I needed to work through it before I could go on to become a Reiki Master.

Days passed, and I didn't feel any different. I thought maybe I had healed already. After all, I had been doing work for the last seven months. Maybe I was healed. Maybe I didn't have to *fix* anything else. Maybe I was finally okay. I wasn't crying, but I was outraged. Everything made me angry. People, my kids, Kate, work, and Mom, made me angry. *Everything.*

I had expected to be sad, but my emotional work was with anger. I tried to stay away from people so I didn't say or do anything I shouldn't. Anger is a secondary emotion, so I looked past it to find the emotions it was hiding. The anger soon turned to sadness. All the thoughts of all of the people and time in my life I had lost kept coming back to me. Life was not fair. There were too many times where I was being tested. I didn't want to be tested anymore—I wanted to live. I wanted to live like all of the rest of the world. The thoughts circled in my head. Round and round. Self-pity. Self-hate. Self-pity. Self-hate. If I allowed it to continue, it could have consumed me.

When I realized what I was doing and the path I was headed for, I took a step back. I thought about many things. I looked deeper than the surface. There was no denying bad things had happened to my kids and me. There was also no denying good things happened too. I could dwell on the bad or I could be grateful for the good. I could be sad and angry I lost Gram, or I could be thankful I was given her and had her in my life. I could be mad

Ruby was victimized by Chuck, or I could be grateful I was able to protect her and believe her. I could be angry and hurt Mom didn't protect me, or I could be thankful for the lesson it taught me. Every situation in my life could be looked at the same way. It was all in perspective. The gray clouds that followed me soon began to have rays of sunlight shining through.

CHAPTER 42

*I*t had been seven years since my world forever changed. Seven years of sadness, depression, and numbness. I died the day Gram did. There really was no other way to explain how the experience altered my existence. I detached myself from the people I loved. I didn't allow myself to get close to others because I never wanted to feel that pain again. Not a day went by without thinking about Gram. I needed her so many times. I needed to talk to her, to know she was there, and I needed her love.

For seven years, I actively grieved her loss. Each day, the pain came. At work, I helped patients and families say goodbye as they neared their last days. Each loss was a reminder of my loss. Their pain became my pain and helped keep my wound from healing.

Through my healing journey, I began to look at the loss differently. I thought about what my life could have been like if she had died when she was given the two weeks to live. We had seventeen more years together. She helped me through my childhood and into adulthood. She met and held each of my children. She had enough time to make a lasting impact on them. They have memories of her, and they love her.

Gram loved me as much as I loved her. I owed it to her, to my children and to myself, to own the grief and to live again. It was up to me how I was going to allow her loss to affect me. She was always there when I needed her. She taught me many valuable lessons and helped shape me into the woman I am. Her body was gone, but she was not. She was still providing me with love and strength, and that would never change. Those thoughts transformed into genuine healing. The pain on my heart lifted, and her death was not who she was anymore. Her life, her life with me was who she became again.

Good Friday came and went as did April 10th. They came, and I was okay. I was okay for the first time since her death. I missed her still, but I didn't allow the pain to take over any longer. I decided to live. Part of living included starting a blog about grief and loss. My dream to become a writer was pushed to the front. I wanted to help others through their darkest times and let them know they are not alone.

As I worked with Roxy, I felt a shift within myself. Part of living was forgiving. Mom and I were never close, but I was ready to let go of the pain of the past and move forward. I loved Mom, and I knew she loved me. Her love may not have been the love I longed for, but it was the best she had to offer. In that shift, an overwhelming sense of peace flooded throughout my body.

A few days later, the call came that Mom was sick. She had what they thought was a stomach bug. She hadn't been able to keep down any food or water for days. Mary reached out for help from her medical provider several times and was told Mom was okay and to have her continue to sip water. The water she was able to keep down made her stomach bloat. I offered to help but was told there was nothing I could do. However, Mary said Mom would love a visit.

That Sunday was April 17th, and I had to take Ruby to the on-call pediatrician to look at a probable tick bite. We were going to see Mom afterward. When the visit was over, I saw a message from Kate. Mom was headed to the hospital by ambulance. The visit was right next to the hospital.

Ruby and I waited in the parking lot for the ambulance to arrive. There were no lights or sirens on. I rushed out of my car and ran to the ambulance. Ruby was right behind me. Kate got out of the front seat, and the doors opened. I got into the back of the ambulance. "Mom?"

Her eyes rolled to the back of her head. "Huh?"

Her tone stung as it hit my ears. She was angry with me and didn't want to see me. I got off the ambulance and realized Ruby had gone in after me. "Hi, Grammy Wendy."

"Hi." Mom tried to lift her hand to wave.

I took Ruby off the ambulance. Mary arrived soon after, and we all followed Mom into the emergency department. Mom had lost a hundred pounds, but she was still close to five hundred, so moving her even on the stretcher was not an easy task. The room they put her in was the same room Gram was in seven years before. An eerie feeling came over me. I hated that Mom was so sick, and I hated her being in *that* room.

A nurse came into the room and told us Mom could only have two visitors at a time. Ruby and I went out to the waiting room where I called Greg to let him know where we were and what was happening. He offered to come get Ruby since we didn't know how long this was going to take.

Kate and Mary soon came out to the waiting room because Mom had to go for x-rays. An hour passed, and they told us the x-rays were unsuccessful because of Mom's size, and they had to try again. Ruby's patience was lost as the clock kept ticking. Greg arrived soon after and took Ruby home.

Mary, Kate, and I sat in the waiting room as the afternoon turned to evening. A nurse came out and guided us back to Mom's room. When we arrived at the room, the doctor told Mom she had a possible small bowel obstruction, and they would have to insert an NG tube to help empty her stomach. Mom asked Kate and me to leave the room while they did this. Mary stayed with her.

In the waiting room, I looked up information on small bowel obstructions. The more I read, the scarier it became. If they were wrong, and she had a large bowel obstruction, the outcome did not look good. Causes included cancer. *Cancer!* I texted Greg and told him what I had found. He asked me to stop looking up information and to relax. He said no good was going to come from any information I found online, and I would jump to the worst possible scenario. He was right.

After four hours of waiting, the doctors decided to admit Mom. When we got upstairs to Mom's room, I stood back and watched the nurse take her vital signs. I watched as her blood pressure read at 77 over 44, and as the nurse rechecked it, only a few numbers were different. A new doctor came in and started asking questions. Mom answered them, for the most part, accurately. "It says here you have a urinary tract infection. What's the NG tube in for?" We told her the doctors in the emergency room concluded Mom had a small bowel obstruction.

The nurse spoke up, "I got two low readings on her blood pressure."

The doctor looked at Mom and then at us. "This is a surgical patient. I am a medical doctor. She needs to get out of here. She needs surgeons, not me."

Mom was moved to the Intensive Care Unit until they could get her transferred to another hospital. I sat crouched down against the wall as this all happened, and it hit me. It was the seventeenth of April. Seven years ago, we were at Gram's funeral. Seven years to the day. I couldn't hold back my tears. I had to leave before Mom saw me crying. I walked down to the waiting room and sent Peter a text to let him know Mom was at the hospital and very sick. He replied back a few minutes later he was out of town and couldn't make it there. He said he was really sorry and wished he could be there. It had been over two years since he had seen Mom and at least a year since I had seen him.

Once they moved Mom to the ICU and had fluids started, they told us her blood pressure was going back up, and she was just dehydrated. The doctor said she was on the phone with Dartmouth to try to get her transferred, but they did not have any beds available, and their equipment could not accommodate her size. Boston or New York were Mom's only options.

Mom's vital signs continued to improve, and they allowed us to see her. Mom said she was tired, and she wanted us to go home. The doctor told us as long as she kept improving, they would not transfer her.

Mary, Kate, and I left for the night and agreed to meet back at the hospital the next day. Since it was spring break, I let the kids sleep in before they got up and ready. We stopped, and I got them snacks for the waiting room. When we arrived at the hospital, I had a bunch of messages from Kate asking me where we were. When I got upstairs, I found out Mom's blood pressure had started to drop again, so they were increasing her fluids.

The doctor told us she was trying to get Mom a bed in Boston or New York, and as soon as they had a bed, they were going to transfer her. The doctor told us they would have to give her medication to speed up her heart to try to raise her blood pressure. I looked at her with obvious fear in my eyes and said, "What about her heart? That'll kill her."

"We don't have any other option."

As soon as the nurses said I was able, I went in to see Mom. I looked down at her and started to cry. Her dark brown eyes looked up at me. "I'm not going to die."

I sat down next to her, not knowing what to say. "Are you scared?"

"No. Too tired."

"Are you in pain?"

She smiled. "No. Too tired."

For the first time in many years, I said, "I love you, Mom."

"I love you too."

I started to cry again. I chased her love my whole life. I tried so hard to make her love me, to make her see me. As our eyes connected for the first time in many years, I knew she saw me. I knew she saw how scared I was at the thought of losing her.

I sent Kate and Mary in to see her and went back to the waiting room with the kids. I sat down and opened up a pack of peanut butter crackers. I took a small bite off one corner when the door flew open. Kate and the doctor were there. "Kids, stay! Jess, get in there *now*." I threw the crackers on the table and raced into her room. She was having a heart attack, moaning with each breath. "Get in there and tell her goodbye." I ran past everyone, grabbed her arm, looked her in the eyes, and said, "I forgive you, Mom. I love you."

"Good... I love you."

They pushed us out of the room as the team of nurses and doctors started working on her. I paced back and forth and stopped at the nurses' station. I banged my fist on the counter and yelled, "Why is she *still* here? You *kill* people here! Get her out of here!" I screamed through my tears. The Chaplin looked at the nurse and asked if she could answer me. The nurse said they do good work there, and what I said was untrue. I screamed back, "You *kill* people here! My best friend's husband came here having a massive heart attack, and you sent him home!" As I turned around and headed back to the waiting room, the heavy door slammed open into the wall.

My whole body shook as I tried to call Greg. I couldn't get my fingers to hit the right buttons. He was at work and wasn't able to answer right away. I managed to text him "I need you. She's... Mom's dying." I sent a text to Peter as well and told him she was dying. Peter said he would be there, but then said he didn't have his keys to his truck and wouldn't be able to get there. Greg called me back to tell me he was on his way.

Kate came back in and said Mom was stable. The team was going to put her on a ventilator. I went back in with her. We were told to tell her goodbye again in case they were unable to insert the ventilator. I walked over, kissed Mom on the forehead, and told her I loved her. Kate and I sat in the hall next to Mom's room while the team inserted the ventilator, and Mary went to the waiting room with the kids to have lunch with them.

Boston hospital called, they had a bed for her. Fear turned to hope—Mom might have a chance in the right setting. The doctor said Mom was very sick but stable enough to make the trip.

Greg arrived soon after. He sat in the waiting room with us as we waited for the ambulance to arrive. I texted Peter again to let him know what was happening. He said he wished he could come, but he had no way to get there. I asked Greg to take the kids home, but he wanted to wait to make sure everything was going to happen as planned. After a two-hour wait, the ambulance crew arrived, and Greg left to get the kids home.

They began the transfer process only to find out they didn't have enough medications to make it to Boston. The Boston Marathon was happening that day, and they were afraid they would be held up in traffic. The three-hour drive could turn into five or more. Kate, Mary, and I watched as the crew worked to get everything ready to go. I stood at the nurse's station and felt dizzy. I hadn't had anything to eat or drink that day, and it was catching up to me. Kate and I decided to get gas before the ambulance left so we could try to follow them.

As I started pumping the gas, I started having chest pains. I finished pumping the gas and went in to get drinks and snacks for the ride. I was terrified of the drive to Boston. Traffic and night driving were two of my fears, but I had to face my fears and make the trip. We wouldn't reach Boston until well after dark. Kate noticed as I clenched my chest, and she was upset I was going to be sick too.

"Just anxiety…I'll be fine." *I hoped.*

When we returned back to the hospital, we were told the plan was to stop along the way to get the needed medications to make it to Boston or stop at Dartmouth if Mom became unstable. Mom was ready for them to load her onto the stretcher. Due to her size, they had to find more men to help transfer her from the bed to the stretcher. When they got her loaded on the stretcher, a group of eight men headed for the ambulance. Kate, Mary, and I waited in the parking lot as the crew in the ambulance got Mom ready for the ride. The eerie feeling I had the day before returned. I was worried something was going to go wrong. Rain began to fall as the ambulance pulled away. I followed closely behind with Kate and Mary.

My foot was pressed to the floor to keep up with them. Less than five minutes into the drive, the ambulance pulled over on the side of the interstate, and I followed. Kate said she thought they were going to tell me to stop following them, but they didn't. Through the back window, I saw the EMTs doing chest compressions. Adrenaline ran through my veins as I watched. The ambulance soon started back on the interstate, their directional signal on to get off at the exit. I followed. As they began to turn to get off at the exit, they sped up and stayed on the interstate. I tried not to focus on what might be happening in the back of that ambulance and focused on the drive.

I was going at least fifteen miles over the speed limit to stay with the ambulance. I passed cars as they did. They passed a trac-tor-trailer, and I followed. I noticed the truck was beginning to change lanes—into the lane we were in. I hit my brakes, hoping we were going to be able to get out of the way in time. We made it—barely. My nerves were shot, my heart was aching, and I was still dizzy. I wasn't fit to drive, but I had no other option. After the initial shock of almost dying, I sped back up and was able to catch the ambulance. I continued to follow the ambulance, getting off the interstate with them and driving through town. The speed limit was marked at thirty-five miles per hour. I was doing sixty-five to keep up. I turned on my hazard lights hoping to keep from getting a ticket.

Through the turns and stoplights, we made it to the hospital to get the medications. I followed the ambulance until I saw the sign "Ambulances Only." I found a parking space and ran to the ambu-lance. Greeted by a female EMT, she told me Mom needed to stabi-lize before the trip to Boston. Mary, Kate, and I went inside and filled out the required paperwork to get Mom registered. We sat in the waiting room, waiting to hear when we would hit the road again.

Two doctors came out. "Aiken family?" We all stood up, and they asked us to follow them. They sat us in a room and asked, "Have you been told what is going on?"

I replied, "Yes, my mom is getting stabilized for the rest of the trip to Boston."

They looked at each other, and one responded, "Your mom is very sick. She has been coding all day. She had multiple heart attacks on the ride down. The guys restarted her heart each time. She will not make it to Boston. She most likely will not make it through the night." I began to shake, and I felt sick to my stomach.

He went on, "We have two options, neither good. We can let her go the next time she has a cardiac event, or we do emergency surgery to see what is going on in her stomach area. We don't know if that's where the issue is, or if it will help. We don't know if she will make it through the surgery. She has less than a one percent chance of surviving the surgery."

I looked at Mary and Kate, and I said, "Do everything. She doesn't want to die. Please try. Please try anything you can." Mary and Kate agreed. We gave our permission to start surgery, and Mary signed the needed forms. The doctors told us we could go see Mom before she went into surgery.

What I saw next will never leave my memory. I walked ahead of everyone and saw Mom, unconscious on the stretcher with what looked like half of her top lip ripped off, blood all over her face and the pillow. Her skin was purple, and she looked like she was already gone. I patted her arm and said, "I love you, Mom." I rushed away unable to catch my breath. Kate grabbed hold of me to hold me up. Mary rushed past us to see Mom. Kate took me back into the room, and the social worker came in to sit with us. I started to hyperventilate, and Kate asked her for a paper bag. The social worker brought some in, as well as water and told us it was important we stay hydrated.

After she left the room, I started sobbing, "She doesn't know I love her. She thinks I'm mad at her. We never got to talk. I never got to tell her all the things I needed to say to her. She thinks I hate her. I haven't been to visit her in a few weeks. It's not fair. *It's not fair!* I need her. She is all I have left. She can't die."

Kate and Mary both tried to comfort me. They said Mom knew I was busy, and I was going through a lot to keep my kids safe.

Kate reminded me I was there all the times it mattered and told me anytime Mom needed something, I made sure she had it. Mary reminded me when Mom was no longer able to leave the house for holidays, I made sure she had food so she could have a meal at home. "She knows you love her."

But I didn't know that she loved *me*. I had been waiting to talk to her to go over the things from the past. I was waiting to tell her I understood she did her best, but it still hurt. I had so much to say to her, but I held it in because I didn't want it to be our last conversation. I had always said I would be sad if Mom died, but I would get over it quickly because I had never really had her. I was wrong. As I faced the reality that she might not survive the next few minutes, my world began to shrink. Mom was my oldest living relative. If she were to die, I would become an orphan. *An orphan.* I never thought in those terms before. We may not have been close, but *she was my mom*.

The social worker walked us upstairs to the Critical Care waiting room where they told us a doctor would come out to let us know what was going on and how things were going. Kate, Mary, and I sat in the waiting room holding on to hope Mom would beat the odds and make it through surgery.

After an hour of waiting, one of the surgeons we'd met downstairs came out and told us, "She's still with us, but she's the sickest person in New England. We found a mass in her colon, and all of her large and most of her small intestines are dead. Right now, she is critical but stable."

Relief flooded me. She was still alive.

"She is not out of the woods. There are many more surgeries in her future. We will leave her abdomen open while we wait for the next surgeries. There is no way of knowing what will happen over the next twenty-four to thirty-six hours."

We went back to the waiting room with the new information.

There was little hope. However, they had only given her a one percent chance of survival before they started the operation, and she was still with us. She beat the other ninety-nine percent of the odds. With that information, we held onto hope that she was a fighter, and she would beat this. She wanted to live, and she was working hard to do so. We clung to hope. It was all we had. I knew the reality of the situation, but I couldn't believe it. I feared if I gave that thought energy then she wouldn't make it.

A couple more hours passed, and the second surgeon came out again, he told us how sick Mom was. He told us it would be best if we went home for the night since Mom was stable. They would prep her for the next surgery as soon as they could.

I updated Peter to let him know what was happening. I let him know we were going home for the night, but we would be returning the following day. I told him how sick Mom was and that she may not make it. I asked him, "Please call and have them tell Mom you love her." I knew it would be important for her to hear those words. I knew Peter loved her, but it was just a hard relationship to maintain.

Greg had told me he didn't want me to drive Kate and Mary home. He said to come home, and he would drive them the rest of the way. I agreed I wasn't in any shape to drive. I arrived back at twelve-thirty in the morning, and he completed the trip for me. I was exhausted as I waited for him to return home, but I couldn't sleep until he was home safe. I was so scared I would lose him too, fearing I would lose everyone. He arrived home at two-thirty, and we talked for the next couple of hours. I couldn't sleep. I had seen and heard way too much over the last twenty-four hours. My mind would not stop racing. I wanted to know Mom would be okay. I wanted to know that tomorrow they would say she was improving and things could go as planned to get her on the road to recovery. A few hours after I finally fell asleep, my phone woke me up.

The first message was from Peter. He said he had called the hospital and asked them to tell Mom that he loved her. He said he left work because he couldn't handle it. He wanted to go see Mom but had to wait until his wife got home, and then asked me if I would take him. The following message was from Kate who wanted to know what was going on. She said Mary was going to stay home to take care of the animals and was planning to go visit Mom later. Kate wanted a ride to the hospital as well. Greg offered to get her and Peter and bring them to me so we could make the trip together.

When Greg arrived at the house, Kate, Peter, and I started out for the hospital, the same scenario as it had been the day before Gram died. That thought lingered in the back of my mind, but I tried to push it away. I didn't want this to be a repeat of that. Mom *was* going to survive this—she had to. Peter, Kate, and I talked about old memories and tried to kill the awkward silence. The three of us were never close. I was always available for both of them, but there was always some sort of conflict.

When we arrived, we were sent to the Critical Care Unit on the third floor, right next to where Kate, Mary, and I had waited the night before. Mom was only able to have two visitors at a time. Peter stepped back and said Kate and I should go in while Kate said Peter and I should go in. I said I wanted Peter and Kate to go in. They tried to fight me, but I told them I couldn't go in yet. A few minutes later, Peter came out through the doors of the Critical Care Unit. His head hung low, his face pale. "I didn't expect to see that. It...she... didn't look like Mom." He sucked back his tears and let out a sigh. "You should get in there. She gripped my fingers...and opened her eyes when I told her I loved her." He ran his fingers through his dark brown hair. "Fuck, this is hard."

After Peter settled into a chair in the waiting room, I went in to see her. Peter was right—I was not expecting what I saw. They had cleaned the blood from her face, but there remained a small amount of dried blood near her nose. She was very puffy and bloated. Her lips were so fat and blue that she looked like a blow-fish. Her eyelids were just as puffy. I took her hand and started talking to her.

"You're so strong, Mom. Keep fighting. You're doing such a great job. I love you." I was trying not to cry, but I had no control over my tears. "Mom, I know you did your best. Thank you for that. I'm a mom now too, and I know how hard it is. Thank you for doing your best. I am proud of you, and I know you are proud of me." With that, she pushed her eyes open and looked into my eyes. "I love you, Mom." She squeezed my fingers. "I forgive you, Mom. I understand it all. It's okay. You're the reason I went to college. You showed me I could do it. I know you love me, Mom." The words poured out through the tears. I wanted to tell her all of the things I had been holding onto in case I didn't get the chance again.

The nurse said the neurologist was coming in to work with Mom and asked us to go to the waiting room. Kate and I left the room and went to sit with Peter. A little while after sitting in the waiting room, a doctor came out. He took us into the same room as the doctors did the night before. He said, "I have some good news, but mostly bad news. The neurologist said your mom didn't lose function of her brain. She was able to move one side of her body and open her eyes as directed. That is great news. However, it is the only good news I have for you."

He went on to talk about the other parts of her body, going from her head down. He said her heart was not functioning properly and was on almost the maximum medication to keep her alive. The intestines remaining would have to be stretched to fit an ostomy bag, and she would have to have IV nutrition and hydration for the rest of her life. She would never be able to eat again.

Her liver wasn't working as it should, and neither were her kidneys. She would have to be on dialysis the rest of her life.

I sat in the middle of Peter and Kate, and they both tried to comfort me. The doctor continued. "Your mom has a ten percent chance of living, and there are many more surgeries she will need to go through... each one with its own risks. I have already talked to Mary and let her know all of this information."

He had to be wrong. Mom was a fighter—she could beat this. There were many struggles ahead of Mom, but she could do it, she had to.

"What do you guys want to do?"

Peter, Kate, and I looked at each other. Peter spoke up. "The life he just told us about is not one worth living." He caught my eyes as I stared through him. "Jess, I know this is hard. I don't want her to die, but she would be angry if she had to live with so many restrictions."

Kate said, "Mom wants to live. She's like a little kid, she just wants to live."

I told the doctor, "There's still a ten percent chance she will make it. I don't want to give up on her. I want to keep trying."

He replied, "Yes, however, with a ninety percent chance of not surviving, the odds are not in her favor."

"Please, keep trying. She doesn't want to die. There is a chance she will make it. Ten percent, but it's all we have."

We called Mary to tell her Mom was able to hear us and opened her eyes. We told her it was important for her to come down. Mary said she would be there as soon as she could. Kate went back in with Mom, and Peter and I went to have lunch at the food court. We talked about what we heard and what we thought. Peter said, "I want Mom to live, but what he just said isn't living. Even if she makes it, she'll never be able to live again."

"I guess we are being selfish. I know she's not ready to die and she's afraid, but we have to let her go. Do you think the other two will agree?"

Peter responded, "I don't know, but I hope so."

"I was really hoping all of our hope was going to save her. I know she's fighting hard. I hope she isn't scared. The machines are the only thing keeping her alive...that's no way to live. We *are* being selfish now." I fought the tears back as the words I'd spoken circled throughout my head. *She was not going to make it.* No amount of hope was going to keep her with us. Her time on Earth was up, and we had to be strong enough to let her go.

"I didn't want to come today," Peter said. "I was afraid this would be a repeat of what happened with Gram."

"I know. I had the same thought," I told him. "This is all happening like it did with Gram. I mean not exactly, but close. Mom was in the same room Gram was in at the emergency room, and then she gets transferred to Dartmouth...and then the three of us come together to..." I paused because the words were too painful. "...to say goodbye." I looked at him with tears in my eyes, "You know, when Mom got sent to the hospital, it was seven years to the day that we had Gram's funeral. The timing is too much. *Seven years.* That must mean something—it has to."

"Wow, really...to the day? That's messed up." Peter looked at me and saw that I was crying.

When I could manage to speak, I told him, "I just miss Gram so much. This was the first year I was actually okay on the anniversary. For the last seven years, I have been so sad, and when I'm finally okay...this happens. I just don't get it. Gram was all I had, and when I lost her, I lost myself. I'm not ready for this again. I never got to talk with Mom about all the things I wanted to. I know she never liked me—she loves me, but she never liked me."

He nodded his head, as to agree with what I had said. "I'm

really sorry I wasn't there for you...you know...when all that stuff with Bill happened. I'm sorry I didn't stand by you."

"It's okay, I'm over it. Don't worry about it. We both had a really screwed up life, and we both had a lot of shit happen to us. We're lucky we're not more fucked up than we are!" We both laughed. "I know Mom did her best. Her best might not have been good, but it was her best. She was so childlike. She did good for being a kid."

Peter agreed. "Yeah, she did her best. I have a lot of good memories too. It wasn't always bad. She just became whoever she was with. She stood behind her man. It must have been hard to be with such assholes."

"I feel bad saying bad things about her when she's up there dying. I feel guilty, but she really hurt me, hurt us. I mean, Kate had it easiest, and her life was fucked up too, but at least she was Mom's favorite. I told Mom I forgave her...it was the last thing I said to her before she lost consciousness and I told her I loved her. Her last words to me were, *I love you*." I pushed back the tears. "I don't want to say bad things. I just want to be honest. This is really hard."

We went back upstairs and waited for Mary. When she arrived, she gave Peter a hug and said she was here for us if we needed her. We walked upstairs, and I walked Mary back to Mom's room. Kate came out so I could say goodbye to Mom. As I walked into the room, I saw the reaction Mom had when she heard Mary's voice. She nodded her head to the sound of Mary's voice, and her body twitched. I knew at that moment how much Mom loved Mary. I left the room without disturbing them and found Kate. I wrapped her in a big hug and told her Peter and I were leaving.

"Please tell Mom I love her and goodbye for Peter and me. I just saw how she responded to Mary, and I don't want to interrupt that."

"Wow, that's the first time you hugged me in I don't know how long," Kate said as she laughed. "I'll tell her. I love you, Jess."

"I love you too." I cried as I walked down the long winding hall back to Peter. This may be the last time I see Mom alive. The thought was too painful. This wasn't fair, but that thought wasn't going to save her. Nothing was going to save her.

I asked Peter to drive us to his car because I didn't feel I could make the trip. I felt so dizzy and out of place. It was the same feeling I had each time something traumatic happened. Unfortunately, it was a feeling I was familiar with. It is the feeling you are in your own world, where other people can see you, but they don't know. They don't know what you are going through. They don't know your world has been shaken up and your reality altered. I imagine the feeling to be similar to when you first die and you are between here and there. No one can see you or hear you, but you are still there. No one will ever understand what trauma feels like until they experience it. There are no words that describe it—only raw, aching emotions that replace all you have known. In those moments of trauma, your life becomes forever changed.

Peter and I talked the whole hour drive back to his car. We shared funny memories and reminisced about our childhood—the good, the bad, and the ugly. We talked about how young our dads were when they died and about how life could have been different had his father lived and taken care of us.

"We'd probably still be screwed up." He laughed. "My dad was my friend, not really a father, and Mom, well, Mom was just a kid. I guess that wouldn't have worked out very well either."

"We're lucky we had Gram for as long as we did," I told him. "She's the only reason I'm alive."

He agreed. "There has always been someone or something looking out for us. Every time I am down and out or get in a situation where I should've died, there's something there that helps me.

I had two car accidents, and I should've died, but I walked away both times. And every time I need money to pay a bill or something, money always shows up unexpectedly."

I looked over at him. "You're right. When we were living in Westville, I heard this woman's voice call my name. I got out of bed and looked in Mom and Ralph's room, and then in yours, and you were all sleeping. I didn't know who it was, but I felt safe. And the times Chuck beat me so bad—he could've killed me, but something was there making me fight back. And the money thing happens to me too, something always makes it okay."

"I know it's not Gram. It happened before she died. I think it's an angel or a guide or something," he said.

We agreed we had someone or something helping us through life and enjoyed our last few moments together until we reached his car. Peter told me he loved me and to call anytime I needed to talk. I said the same. We left knowing we'd be okay. Our bond strengthened that day as we realized we would always be connected. We drove off in different directions toward our own separate lives as the world kept spinning.

My drive home was only twenty minutes, but it felt like forever. I couldn't hold the tears in. There was nothing that could stop what was happening. Memories flooded my thoughts as tears streamed down my cheeks. As I neared home, a warm sensation started at my ankles and flowed through my body. As it reached my chest, I knew what it was—Mom was passing away.

CHAPTER 43

*W*hen I got home, Greg and I talked. I told him about the warm sensation that filled my body. "I don't want to be there when she dies. I don't want to see her body. I don't think I am going to go back." The reality of what I said hit me, and he hugged me as I sobbed.

A couple of hours later, Kate and Mary called me. They said we had some important decisions to make. I interrupted them, "We have to let her go. It's not fair that we are keeping her alive."

Kate said they agreed, and they wanted to make sure that I did as well. Mary said they asked to make Mom a Do Not Resuscitate (DNR) and see what happened overnight. I told them we should give her the pain medications and let her go comfortably. Mary said she wanted to give it the night to see if by chance she improved. If not, we would talk in the morning. The thought of Mom being alone in her room and in pain bothered me. I didn't want her to be afraid. The last couple of days had been hard on us, but what was it like for her? The time passed so slowly for us. I couldn't even begin to imagine how time was passing for her.

I couldn't stop thinking about it and how it was all unfolding. I sent messages to Amber and Amethyst asking them to send Mom distance Reiki and told them she was dying. Amber asked me to call her. When I called, I couldn't stop crying as I talked to her. "You need to ground yourself and breathe."

"I'm trying."

"You need to gather pictures of her ancestors. If you don't have pictures, write their names down and place them on an altar. Doing this, you are summoning your ancestors to help her cross over."

"Okay." I wrote down the instructions as Amber went on.

"Light a candle and give an offering of food to the ancestors. Sit with a picture of her in front of the candle and sing to her and let her know it is okay to go."

After we hung up, I gathered the photos, food, and candle. I set up an altar with pictures of Gram, my grandfather, Uncle Doug, and Mom. I put a sand dollar I had found on the beach soon after Gram died, a blue glass ashtray that belonged to Gram that Mom had given to me the past Christmas, and a small dish Ian made at school. I placed saltines in the dish and grapes in the ashtray. I lit a small white tea light and a blue candle Amethyst had given me to help with peace and harmony. I held the picture of Mom and began to hum to her. I had a hard time making any sounds through the tears. My humming turned to words, "Where Have All the Flowers Gone?" Over and over again, I sang the song she sang to us as children. As I sang the words, I began to sob. I looked at Mom's picture and told her she could go, and she didn't need to be afraid.

I heard a notification on my phone. I didn't want to stop my ceremony, but I also didn't want to miss news about Mom. When I looked at the message, it was from Amethyst. I had messaged her earlier telling her Mom was afraid and needed help. Amethyst said, after she heard from me, she spiritually journeyed to visit Mom, and she wasn't afraid. Mom had many people with her ready to help her cross over. Mom knew she was dying, but she needed to know it was okay to go. She didn't want to let us down. She said Mom was dancing and was happy to be free but hanging on because she didn't want to hurt us. Amethyst said once Mom knew we were okay, she'd send a kiss and be gone. I thanked Amethyst, went back to the altar, and told Mom she was not letting us down. It was okay to let go and be free.

I heard a knock at the door, and Ruby yelled, "Mommy, are you in there?"

"Just a minute." I blew out the candles, turned on the light, and opened the door.

"What are you doing? How's Grammy?" Ruby looked around the room.

"Grammy's very sick, honey. I don't think she's going to make it." Ruby grabbed onto me and started to sob. "It's okay, though, Ruby. Grammy's okay. You know what? Amethyst talked to her, and guess what? She said Grammy is dancing."

"But I don't want her to die, Mommy. I miss her. I didn't get to say goodbye."

"I know, honey, but she can dance now. We don't want her to be sick and in a wheelchair. We want her to dance and be free. She's happy, Ruby. She doesn't want to leave us, but she can dance, honey. She can dance."

"She's really dancing? I want her to dance, Mommy."

I ran my fingers through Ruby's hair as we hugged. "She's going to be with God, and she will be safe and happy and free. She'll always be in your heart."

Ruby went to sleep thinking about her grammy dancing and was happy for her. It was heartbreaking to see Ruby so sad, but I hadn't wanted to lie. I wanted her to know what was happening. I didn't want to tell her Mom would be okay only to tell her later that she had died. I didn't want her to hurt, but I didn't want her to be afraid either. I wanted her to know death is not scary, and it's okay to be sad and happy—to feel anything and everything.

I wasn't able to sleep that night as I waited for the phone to ring—to get "the call." The phone never rang. Early that morning, Mary sent a message that said she had talked to the doctors, and she was on her way to get Kate. Mary said she didn't have time to explain what she was told, and we needed to get to the hospital as soon as we could. Greg got up with me and said he would drive me to the hospital. He didn't want me to drive alone. I tried to talk him out of it, but he knew better and insisted on taking me.

I threw on clothes, a purple shirt—Mom's favorite color to comfort her. I found my moonstone necklace, added a rose quartz pendant to the chain, and then took a deep breath. I sent Peter a text to let him know what was happening and sent a message to Kate to tell her about what I learned the night before—that Mom was dancing, and we had to tell her it was okay to go. I called the hospital and talked to her nurse and asked her, "Please, tell my mom it's okay to go, I love her, and she has my permission." I also asked her to please give her pain medicine if she is in pain. The nurse said she had spoken with Kate, and she told her the same thing. Mom was resting comfortably. I told her I was on my way but to please give Mom my message. She said she would. I woke the kids and told them we had to get to the hospital, and we'd be back as soon as we could.

Greg and I started on the hour drive to the hospital. Half way through the drive, we passed Mary and Kate. I texted Amethyst and Amber on the trip to tell them what was happening. Amber and Amethyst both said they would send me Reiki to help keep me grounded. Amethyst asked me to call her so she could help walk me through what I needed to do. I called her, and she told me it wouldn't be long before Mom left, and I needed to tell her it was okay to go. She told me I needed the doctors to switch to comfort mode, taking her off all of her medications and the ventilator, and to make sure they gave her morphine and Ativan to be sure she passes peacefully. She told me to do Reiki on her and go to the spot I felt she was connected to her body.

I told her, "I don't think I can. I'm a mess. I don't think I can tell her what I need to."

"You can do this, Jess. Breathe and give yourself Reiki...I'll send you some too. There are spirits with her, and they are ready to help her cross over."

"I'll try."

"I may be in the area later. What is the room number?"

I sent Amethyst a message with the room information. I put the phone down, placed my hands on my upper thighs, and focused on grounding myself. I wanted to be able to be strong for Mom and for the others. I needed to be. I watched out the windows as buildings and people passed by. People were living their lives as though nothing was happening, and my world was falling apart.

When we arrived at the hospital, my heart began to beat faster. I wanted to stall this. I wanted more time. I asked Greg if I should wait for the others. He told me I needed to get into Mom's room as soon as I could. He stayed in the waiting room to wait for Kate and Mary.

As I walked down the hallway to Mom's room, I couldn't control my tears. I was about to say goodbye to my mother, to tell her she could let go and give her permission to be free. I was about to tell the doctor it was okay for Mom to die. How could I do that? How could I do any of that? How could I stop crying to do what I needed to do? A million questions buzzed through my heart and mind.

When I entered Mom's room, I felt a rush of peace come over me, and my tears stopped. My heart stopped racing, and my mind was clear. I walked over to her bedside where she seemed to rest peacefully. All the machines were still running and making noises. She was unresponsive. Her heart monitor was on, and she was still alive, but her blood pressure was very low. She was on the maximum dose of all medications now, and it was not helping her. I saw the doctor and told him, "We are ready to let her go. Once my sister and Mary get here, we will be ready."

"Take your time. I'll be available when you're ready."

I walked over to Mom, placed my hands on her arm, and said, "Mom, I love you. I know you love me. You fought so hard, and I'm so proud of you for all you have done, but you don't have to fight anymore. Mom, you can dance." I looked down at my hand on her arm and saw Gram's jade ring. I smiled as I thought about her helping Mom cross over and helping me help her. We were working as a team, even now.

I continued talking to Mom. "Mom, I know why things happened the way they did. And you fought so hard to live. You gave us such a gift to be able to have time to say all the things we needed to say. I love you, Mom. It's your turn to be free. I'm so jealous of you. I cannot wait for my turn. Your life was hard, but you can be free and live. Mom, you can finally live."

I focused on helping her release from her body as I continued to give her Reiki. "It's time for your next journey. You get to do all the things you wanted to do. You're not a prisoner to this life anymore. Let the people you love guide you."

The warmth of her skin under my hand brought me closer to her. "You don't need to worry about us anymore. We'll be okay. Tell Gram I said hi and I love her."

Mary and Kate arrived, and I told them I had let the doctor know we were ready. Kate and Mary both told Mom it was okay to let go, and they would take care of each other. I moved to Mom's feet, uncovered her left foot, and started giving her Reiki. When I kneeled down to work on her foot, I noticed the purple DNR bracelet—the same bracelet I fought with Gram to take off seven years before. I kissed the top of Mom's foot and asked Kate and Mary to kiss her as well. I stood at her feet and continued to tell her it was okay to go. Kate took over the talking, and Mary sat by the bed and cried. I asked Kate to sing to her and told her it would help make Mom's transition easier.

"I don't know what to sing," Kate said as she looked at me.

"Sing anything. Sing the songs she sang to us," I said hoping it would help take her mind off what was happening. Kate began to sing, "Where Have All the Flowers Gone." The words brought me back, but I remained grounded. I remained calm and was able to focus on what was happening. We had minutes left with Mom, and I wanted the memories to be something we could think back to and smile. I didn't want any of us to leave feeling like we hadn't done our best.

I asked if they were ready to tell the doctor, and they both agreed they were. We told the nurse, and she got the doctor to come into the room. We told him we wanted to switch over to comfort mode, and I asked that they give her morphine and Ativan.

"I cannot speed the process up."

"I only want to make sure she's comfortable."

Two nurses came into the room. First, they shut down Mom's heart monitor and all of the machines, and then they injected morphine into the line in her neck. The nurse turned off the medications and then the ventilator. They attached a blue balloon-like bag where the vent was, and it filled with air. I continued to do Reiki on her foot, and Kate kept singing.

"It's your time to be free, Mom. We'll take care of each other. I love you, Mom. Be free. Walk towards God and take Gram's hand. You are free." The voice leaving my mouth was not mine. It was a voice I had never heard before. Moments later, I stood up. *I knew*. She was free.

I stood quietly with my hands at my side and watched Kate sing and Mary cry. I felt it as Mom left her body. I felt the warmth I had felt the day before. This time it was a warm sensation in my upper body, almost as if someone was hugging me. My shoulders and arms were warm, and so was my heart. I was at peace, so calm. It was magical. Mom allowing us the chance to be at her side to help her transition to the next phase of her journey was the best gift she had given me—aside from life.

A doctor and nurse came in. The doctor put a stethoscope on, listened to her heart and lungs, and then looked at the nurse and up at the clock. I followed his gaze. 11:23 a.m. She was gone. My eyes met his, and we nodded together confirming.

"Is she gone?" Kate asked through tears. The doctor nodded. Kate began to sob. "I didn't want her to see me cry. But she's gone now so it doesn't matter." She let go of Mom's hand and continued to cry.

I hugged Kate tight and told her, "She's not gone. She's still in the room. She heard you singing. You helped her make this so much easier. You brought her peace."

After I let go of Kate, I told them I wanted to go see Greg to let him know what had happened. As I walked out of the room, and down the long hallway to Greg, I began to cry. I didn't have to be strong anymore, and the reality of what happened hit me. My mom was dead. *She was dead.* I couldn't wrap my mind around that thought. Now what? There was so much to think about, and so much we needed to do.

When I reached Greg, I told him, "She's gone. She just went." He hugged me as I cried. I said I needed to go back in with them and talk about the next steps.

As I walked back through the doors of the Critical Care Unit, the calm I had experienced earlier returned. When I arrived back to Mom's body, they had pulled the curtain, and a picture of a daisy with a fallen petal was clipped to it. I pushed it back and found Kate and Mary looking at each other in shock. We all left the room, and a nurse walked us down the hallway of patients to a room behind the nurse's station. She turned the light on and asked us to have a seat while we waited for someone to talk to us.

While we waited, I looked over at Mary and asked her, "Do you know if Mom wanted to be buried or cremated?"

"I don't know. We talked about it, but I don't remember. There's a document back at the house that says what her wishes are." Mary blew her nose and said, "I just don't know. We didn't expect this to happen so soon."

I went on to explain, "I know it shouldn't be a money thing, but cremation is much cheaper. I don't know with her size if that makes it cost more or not. Funeral homes cost more, but there is a cremation society that is usually the cheapest."

Kate added, "With her size, she probably needs to be cremated. I don't think there are caskets that big, and if there are, they're probably expensive. I mean, they probably have to cut her up to cremate her."

I butted in. "Please stop! I don't want to think about that. We do need a plan though, but let's leave those details out of it."

There was a knock at the door. The Critical Care social worker came in and offered her condolences. She gave us options and talked about the next steps.

Mary told her, "Jessica does this for work. She has been telling us our options." The social worker said she would give us numbers of places and would give us all the time we needed to figure it out. Kate suggested I get Greg since we weren't in Mom's room anymore. The social worker walked me out to go get him. As we walked down the long hall, I told her I was a hospice social worker, but there was no way I would be able to return to work right now. I told her I had lost my gram seven years ago, so everything was all so similar, and many memories were coming back. She agreed I should heal before I helped others go through what I had.

When we got to Greg, I asked him to come with me so we could figure things out. When we got back to the room, I asked Mary, "Do you think you want to go with cremation?"

She nodded her head.

"Do you want to go with a funeral home that will handle everything, but cost more or do you want to go with a cremation society that will be cheaper but will give you less help?"

"There's so much to do and so much to think about, I—"

"I know, but right now, we need to know what to do with her body. I'm not comfortable leaving her here without a plan. I know it's just her body, but it's still my mom. I don't want to think about her being here alone..."

Kate cut me off, "Where do they...uh—"

"Keep the body? In the morgue," I knew what she was trying to ask and answered her before she finished. "I just don't want her in the morgue with no plan. We need a plan before we leave here." I asked Mary again what she would prefer.

She hesitated and said, "I know it's awful, but I have to do what's cheapest. With her gone, I lost her income and mine. We didn't plan for this." She paused. "I guess I need to make a bunch of phone calls to see who will do what we need the cheapest. I just don't think I can do it right now."

"I'll make the calls. I will take care of it."

"Thank you, Jess."

They gave us a card for the "Deceased Patient Coordinator" and were told to call them when we knew what we wanted to do, and they would take care of the rest. We decided we had done all we could there, and it was time to go home. We said goodbye to each other. I told Mary she never had to second-guess herself. She should always know she did everything she could for Mom and it was Mom's body that decided it was time to go. I wanted her to know there was nothing more we could have done. We tried everything to keep her alive, but it was out of our control.

As we walked down that long hallway of the Critical Care Unit one last time, none of us spoke. When we got to the parking lot, we hugged, and I told Mary, "You're my only mom now. I love you. Thank you for all you did for her." She cried and said she was lucky to have me, my family, and Kate in her life.

When Greg and I got to the car, I looked down at my phone and noticed a missed call from Amethyst. I called her back, and she said she was in the area and came to check in on us. She was still in the hospital, so we headed back to meet her. My heart filled with love as I thought of how much support and love she had given me.

We met in the parking lot and walked toward the car. We stopped at the corner of a crosswalk, and I told her how it all happened. She pulled out a bag of stones and a vial of oil. "Give these to the funeral home and ask them to put them with her ashes."

"She's going to the cremation society, so I don't know how to get them there. Will the hospital give them the items?"

"Probably not."

"Is it too late for me to put the oil on her now?"

"No, let's go."

We walked back up to the desk to ask to see Mom's body. We were told we were probably too late, but he would check. The receptionist called back and they said they were still cleaning her up. I spoke up and said, "I want to clean her body." Amethyst told him it was my religious belief, and he repeated the words back to the person on the other end of the phone. He rolled his eyes as he hung up the phone and agreed to let us back.

As we walked down that long hallway to where Mom's body was, Amethyst told me the woman who was with Mom the other night was my gram. When we entered the room, Amethyst said Mom and Gram were still in the room. Mom was sitting by the window. I walked over to her body and looked at her. The machines were off her face, and the bloating and puffiness she had earlier were gone. She looked like Mom again.

I dabbed a little of the oil on one finger and began to rub it on the side of her forehead. I couldn't hold back the tears. Amethyst asked for a washcloth, but all I could find were paper towels. I handed her a few and went back to dabbing the oil on Mom's forehead around her hair. Amethyst got the paper towels wet and washed off the dried blood on Mom's face from where the machines had been. I watched as she gently cleaned her off. She took the oil, dumped a large amount into her hand, and began to rub it on Mom's body. I put more oil in my hands and rubbed it on the side of the body I was on.

I stopped in between rubs to look at Mom's body and *really* look at her. I kissed her forehead and inhaled her smell. The smell brought me back to when I kissed Gram's head seven years before. I watched as Amethyst placed crystals above Mom's head and draped a shawl over her body. She did Reiki on her and helped Mom detach from her body. Amethyst smiled as she finished. "She was ready. She has totally let go. She said she's done here and is out there enjoying the sun."

It had been years since she was able to be outside and enjoy the warmth of the sun on her skin. I looked at Mom's face, ran my fingers under her lips, and I saw Ruby. I saw a little girl resting in that bed. Mom was childlike my whole life, and as her body rested there, I understood she *really did* do her best. She was free now. She was free from the prison of her body and mind. She was free from the physical and emotional pain. She was free from the monster that had eaten her. I smiled as I thought about the future ahead of her. How could I be sad when everything was so much better for her now? I couldn't. I was so happy for her. My heart swelled with love.

As I looked at Mom's body, I tried to imagine the grand adventure she was about to take. Amethyst took some scissors, cut a lock of Mom's purple hair, and handed it to me. I was so happy to have this keepsake—a part of my mother.

The time with Amethyst and Mom's body was a blessing. It was healing as I watched the woman who caused me so much pain become just a shell. I understood it all, and I could see why things happened the way they had. She was wounded. Her life was much like mine. We shared that. She wanted to be loved as desperately as I did. She did her best, as did I. I never saw her as vulnerable until that moment. She was someone I wanted love from so badly that I just saw hurt and disappointment. I always felt like a timid child trying to get my needs met around her. I wanted her to love me and be proud of me. Seeing her as a whole, *I got it*. I was finally able to see the big picture.

The love I had been searching for my whole life—I finally received. Her last days on this Earth she granted all of my wishes. She gave me the love I had longed for my entire life in the last few moments of hers. She fought and clung to life to be sure I had closure. I was able to tell her all the things I needed to. Years of hurt and rejection were healed as I was able to connect with her. The love she gave me as she ended her life made up for what she had not been able to give me for so many years.

With her freedom, came mine. Released together to travel our different journeys, I will spend the rest of my life knowing she loved me.

With love comes strength to continue on.

If you or someone you know is struggling please know there is help.

Domestic Violence Hotline
www.thehotline.org
1-800-799-7233

National Suicide Prevention Lifeline
www.suicidepreventionlifeline.org
1-800-273-8255

Child Abuse Hotline
1-800-4-A-CHILD

National Alliance on Mental Illness (NAMI)
www.nami.org
1-800-950-NAMI (6264)

ACKNOWLEDGMENTS

This book would not have ever been possible without the love and support of my fiancé, George. It was he who believed in my dream to share my story, it was he who encouraged me along the way, and it was he who held me up when all I wanted to do was fall down. He believed in me when I could not believe in myself.

My children, who know some of this story better than I do, but I wish they didn't. They gave me the push to be my best self. My love for them is unconditional, and my hope for them is to be safe and happy and reach for any dream in their heart.

My gram for loving me unconditionally, and even still, providing me with love and support. My mom for teaching me how to survive and how to see the person under the diagnosis. My brother for sharing some of the most traumatic events with me and loving me through it all. My sister for believing in me. And to Myscha for loving my mom and accepting us as her own.

I owe more than I could ever measure to the people who came to me at all the right times and helped me when I needed it most. My mentors, M-E and Hutch, surrounded me in love and acceptance when I had given up on believing good people still existed. The cohort at Springfield College, who soon became family, pushed me to find who I really was. The Crow Sisters healed many, many years of pain and suffering and helped me understand some of the "whys." Rhonda, who listened without judgment. Heather and her family, who became my family when I needed it most, and still, all these years later, love me like blood. My tenth grade English teacher, Jodi Gonyaw-Worth, who believed in my writing and gave me hope when I felt lost in the world.

Tom Petty and the Heartbreakers for giving me words when I couldn't find them, for speaking to parts of me that make me feel alive, and most importantly, for being there when it felt like no one else was.

I want to thank the people who helped shape *The Monster That Ate My Mommy* into what it is today. Alice Peck, who took my raw emotions, read them with grace and guided me with patience. Julie, who read all versions and gave honest and gentle feedback, offered support and understanding, and continues to be a cheerleader. Sarah Felix Burns, who beta read for me and gave me expert advice and kind words. Diane Abesse, a friend with a mutual love for Tom Petty, who read, edited, and encouraged me through the final process. Rogena Mitchell-Jones, my editor, for putting the final touches on and helping me reach the finish line. AmiLynn Hadley for a beautiful cover that speaks to who I am and helps to tell my story.

There have been many people who have helped me on my journey so far, and I am forever grateful for their love, kindness, and support. Small acts of kindness can mean the world to someone. It is never too small.

ABOUT THE AUTHOR

Jessica Aiken-Hall lives in New Hampshire with her three children, three dogs, and her fiancé. She is a graduate of Springfield College with a Master's Degree in Mental Health Counseling. She is a Reiki Master, focusing her attention on healing. As a social worker, she uses her life experiences to help others in their time of need.

Jessica was a guest on the Dr. Phil show, where some of her story was discussed.

To stay connected with Jessica, she can be contacted at:
Facebook.com/aikenhallauthor
www.aikenhallauthor.com
Aiken-hall.author@outlook.com

Made in the USA
Middletown, DE
01 March 2020